The Age of Hybrid Intelligence

The Age of Hybrid Intelligence

When Humans and AI Merge

Kenan Durveil

Mindful Pages

Published in 2026

ISBN: 9789374594766 (PB)
ISBN: 9789374595480 (eBook)

Published by

Mindful Pages
Imprint of Alpha Editions LLC
312 W. 2nd St #1834
Casper, WY 82601, USA

Content

Introduction

The neurosurgeon watched the cursor shiver across the monitor as if waking from sleep. Electrodes traced faint signals from the patient's motor cortex, translating intention into movement. Think left, and the cursor edged towards the margin; think right, and it followed. The first few words arrived slowly, hesitant as a child learning to form letters, yet unmistakably human in their origin. No keys were pressed. No hands moved. A thought had travelled into text. Minutes earlier, the room had felt like any other clinical lab: disinfectant in the air, cables coiled with dutiful precision, the quiet hum of machinery. Now it carried the hush of something historic. A line had been crossed—not between science and fiction, but between effort and expression, between the body's limits and the mind's reach. The neurosurgeon could not help wondering what it might mean when thought itself became a user interface.

Across the city, a call-centre agent nudged her headset and pressed a shortcut key. Her dashboard split in two: on one side, a customer typing out a complaint in clipped frustration; on the other, a model drafting a suggested reply. It offered empathy first, then troubleshooting steps, then reassurance about the refund policy. She scanned the response like a conductor reviewing a score—adjusting tone here, adding a clarifying phrase there, softening a sharp consonant of corporate jargon. To the untrained eye, she was merely following a script. In truth, she was shaping a duet between her judgement and the system's predictions. Her job had not been automated. It had been reframed into something stranger and subtler: steering another intelligence to amplify her own.

And in a dim student bedroom, a teenager rubbed tired eyes and reopened a revision assistant. The app summarised key concepts, generated flashcards, offered structured practice questions. After a few weeks of use, her marks rose. But something else shifted. Her recall felt thinner, like a muscle used less vigorously. She would explain this to a friend in the cafeteria: "It's brilliant, but I feel... dull afterwards. Like it's doing the thinking for me." She wanted the help, yet feared the cost. This quiet unease—a sense of personal erosion—was not superstition. It was a warning that augmentation is not neutral. Tools that sharpen us can also soften us, depending on how we shape the relationship.

These three scenes sit at the threshold of a new age—an age in which human ability is no longer bounded by biology, and artificial systems are no longer mere tools. They act, suggest, anticipate, and sometimes persuade. They learn from our data, our decisions, our injuries, our desires. They offer potential that feels electric. Yet they also test the integrity of our judgement, our attention, and even our sense of self. The stakes could not be higher, for the challenge is not whether machines will match human talents, but whether we can remain fully ourselves while partnering with them.

This book argues that we can—if we learn to design the relationship with rigour and humility. Hybrid intelligence is not a slogan about man and machine becoming indistinguishable. It is a practical craft: architecting interfaces, agreements, and habits so that artificial systems scale our attention rather than dilute it; supporting human judgement rather than bypassing it; extending capability without hollowing competence. It requires the clarity to define what should stay human, the discipline to structure handovers, and the wisdom to keep our moral bearings when scale tempts us into shortcuts.

To understand why this moment demands a new framework, it helps to recognise a pattern that recurs across history whenever power expands faster than culture catches up. The printing press multiplied knowledge but destabilised authority; factories increased productivity but fractured traditional skills; electricity transformed domestic life while unsettling labour and social rhythms. Today's transformation is subtler. It reshapes not the world around us first, but the workings of our minds. The tools that assist us are beginning to internalise our habits, our preferences, even our emotional cadences. They reflect us back to ourselves with uncanny fluency. And because they speak in human-like language, they invite us to assume they reason as we do—even when they do not.

The result is a paradox. Never has human capability been more expandable at speed; never have the risks of dependency been more insidious. When a system finishes our sentences, retrieves our memories, or drafts our decisions, its convenience can mask its intrusions. Handing off too much too quickly may quiet the discomforts of uncertainty, but it can also deprive us of the friction that strengthens judgement. Craft requires resistance; so does character. Hybrid intelligence, at its best, preserves that resistance while offering leverage. At its worst, it erodes it until we forget it ever mattered.

This book offers a counterweight to that erosion. It provides a playbook for individuals, teams, and institutions seeking to harness AI in ways that expand human talent without compromising human dignity. Its central question is deceptively simple: how do we design partnerships between humans and models that elevate rather than replace, sharpen rather than soften, empower rather than anaesthetise? The answer is not technological. It is architectural, behavioural, ethical, and deeply cultural.

We begin by examining the shift from tools to teammates. For centuries, machines obeyed static commands: pull a lever, receive a force; type a query, retrieve a file. Contemporary models behave differently. They infer intent, adapt to context, and generate options. They negotiate. They guess. They sometimes challenge the user's initial framing. This new agency—partial, statistical, yet undeniably generative—

requires a new vocabulary. Without shared language for prompts, policies, escalations, provenance, and traceability, collaboration becomes error-prone and opaque. But once we articulate the terms, we can design clear decision boundaries: when to delegate, when to collaborate, and when to keep responsibility firmly in human hands.

From there, we turn to the twin engines of learning and feedback. Humans flourish when supported by scaffolds that accelerate understanding yet demand active participation. Models flourish when given structured feedback that tunes their behaviour and reveals their blind spots. Hybrid intelligence emerges in the interplay: a continuous, bidirectional training loop in which human judgement guides model performance, and model suggestions stimulate human insight. This process is powerful—but only if trust is calibrated, not assumed; only if verification becomes a habit rather than an afterthought.

The book then moves inward, towards the frontier where biology meets computation: the interfaces that read and shape signals from the brain. These technologies bring extraordinary promise for rehabilitation, communication, and accessibility. They also carry profound risks when reading becomes surveillance or stimulation becomes manipulation. Navigating this frontier requires principles capable of resisting commercial optimism and political temptation. Consent must be explicit, reversible, and meaningful. Cognitive dignity must be non-negotiable.

Beyond biology, we explore the augmentation of core capacities: perception, reasoning, memory, attention, creativity. The opportunity here is immense. A well-designed search tool can compress hours of trawling into seconds. A structured reasoning assistant can transform messy ambition into executable plans. Yet each augmentation carries a shadow. External memory aids may weaken recall; automated synthesis may flatten aesthetic sensibilities. Hybrid intelligence thrives when we preserve human sense-making at the centre and treat models as catalysts rather than substitutes.

In the workplace, the challenges become even more intricate. A workflow is not simply a set of tasks; it is an ecology of roles, expectations, and tacit agreements. Introducing AI into that ecology without clear handover rules risks confusion, complacency, and failure. Precision matters: what evidence must the system supply? At what threshold should a human escalate? Which outputs must be verified by default, and which may be accepted provisionally? Organisations that answer these questions with clarity gain not only productivity but trust.

Safety and accountability demand equal attention. Hybrid systems inherit human biases and may amplify them with algorithmic confidence. They can also obscure accountability in a haze of automated suggestions and partial oversight. The remedy is not fear-driven paralysis but structured boundaries: tiered permissions, auditable logs, signed artefacts, and a simple rule of responsibility. Systems advise. Humans decide. And where formal delegation occurs, it must be explicit, supervised, and reversible.

Law and norms appear later in the book, not because they are peripheral, but because they crystallise only after culture begins to shift. Before statutes harden, soft law—standards, procurement rules, best-practice frameworks—guides behaviour. Consent emerges as a central theme in both public and workplace settings. Education must adapt as well: assessment must reward thinking, not just recall, and must reflect the reality that assistance is part of modern cognition. Public services must remain legitimate by involving communities in design and oversight. Hybrid intelligence can widen access, but only with transparency and participation.

Identity and culture form one of the book's deepest threads. Augmentation can provoke a sense of internal theft, a suspicion that one's achievements are no longer fully earned. Creative fields, in particular, face an existential question: what distinguishes human craft when synthetic variation is infinite? The answer may lie not in originality alone but in the discernment to choose, interpret, and constrain. Meaning survives not by resisting assistance, but by integrating it into coherent rituals of effort and reflection.

Finally, the book culminates in a practical skills playbook and an organisational blueprint. Individuals learn how to design prompts as briefs, evaluate outputs robustly, manage their data hygiene, and track how assistance shapes their thinking. Organisations learn how to craft charters, rationalise platforms, support adoption without shaming sceptics, and retire tools that undermine trust or dignity. These final chapters translate philosophy into concrete practice. They show that hybrid intelligence is not a distant technological horizon, but a discipline available to anyone willing to engage with it deliberately.

At the centre of this book lies a recurring motif: the handshake. Not the mechanical handshake between code and hardware, but the human handshake—symbol of agreement, of mutual responsibility, of shared understanding. Every hybrid system involves such a handshake, even if we rarely name it. When we rely on a model to search, summarise, propose, or predict, we tacitly enter a contract: we trust that the system has been built with care, that its limits are recognised, that its outputs will not override our judgement. And the system, in turn, relies on us to provide context, oversight, and correction. The handshake must be designed, not assumed. Its terms must be legible and its boundaries clear.

The questions that follow are both urgent and timeless. How do we remain authors of our own choices when assisted at every turn? How do we cultivate competence in a world where convenience is abundant? How do we preserve attention—one of the scarcest resources of modern life—when countless systems compete to anticipate our needs? And how do we ensure that the benefits of hybrid intelligence are distributed widely, not concentrated narrowly?

These questions resist easy answers. But they are not unanswerable. This book aims to equip you with the frameworks, stories, and conceptual tools to confront them with confidence. It draws on cognitive science, engineering, ethics, organisational design, and human experience. It offers not merely critique, but a path: a way to shape the future so that intelligence—human, artificial, and hybrid—serves our highest ambitions rather than our laziest impulses.

The age of hybrid intelligence is not approaching. It has already begun, quietly and unmistakably, in the neurosurgeon's lab, the call-centre cubicle, and the student's bedroom. The question now is how we will inhabit it. Will we allow systems to shape us by default, or will we shape the partnership with intention? Will we drift into dependency, or design for durability? Will we trade depth for speed, or seek a balance that lets us think more clearly, act more wisely, and remain recognisably ourselves?

The chapters that follow invite you to make that choice deliberately. They do not promise certainty, but they offer clarity—a guide to forging a handshake worthy of the future we are building together.

Chapter 1
The Hybrid Turn

The technician watching the factory line noticed it before anyone else. A sorting arm—one of the dependable workhorses of the plant—paused mid-motion, hesitated, then corrected its angle with an almost uncanny subtlety. Instead of following its usual pre-programmed route, it had drawn on live data to anticipate a minor defect in the material and adjust accordingly. Nothing dramatic happened: the belt kept moving, the workers continued their quiet choreography, the machines hummed as they always did. Yet that tiny adjustment marked a profound shift. The arm was no longer simply executing instructions; it was negotiating with its environment, interpreting ambiguity, behaving—within narrow limits—like a partner rather than a tool. In that moment, the technician realised the line was not just automated. It had become, in a small but telling way, collaborative.

That hesitation, that micro-decision, is the signature of the hybrid turn. It is the point at which machines stop waiting patiently for direction and begin to offer suggestions, alternatives, and sometimes corrections. We see it in mundane places: in the email client that proposes a softer phrasing when our writing turns curt; in the navigation system that anticipates congestion and recommends a different route before we notice the brake lights; in the design assistant that supplies a palette we did not think to request. These systems do not merely obey. They participate.

For generations, humans have understood machines through the lens of instrumentality: a hammer amplifies the force of a hand; a spreadsheet magnifies the accuracy of arithmetic; a search engine accelerates retrieval. But contemporary learning systems, trained on vast patterns of human decisions and language, behave differently. They do not just enact our intent; they infer it. They do not simply respond; they anticipate. They propose options that shape how we think about the task itself. And in doing so, they force us to confront a deceptively simple question: when intelligence becomes ambient, probabilistic, and partially autonomous, how do we decide who leads and when?

This chapter traces the origins and implications of that question. It asks what happens when assistance becomes collaborative, and when collaboration starts to blur into delegation. It explores how we distinguish mere convenience from genuine partnership, and why getting that distinction right matters for competence, responsibility, and even dignity.

To understand this shift, we must first recognise that our relationship with machines has always been cultural as much as technical. Consider the mechanical loom, which workers once feared would displace their craft. It did, in many respects. But it also produced new roles—designers of patterns, operators of increasingly sophisticated machinery, coordinators of supply chains. Each technological leap recalibrates the boundary between human and machine capability, often provoking anxiety before enabling new forms of expertise. What makes the hybrid turn distinct is its intimacy. Earlier tools extended muscle or memory; today's systems extend attention, reasoning, and decision-making. They are not strapped to the body or placed on the desk; they are woven into cognition.

Co-intelligence, the central idea of this chapter, names the emerging relationship in which human judgement and machine inference shape outcomes together. It is neither subservience nor surrender. It is a spectrum—a dynamic gradient that stretches from simple assistance to rich collaboration and, in some contexts, to carefully bounded delegation. On one end, the system offers suggestions we can accept or ignore. In the middle, it becomes a thinking partner: surfacing ambiguities, challenging assumptions, enriching our perspective. On the far end, it handles routine or well-defined decisions, freeing humans to focus on work requiring nuance, empathy, or creativity. The challenge is deciding where on this spectrum any task should sit.

One of the simplest tests is this: *who must bear responsibility for the outcome?* If the answer is unequivocally human, then the system must remain advisory. If the answer can be shared, then collaboration becomes possible. If responsibility can be formally delegated—accompanied by oversight, safeguards, and reversibility—then parts of the task may move towards automation. This test is not merely procedural; it reflects a deeper ethical truth. Responsibility cannot be abdicated simply because a system is capable. It must be allocated deliberately, with clarity about who acts, who decides, and who answers when something goes wrong.

Why this hybrid turn is happening now is equally important. The popular narrative credits a sudden leap in ability—a new generation of models speaking in fluent prose and generating persuasive designs. But beneath that narrative lies a longer story shaped by three forces. First, the cost of computation has fallen dramatically, allowing models to run at scales once reserved for national laboratories. Second, data from decades of digital life—texts, images, interactions—has made it possible for systems to capture the statistical structure of human behaviour with astonishing fidelity. Third, interface design has matured. The conversational handshake between human and machine is now smoother, more intuitive, more responsive. You no longer need to speak the machine's language; the machine learns to speak yours.

These forces create a form of intelligence that is, paradoxically, both fragile and formidable. Fragile, because it can misread context or hallucinate confidently. Formidable, because it can generalise across domains, seek patterns humans overlook, and supply insights at speeds no individual could match. This combination is precisely why hybrid work will outlast any particular model or release cycle. The underlying drivers—cheaper prediction, richer datasets, more natural interfaces—are structural. They are not going away. Whatever the next breakthroughs bring, the need for human judgement in partnership with machine inference will remain.

Yet the hybrid turn demands boundaries. Not all tasks benefit from delegation, and some should remain unequivocally human by default. Responsibility, consent, values, and exception handling form a quartet of domains that require human stewardship. Consider a hospital triage system: it may sort symptoms rapidly, highlight risk factors, and suggest priorities. But when a case falls into grey territory—a patient who describes discomfort in halting phrases, or a constellation of symptoms that defies tidy categorisation—clinician judgement must prevail. The machine can streamline, but the human must decide. This preserves not only safety, but trust. Patients want speed, but they also want assurance that someone capable of empathy and wisdom is ultimately accountable.

To navigate these boundaries, we need a shared vocabulary for co-intelligence. Without one, teams talk past each other, policies become ambiguous, and errors proliferate silently. Terms like *prompt, policy, escalation, provenance,* and *trace* might seem technical at first glance, yet they are as essential to hybrid work as verbs are to language. They help us specify intent, define constraints, document decision paths, and diagnose failures. Imagine a hiring team auditing an AI assistant that screens applications. Without clear vocabulary, they might describe a problem as "the model feels biased." With proper language, they can examine the training data's provenance, inspect traces of specific decisions, adjust prompt constraints, and raise an escalation when outputs violate policy thresholds. Clarity is not mere precision; it is the foundation of accountability.

As we proceed through this chapter, we will explore how machines have moved from instruments to teammates, why their new role alters the fabric of work, and how to design human–machine partnerships that enhance capability without fracturing responsibility. We will interrogate the mechanics of collaboration: how shared agency emerges, how ambiguity is negotiated, how trust is earned rather than assumed. We will confront the psychological dimension too—the subtle shifts in identity and autonomy that occur when systems anticipate our needs before we articulate them.

The hybrid turn is not a technological curiosity. It is a cultural hinge. It asks us to redefine competence, redraw boundaries, and rethink what it means to work well with another intelligence—one that is statistical, tireless, occasionally brilliant, sometimes brittle, and increasingly omnipresent. The way we answer will determine whether we gain leverage or lose grounding.

As you move into the chapter ahead, consider this question: if machines are learning to meet us halfway, how do we decide where halfway should be? The possibilities are exhilarating; the risks are real. And the decisions we make now will shape not only our workflows, but our sense of ourselves as thinkers, makers, and moral agents. The hybrid turn has already begun. The challenge is to navigate it with clarity, courage, and a commitment to keeping the human at the centre of the handshake.

From Tools to Teammates

On 14 March 2016, in Seoul's Four Seasons Hotel, DeepMind's AlphaGo faced Lee Sedol, one of the most accomplished Go players of his generation. The cameras captured a moment that would echo far beyond the tournament room. Midway through the second game, AlphaGo produced a move so startling—so seemingly ill-judged—that Sedol stood up, walked out briefly, and returned with a faint smile of disbelief.

The move was later analysed across thousands of commentaries; professionals noted that no conventional human training would have produced it. What mattered was not the victory that followed but the nature of the interaction itself. Sedol adjusted his strategy in real time, probing the system's logic, inferring its strengths, testing its flaws. The encounter resembled less a duel with a tool and more a negotiation with a strategic partner. Five words from a commentator captured the shift: *The machine is playing differently now.*

That moment helps illustrate a broader truth. When systems begin to anticipate rather than merely react, the relationship subtly tilts. The hammer does not analyse the nail. The spreadsheet does not propose a new model. But contemporary learning systems—spanning language, perception, and planning—offer suggestions that shape human decisions before we notice. An email client hints at a tone adjustment. A medical imaging model highlights an ambiguous region of a scan. A legal assistant surfaces a precedent that reframes the lawyer's initial argument. These are not mechanical extensions but conversational invitations. And that invitation raises a question that this chapter keeps returning to: *when a machine proposes, who leads?*

Co-intelligence is the working answer to that question: a partnership in which human judgement and machine inference steer outcomes together. Before we dissect its architecture, it helps to observe how the shift looks in practice. In January 2023, the UK's National Archives piloted a classification assistant in Kew to process incoming digital records. Staff noticed a striking pattern. Instead of labelling documents strictly according to pre-defined taxonomies, the system offered alternative clusters that reflected thematic relationships not captured by the official categories. The archivists did not simply accept these suggestions; they debated them, amended them, rejected some, and refined others. What emerged was not automation but a joint curation process. The tool behaved like a teammate—one whose proposals demanded scrutiny rather than obedience.

Naming this shift matters. For much of industrial history, machines served as instruments: levers of amplification. Assistance was the default mode—machines extended human effort without altering its direction. Yet the rise of probabilistic models introduces behaviours that feel collaborative. They fill gaps, reveal assumptions, and widen or narrow decision frames. In research teams at CERN in 2022, anomaly-detection models flagged data distributions that physicists later described as "plausible but non-obvious." Their notes revealed a quiet recalibration: the model had taken the first pass; the researchers used their expertise to interrogate it. Agency had shifted from singular to shared.

To distinguish assistance from collaboration and delegation, we must first look at agency—the locus of direction, not merely of action. Assistance retains human primacy. A radiologist reviews a scan, while an AI highlights features; the decision flows one way. Collaboration occupies the middle ground: a designer sketches an idea, a model produces variations, the designer chooses, the model refines, and the cycle continues. Responsibility stays human, but influence oscillates. Delegation appears when a system is authorised to act within defined limits. In 2019, Heathrow Airport's gait-monitoring programme used machine vision to identify wheelchair assistance needs from passenger movement patterns. Staff retained escalation rights, but within bounded thresholds, the system initiated support. Delegation in this context is neither abandonment nor abdication; it is a controlled transfer with explicit boundaries.

However, a limitation complicates the spectrum. Machines can mislead through an illusion of fluency. A system generating a polished explanation may mask uncertainty more effectively than a faltering human. The risk is not error alone but misplaced confidence. This phenomenon surfaced in

Stanford's 2023 evaluation of biomedical language models, where syntactically perfect summaries sometimes omitted critical qualifiers. Some critics argued that such cases undermine the whole collaborative premise. But this objection, though valid, does not negate co-intelligence. Rather, it exposes the necessity of role clarity. A teammate's fluency should prompt scrutiny, not deference. Collaboration succeeds when humans treat suggestion as stimulus, not verdict.

Agency becomes meaningful only when tied to a visible decision. Consider a simple threshold: *who must answer for the outcome?* If the answer is unequivocally human, the system's role must remain advisory. This test, applied across sectors—from journalism to urban planning—constrains delegation without freezing innovation. In the BBC's 2021 trial of automated metadata tagging, journalists retained responsibility for final classification. The system's suggestions saved time but did not alter editorial accountability. The threshold is not philosophical; it is operational. It identifies the inflection point at which a proposal becomes a commitment.

Behind all these examples lies a quiet motif worth keeping: the *handshake*. Every hybrid interaction forms a handshake—implicit or explicit—between human and machine about role, direction, and bounds. The quality of the handshake determines whether the partnership elevates or distorts. A weak handshake leads to over-reliance or unnecessary suspicion. A strong one produces clarity: who initiates, who reviews, who finalises.

A second example deepens this further. In December 2021, at the Mayo Clinic in Rochester, a pilot decision-support tool analysed early stroke indicators from patient records. Clinicians reported that while the model flagged cases with commendable sensitivity, its greatest value lay in prompting them to revisit borderline symptoms. This behavioural shift is measurable: clinicians increased documented differential diagnoses by an observed margin of roughly 18%, according to the internal audit. The system did not replace expertise; it widened the space for expert reflection. The handshake in this setting was advisory but catalytic. The machine's role was suggestion; the clinician's role was synthesis.

The distinction between suggestion and synthesis illustrates an important boundary. Machines excel at pattern synthesis across vast data landscapes, but humans remain unmatched in contextual interpretation—pain, hesitation, cultural nuance, political constraint. Yet even here, a counter-example sharpens our thinking. In 2020, the Estonian government introduced an automated eligibility check for certain welfare services. The system, trained on administrative records, performed consistently well and reduced processing times. Advocates claimed it demonstrated that contextual interpretation could be automated. Critics noted that the context was narrow: rules-based thresholds, not the lived experience of applicants. The counter-example is instructive: delegation thrives where rules are stable and outcomes auditable; it fractures when ambiguity demands human discernment. The reconciliation is clear. Delegation is not universal; it is conditional on clarity, reversibility, and robust oversight.

The shift from tools to teammates also alters what counts as evidence of competence. In traditional settings, skill is measured by personal output: the engineer who writes elegant code, the analyst who constructs meticulous models, the teacher who crafts compelling lessons. Hybrid work reframes competence as orchestration: the capacity to design the handshake, specify the task, interpret the model's rationale, and decide when to override. This is not less demanding. If anything, it requires a higher standard of judgement. A teammate's suggestion is only as good as the human's ability to contextualise it.

This reframing forces reconsideration of trust. Trust, often invoked abstractly, takes shape as behaviour: whether a pilot checks instrument readings against experience; whether a lawyer scrutinises a generated draft against statute; whether a scientist probes an outlier instead of dismissing it. Trust becomes calibrated rather than assumed. In April 2022, the European Molecular Biology Laboratory in Heidelberg observed that researchers using automated analysis pipelines were more likely to examine flagged anomalies when the interface transparently displayed model confidence intervals. That transparency—an architectural choice—encouraged scrutiny, not complacency. The handshake improved because both sides revealed more of their reasoning.

The implications ripple into education and professional development. Students accustomed to outsourcing initial ideation to assistants may struggle to distinguish a promising direction from a superficially coherent one. Coaches and supervisors report a quiet shift: the challenge is no longer generating options but discriminating among them. The machine offers breadth; the human must supply depth. The distinction matters because delegation at the wrong stage hollows rather than strengthens expertise. Expertise grows through friction—the skilled confrontation with uncertainty. If friction is removed too early, depth erodes.

This relationship, though promising, carries a further tension. Machines are predictable in aggregate yet unpredictable in specifics. They follow statistical gradients, not internal world models. When they produce an unanticipated suggestion, humans may incorrectly attribute intention. The danger is anthropomorphism: assuming a teammate's mind where none exists. In July 2022, a widely discussed incident at Google involved a model producing emotionally resonant dialogue. Some commentators inferred consciousness. Engineers emphasised that correlation, not sentience, drove the responses. The incident illustrated a perennial risk. A teammate-like surface invites over-ascription of agency. The reconciliation again lies in the handshake: explicitly treat the system as pattern synthesis, not moral agent.

This subchapter has introduced the architecture of the spectrum—assistance, collaboration, delegation—and shown how naming roles clarifies responsibility. Yet beneath the framework rests a single guiding tension. When a machine proposes, the human must decide whether the proposal is stimulus or direction. The decision is never trivial. It shapes not only outcomes but capability. Each acceptance or override subtly trains both sides: the model via feedback, the human via habit.

The forward test is simple, though not easy. When a system offers a path, ask: *does this proposal sharpen my judgement or dull it?* The answer marks the line between tool and teammate.

Why This Is Happening Now

In June 2020, at the University of California, Berkeley, a research group led by Rediet Abebe examined a language model's ability to classify social policy abstracts. The model processed thousands of texts in minutes, clustering themes that previously took doctoral researchers weeks to map. The outcome was modest in one sense—a reorganisation of academic literature—but profound in another. The team noticed that the model did not merely speed their workflow; it shifted their starting point. Instead of beginning with preconceived categories, they began with patterns surfaced by the system. A familiar rhythm broke. Human reasoning no longer led alone; it entered a duet shaped by computation. Five words apply here too: *the work is starting differently now.*

The change was not a surprise. By 2020, the cost of running large-scale models had already fallen sharply, and the lab had access to cloud resources unimaginable a decade earlier. What startled the researchers was the quality of the conversational handshake between themselves and the model. They could ask exploratory questions in plain language and receive plausible pathways in return. That fluency was new. The line from tool to partner had crept closer, one interaction at a time. And the question that emerged in their debrief session in Berkeley—*why now?*—has become central to understanding the hybrid turn.

Three forces anchor the answer: the collapse in the cost of prediction, the saturation of digital life into tractable data, and the quiet revolution in interface design. Each force is structural. Each alters what work feels like at the level of the individual task. And each explains why hybrid work will persist far longer than any particular model generation.

The first is computational cost. The curve is not aesthetic; it is measurable. In 2011, training a model with 100 million parameters required dedicated hardware and substantial institutional backing. By 2023, models with tens of billions of parameters could be fine-tuned on rented clusters for a fraction of that cost. The shift resembles what economists describe as a "general-purpose technology shock"—a drop in price that unlocks new behaviours. A visible example came from OpenAI's January 2021 release of DALL·E's initial research preview. Artists in London, New York and Sydney began experimenting with image generation not as an exotic tool but as part of daily exploration. The behaviour to watch was not uptake; it was iteration speed. Ideas that once died on the sketchpad because they were too slow to test became viable. When iteration accelerates, conception itself changes.

Compute alone, however, explains little without data. Digital life has matured into a dense archive of human patterns—contracts, medical notes, public conversations, transport flows, supply chains, creative works. The phenomenon is mixed in its consequences but undeniable in its scale. Wikimedia's 2022 transparency report documented over 6.5 million edits per month across its language projects. GitHub's activity logs in the same year reported more than 90 million pull requests. These are not random artefacts; they are structured expressions of what people know, build, argue, and maintain. Models trained on such data inherit a statistical map of collective behaviour. They do not understand intention, but they capture regularity and variation with granular accuracy. The implication is practical: systems can produce plausible next steps because they have observed countless prior ones.

A second example illustrates how data expands capability. In August 2019, the Royal Free London NHS Foundation Trust evaluated a machine-learning tool to detect acute kidney injury from patient records. The model flagged anomalies earlier than manual review, prompting clinicians to revisit borderline cases. The behavioural metric was unambiguous: earlier intervention occurred in 11% more flagged cases, according to the Trust's audit. This improvement relied not on abstract "intelligence" but on the mundane accumulation of digitised clinical signals. Data density became predictive power.

Yet a limitation tempers this enthusiasm. Data can reproduce systemic fragilities. When Amazon famously halted its experimental hiring model in 2017 after discovering biased patterns, the lesson was clear. Rich data is not inherently good data. Saturation does not mean fairness. The limitation, however, does not negate the structural forces driving hybrid work; it refines them. It signals that the move from tools to teammates demands curation, not blind acceptance. When the dataset is skewed, the handshake falters.

Alongside compute and data sits the third force: interface design. This change often hides in plain sight. Command lines have given way to conversational agents; rigid dashboards to adaptive canvases; modal alerts to contextual cues. If one wants to see interface transformation in sharp relief, consider the December 2022 introduction of GitHub Copilot's chat mode. Developers in Toronto and Singapore reported that their "debugging posture" shifted. Instead of toggling between documentation, search engines, and code, they held an iterative dialogue with the assistant directly inside the editor. The visible behaviour was subtle: fewer context switches, more in-flow problem solving. But the cognitive effect mattered. The machine stopped being a peripheral adviser and became a proximal collaborator.

Interface matters because it shapes agency. A system that sits at arm's length demands translation; a system that sits inside the workflow participates. And participation alters perception. Designers at Google's Zurich office noted during internal trials in 2021 that users were more likely to probe a model's uncertainty when confidence scores appeared dynamically rather than in static reports. A small interface choice—progressive disclosure of uncertainty—improved interpretability. The handshake strengthened because the system revealed more of its internal gradations.

The motif of the handshake threads through each of these forces. Compute lowers the cost of extending a hand; data thickens the palm with patterns; interfaces determine how the grip feels. The handshake becomes firmer or weaker depending on design. And its character matters because hybrid work is not merely technical coordination; it is a behavioural contract. When a researcher in Mumbai asks a model to test a hypothesis outline, the question is not only whether the system produces a coherent structure; it is whether the researcher can sense where the system's boundaries lie. A handshake clarifies boundaries.

The durability of hybrid work becomes clearer when viewed against historical counterpoints. In the early 1990s, expert systems promised a wave of knowledge automation. They did not deliver because rules-based logic struggled with messy reality. Tasks involving subtle cues or tacit knowledge slipped through the brittle structures. The counter-example is often raised as evidence that the current wave will fade similarly. Yet the comparison is weak. The brittleness then stemmed from limited pattern recognition; the capacity to generalise from data was shallow. Today's systems, while imperfect, synthesise patterns across domains rather than rely on enumerated rules. Their failure modes differ in nature and require different forms of oversight.

A second counter-example comes from the cryptocurrency boom of 2017. Enthusiasts proclaimed decentralised finance as the future of all transactions. Much of the infrastructure proved speculative, brittle, or unsuited for everyday use. Critics invoke this example to cast doubt on AI's staying power. But again, the analogy misfires. The drivers of hybrid intelligence—cheap prediction, ubiquitous data, naturalistic interfaces—are not speculative bets. They are embedded features of digital infrastructure. They behave more like electricity or fibre-optic connectivity: enabling conditions rather than isolated innovations.

The core development of hybrid work lies in how these enabling conditions reshape behaviour. When predicting the next word costs fractions of a penny, people draft differently. When image interpretation is available on handheld devices, clinicians triage differently. When developers can query ambiguous errors conversationally, debugging changes. These are not personal quirks; they are structural shifts in practice. And practice shapes norms.

Consider two contrasting examples. In April 2022, the Financial Times newsroom in London tested an internal summarisation assistant. Reporters described using it to surface angles during early-stage research but emphasised that final narratives remained stubbornly human. The assistant widened possibility but did not define direction. Contrast that with a 2023 study at the Wharton School observing customer-support agents using generative assistants. The agents not only answered faster; they converged on stylistic patterns seeded by the model. Behaviour shaped by prediction became standardised. The implication is not uniformity but tension. Hybrid work amplifies both divergence and convergence; it depends on how humans steer the handshake.

The tension deepens when we examine decision-making. Efficiency is not an abstraction; it shows up as shorter queues, fewer revision cycles, quicker synthesis. Risk, too, becomes visible. A model that confidently supplies a flawed argument can nudge decisions off course. The behavioural metric here is override frequency—how often a user rejects a model's proposal. In internal logs at an academic publisher in Oxford (2023), editors overrode automated fact-suggestions in 27% of flagged cases. Override frequency is a crude but illuminating indicator of hybrid health. A low override rate may mean high accuracy; it may also mean uncritical acceptance. The distinction is behavioural, not philosophical.

This raises a harder question: why will hybrid work outlast any individual model? The answer lies in feedback loops. Every interaction—whether prompted, revised, or overridden—feeds back into organisational behaviour. Teams begin to shape tasks to suit the strengths of their systems. Universities revise reading lists knowing students now consult assistants for summaries. Law firms adopt drafting templates that integrate suggestions directly into workflows. These structural adaptations persist even when models change. The handshake survives the hand.

Two additional examples underline this continuity. In November 2021, the Estonian Ministry of Economic Affairs logged citizen interactions with its automated advisory system. Even when upgraded versions rolled out, citizen behaviour remained consistent: people treated the system as a first pass, not a final authority. A cultural pattern emerged. Meanwhile, in March 2022, a publishing start-up in Copenhagen integrated a writing assistant into editorial pipelines. Staff reported that even after switching vendors, the structure of collaboration—draft, propose, refine, verify—remained stable. Tools changed; habits endured.

A limitation deserves attention. Hybrid work can entrench over-reliance if humans disengage from difficult steps. A Stanford study (May 2023) found that students using summarising assistants produced more coherent essays but struggled to recall key arguments days later. Delegation reshaped effort. The counterpoint is not to reject hybrid work but to refine it. When the handshake becomes limp—when the system takes more than the human intends—the result is skill atrophy. The reconciliation is architectural. Systems must expose uncertainty, not mask it; humans must remain responsible for the interpretive core. Hybrid work persists because it can be designed, not because it is inevitable.

As these forces converge, the question becomes sharper. When prediction is cheap, when data is abundant, when interfaces are fluent, how should humans shape the handshake? The tension is visible in every workplace experimenting with assistants: should the system propose first, or should the human? Should the model narrow options, or widen them? Should speed trump exploration, or should exploration remain sacred?

A forward test emerges from these tensions: *when you invite a system into a task, does it stretch your thinking or compress it?* That question—answered repeatedly, case by case—will determine whether hybrid work enriches judgement or erodes it.

What Should Stay Human by Default

In July 2017, at the Royal Free London NHS Foundation Trust, a junior doctor stood over a patient's bed with a phone in her hand. The device buzzed with an alert from Streams, the acute kidney injury app developed with DeepMind. The screen showed a risk score, trend lines, creatinine values, recommended urgency. The numbers looked worrying. Yet, before ordering fluids or changing medication, she did something simple and telling. She put the phone in her pocket, pulled back the curtain, and spoke to the patient. The conversation took less than a minute, but it changed her decision. The man was more stable than the graph suggested, and there was crucial information in his voice, his posture, his hesitation when describing pain. The app had triaged. The clinician still decided. The final say remained human.

That same month, the UK Information Commissioner's Office concluded that the data-sharing arrangement underpinning Streams had breached data protection law. The investigation did not allege harm to patients, but it drew a sharp line: even well-intentioned AI in a hospital must respect consent, fairness, and transparency. The message was clear. Speed and sensitivity matter in triage. Yet the authority to initiate, the duty to explain, and the blame for failure still rest with people who can answer for their choices.

The scene in that ward captures the tension at the heart of hybrid intelligence. When systems can monitor thousands of patients, scan millions of documents, or model complex risks, the temptation is to ask: *why not delegate more?* The better question is narrower and more demanding: *what must remain human by default, even when machines are competent, fast, and cheap?* The answer defines not just a safety policy, but a boundary around dignity.

Start with responsibility. Responsibility is not an abstraction; it shows up in signatures and names. It is the consultant who signs the discharge letter, the regulator who approves a safety case, the chief executive who appears at the press conference when something goes wrong. Hybrid systems muddy this line if we let them. A model suggests a course of action, a person clicks "approve", and when harm occurs, each side points to the other. That diffusion feels convenient. It is also corrosive.

The Royal Free example shows responsibility in action. The Streams app could escalate cases, yet it could not admit a patient, order treatment, or talk to a family. Those decisions required a clinician who could look the patient in the eye and justify the trade-offs. The implicit rule was simple: no alert without an accountable human ready to interpret and, if necessary, resist it. Name that rule clearly and it becomes a default-human domain: *ultimate responsibility for consequential outcomes stays with people.*

The explanation is straightforward. Only humans sit inside moral and legal frameworks that can hold them to account. Only humans can stand in a courtroom, write an apology, lose a licence, or change career because of a decision. A system can be patched or retired; it cannot feel remorse. The implication is practical. Whenever a task carries irreversible impact—sending a child into care, denying life-saving treatment, authorising a weapons release—there must be a named human responsible, even if a model contributed heavily to the analysis. The last signature belongs to someone who can be questioned.

The second default-human domain is consent. Consent is not a banner statement on a website; it is a sequence of behaviours. A person is told what data will be used, for what purpose, and with which consequences; they have a meaningful choice, and they exercise it. Cambridge Analytica's use of Facebook data, exposed in 2018, illustrated the opposite. Millions of profiles were harvested and inferred upon without explicit, informed permission. People discovered, years later, that their preferences had fuelled political micro-targeting they never agreed to participate in. Whatever one thinks of the electoral outcomes, the consent relationship was broken.

Contrast this breach with the approach of some Scandinavian health authorities. The Norwegian Directorate of eHealth, for example, has emphasised granular, revocable consent for secondary use of patient data since the late 2010s. Patients can see which research projects their records support, withdraw consent, and track access over time. The behaviour that embodies respect here is visibility. Patients can log in and check. They can say *no more*.

Consent becomes especially fraught when models infer sensitive attributes from apparently mundane traces. An advertising system that guesses pregnancy from search queries, or sexual orientation from browsing patterns, may never show its workings. Yet its predictions alter what a person sees, what prices they pay, what opportunities appear. Delegating those inferences without robust consent erases a crucial human prerogative: the right to decide who may draw conclusions about one's intimate life. The implication is stark. In domains where inference touches identity—health, sexuality, political belief—consent should default to human-controlled and explicit, not buried in a terms-of-service clause.

The third domain is values. Values surface whenever rules do not suffice. They appear in the judge's sentencing remarks, the ethics committee's deliberations, the editor's choice of what to publish and what to omit. They also lie behind apparently technical parameters: the acceptable false positive rate in a fraud system, the weight placed on different types of error in a diagnostic model, the threshold for "harmful content" in a content filter.

One named example brings values into focus. The Dutch childcare benefit scandal, which culminated politically in 2019 and contributed to the resignation of the Dutch government in January 2021, centred on an algorithmic risk system used to flag possible fraud. Thousands of families—disproportionately from minority backgrounds—were wrongly labelled as fraudulent, leading to severe financial and psychological damage. The system did not invent discrimination; it amplified biases embedded in data and institutional priorities. Crucially, the value choices—what counted as suspicious, what warranted aggressive recovery—had been framed as neutral administrative settings. No one signed their name next to them.

The scandal's implication for hybrid intelligence is not simply that "algorithms can be biased". It is that value-laden decisions cannot be outsourced to statistical optimisation without explicit human authorship. Someone must say, aloud and on record: *these are the trade-offs we accept; these are the harms we will not tolerate; these groups we will protect even at cost.* Delegation of calculation is acceptable; delegation of conscience is not. The last signature here is a moral one.

Exception handling is the fourth default-human domain. Systems are good at the median case. People notice the rare, the weird, the almost-but-not-quite. An autopilot holds an aircraft stable through turbulence; the pilot earns their salary when multiple failures combine and the textbook runs out. This pattern repeats across sectors. In 2015, the Boeing 737 MAX's MCAS software became the subject of intense scrutiny after two crashes in Indonesia and Ethiopia. Investigators highlighted how assumptions about pilot behaviour and exception handling had been baked into the automation, without fully accounting for how real crews would respond under stress. Here, the failure was not simply technical; it was a misallocation of who should handle rare but catastrophic scenarios.

Exception handling is visible in small gestures: the customer-support agent who recognises that a distressed caller does not fit the script, the social worker who sees that a family's situation is more complex than the risk score suggests, the cybersecurity analyst who treats a "low severity" alert as suspicious because of timing. If hybrid systems automate away exposure to the unusual, humans gradually lose the feel for edge cases. When the exceptional arrives, no one is ready. The implication is straightforward. We should keep humans in the loop precisely where patterns thin out—where the distribution tails are long, the stakes are high, and the reference cases are few.

The hospital triage setting brings all four domains into a single frame. Automated systems can parse vital signs, lab results, and histories faster than any individual clinician. They can rank patients by risk, highlight subtle trends, and trigger alarms. The benefits are real: reduced time to intervention, more consistent detection of deterioration, better resource allocation. Yet automation cannot replace the bedside conversation that integrates clinical insight with what matters to the patient.

Imagine two patients in the emergency department. The triage system flags both as high risk based on similar biometrics. One is a young parent desperate to return home quickly; the other is an older person with a complex history and an expressed wish to avoid aggressive interventions. Responsibility demands that a clinician, not a model, explain the options and record the decisions. Consent requires that each patient understands the trade-offs in language that respects their fears and hopes. Values determine whether scarce intensive-care capacity goes to likely years gained, suffering avoided, or social circumstances. Exception handling is tested when one patient's symptoms do not match any standard pattern, and the clinician's intuition says, *keep them longer, something is wrong.*

A credible counter-example sharpens the boundaries. Some domains function safely with extensive automation and minimal human input. High-frequency trading systems, for instance, execute orders in microseconds; human traders cannot meaningfully intervene in each transaction. Here, responsibility is managed structurally—through capital requirements, circuit breakers, and regulatory oversight—rather than per decision. Aviation autopilot systems operate much of a long-haul flight without continuous manual control. Pilots monitor and intervene at defined points. These examples show that not every decision can or should be inspected individually by a person. The reconciliation lies in where we place the last signature. For trading, it sits with those who design and approve the strategy and controls, not with the algorithm. For aircraft, it sits with the captain and the safety regulators, not the autopilot manufacturer alone.

The quiet motif that runs through these domains is that last signature. Who signs off? Who stands up? Who can be questioned? Whenever a design choice moves that signature from a person to a system—or hides it entirely—something important is lost. The hospital junior who pockets the phone and chooses to talk; the Norwegian patient who withdraws consent from a research registry; the Dutch official who now has to sign a fairness impact assessment; the pilot who decides to disengage automation during an unanticipated storm—these behaviours are the living proof of human default domains.

This is not an argument against delegation. It is an argument for guardrails built on a simple test. Before you allow a system to act with minimal supervision, ask four questions. *Who will answer if this goes wrong? Who gave permission, and can they change their mind? Whose values shaped the thresholds and trade-offs? Who will cope when something happens that the system has never seen before?* If the answers are unclear, the task belongs, by default, to people.

A Vocabulary for Co-Intelligence

In 2015, at Amazon's headquarters in Seattle, a recruiting experiment quietly stalled. For several years, the company had been testing an internal hiring system that scored CVs and suggested which candidates should progress. By 2018, as Reuters reported, the project was essentially shelved: the model had learned to downgrade CVs that included signals associated with women, such as attendance at all-female colleges. Engineers tried to fix it. They adjusted features, masked certain terms, inspected outputs. Yet when they discussed the system with HR colleagues, the conversation kept slipping into vagueness. Was the problem "the algorithm", "the data", "the rules", or the "way it was used"? Different groups meant different things by the same words. And when bias entered the headlines, the organisation had no shared grammar to describe where it had arisen, who had set the boundaries, or where responsibility ought to rest. Words decide where blame lands.

That episode is often recalled as a cautionary tale about biased data. It is also a story about language. When a system moves from tool to teammate, the organisation needs precise terms for what it asked the system to do, what limits it set, how it reacted when those limits were stressed, and how each decision can be retraced. Without that vocabulary, accountability dissolves into finger-pointing. "The AI did it" becomes a comfortable fiction. The work of co-intelligence becomes guesswork.

Shared language does something more subtle as well. It makes disagreements visible. If a hiring manager says "the model recommended this candidate" and a data scientist replies "no, the model produced a score under this policy", the difference is not pedantry. It is a boundary. One describes a teammate with opinions; the other describes a constrained system applying codified rules. Only when both can point to a clear set of terms—prompt, policy, escalation, provenance, trace—can they see where judgement begins and ends.

The prompt is where the handshake starts. In hybrid systems, a prompt is not just a question; it is a design brief. It encodes the task, the constraints, the tone, the evidence required. When a recruiter writes, "Rank these CVs from best to worst", the system will do so, even if "best" is undefined. When they write, "Identify candidates whose experience matches these job criteria; ignore names, pronouns, and schools; list reasons," they are narrowing the space of interpretation. The difference is visible in behaviour. In the first case, recruiters debate mysterious scores. In the second, they compare explicit

rationales to their own.
Name this clearly and the implication follows. A sloppy prompt creates space for hidden value judgements and historical biases to creep in. A precise prompt forces the team to surface what they care about and what they wish to exclude. The vocabulary here is operational: people do not argue about "bias" in the abstract; they rewrite the instruction that the system sees. The prompt becomes an artefact that can be reviewed, versioned, and audited.

Policy operates a level above. Where prompts are per-task instructions, policy sets the boundaries within which any prompt must sit. A policy might state that no hiring model may use gender, race, or proxies for them as input features; that scores must never be the sole basis for a decision; that certain roles (for example, those involving contact with vulnerable people) require manual review regardless of model confidence. The European Commission's proposed AI Act, published in Brussels in April 2021, reflects this trend by treating some uses of AI in employment as "high-risk" and subject to governance requirements. Policy, in that sense, is not rhetoric. It shows up when a system refuses to run a prompt that violates constraints, when logging is enforced, when escalation is triggered automatically.
Explain policy in those terms and its implication becomes clear. Policy is where organisational values collide with model capabilities. Without a word for it, teams default to ad hoc decisions. With a word for it, they can ask, "What is our hiring policy for this model?" and expect a concrete document, not a shrug. The conversation shifts from "can the AI do this?" to "have we authorised it to, and on what terms?"

Escalation is the bridge between automated suggestion and human override. It answers a simple question: *when should this move up a level?* A content moderation team at Facebook's Dublin office, for example, has long had explicit escalation paths for borderline material—certain combinations of keywords, user history, and complaint patterns send posts to human reviewers. In hiring, escalation rules might dictate that any candidate whose score crosses a threshold but whose CV exhibits unusual patterns—for instance, long career breaks or cross-sector switches—must be reviewed by a human panel. Show escalation in practice and you see it in behaviour: a recruiter clicks "request review" because the explanation feels off; an automated alert routes a case to the diversity officer when demographic patterns deviate from expectations. The implication is structural. Escalation protects exceptions and edge cases from being flattened by averages. Yet without a shared term, teams rely on informal habits. One person escalates out of caution; another never does. Naming escalation allows organisations to measure it: how many cases moved up, from whom, and with what outcomes.

Provenance tells the story of origins. It is the answer to "where did this come from?" In 2016, when ProPublica published its investigation into the COMPAS recidivism risk scores used in Broward County, Florida, one of the central criticisms was opacity. Judges and defendants struggled to know what data the scores relied upon and which historical patterns they reflected. Provenance, if it had been a mandatory part of the vocabulary, would have forced the system's designers to specify sources: which arrest records, which time spans, which jurisdictions, which cleaning steps. In hiring assistants, provenance might describe the training corpus (public job ads, internal performance reviews, historical hiring decisions), the time period covered, and the demographic composition of those examples.
Explain provenance in these concrete terms and the implication follows. Without it, any claim about fairness, relevance, or risk rests on trust alone. With it, critics can argue about specific choices: "Why did we train on pre-2010 data, when our workforce has changed so much since?" or "Why are start-up job ads over-represented relative to public sector roles?" Provenance turns vague discomfort into precise critique. It also gives regulators a handle. When the UK Information Commissioner's Office assessed the Royal Free–

DeepMind collaboration in 2017, one of their concerns was the lack of clarity about which patient records were used and for what purposes. Provenance, if properly recorded, would have made that assessment faster and more transparent.

Trace completes the set. Where provenance describes origins, trace describes the path. It records how a specific output came to be: which version of the model was used, which prompt was sent, which contextual data was attached, which policies applied, which human interventions occurred along the way. Think of it as the flight recorder of co-intelligence. In financial markets, this kind of trace already exists. Regulators such as the UK's Financial Conduct Authority require firms to reconstruct trading decisions: which order was placed, when, by whom, under what strategy. In hybrid systems, trace plays a similar role. When a hiring assistant recommends one candidate over another, trace should allow the organisation to reconstruct the reasoning chain as far as possible. The implication is both protective and cultural. Protective, because trace enables post-hoc review when something goes wrong. Cultural, because the very act of tracing alters behaviour. Managers who know their prompts, overrides, and comments will be visible to future auditors tend to take more care. In many domains, that care is the difference between a system that quietly perpetuates harm and one that can be corrected.

Now bring these terms together in the concrete setting of a hiring audit. Imagine a technology firm in Manchester in late 2023 that has deployed a language-model-based assistant to help shortlist candidates for software roles. Concerns have arisen from staff groups about potential gender and ethnic bias. The leadership convenes an audit team: HR, data science, legal, and a staff representative. Without a vocabulary for co-intelligence, the conversation risks becoming defensive. "The algorithm is neutral." "We only use it to save time." "Recruiters can always override." Each statement hides more than it reveals.

With shared language, the team proceeds differently. They begin with prompts. They collect the actual instructions recruiters have been using: not the hypothetical ones in design documents, but the messy, real-world text. They discover prompts such as "Score higher if candidate has strong cultural fit with our existing engineering team" and "Down-rank candidates with multiple short stints". The first phrase is a known red flag; the second may penalise those with non-traditional career paths. The prompt review makes patterns of bias visible not as accusations but as modifiable text. They move to policy. They ask, "What formal rules did we set for this assistant?" It turns out there is a general corporate diversity statement, but no specific model policy. No explicit prohibition on using proxies for gender or race. No formal requirement that human reviewers compare suggested lists against demographic baselines. Naming policy exposes this absence. The team drafts a concrete model policy: no input fields may capture name, age, or school; the assistant may only operate on skills and experience descriptors; all outputs must include explanatory factors; every hiring cycle must include a demographic review by the diversity officer. Provenance becomes the next focus. The data scientist explains that they fine-tuned the assistant on three years of the company's own hiring decisions—decisions made in a period when women were under-represented in engineering roles. That choice, unnamed, had effectively taught the model to emulate a biased past. Once labelled as provenance, it can be challenged. The audit team decides to augment the training set with external, curated examples that showcase high-performing engineers from diverse backgrounds, and to exclude certain historical decisions that the company now views as misaligned with its inclusion goals. Trace then allows them to select a sample of past hiring rounds and reconstruct why some candidates were rejected. They review the system's top ten recommendations for a particular job, alongside its rationales, the recruiter's notes, and the final hiring decision. They look for visible behaviours: how often did recruiters override the model when it down-ranked women? Did certain teams rely more heavily on the assistant? Did override patterns differ by region or manager? These are not abstract questions about fairness; they are empirical questions about how this specific system interacted with these specific humans.

Escalation rules mature in the process. The team agrees that any candidate flagged as a strong match but belonging to an under-represented group must trigger an additional review if the recruiter decides to reject them. Conversely, if the assistant consistently scores candidates from a particular background lower, that pattern itself must escalate to the oversight committee. Escalation here is not a vague invitation. It is a documented behaviour: when this metric crosses this line, this person must act.

A counter-example clarifies why vocabulary must be used with care. Small organisations sometimes respond to these concepts by over-formalising. A research lab of ten people in Vienna, for instance, might define elaborate policies, logging requirements, and escalation paths that slow experiments to a crawl. The language becomes a bureaucratic shield rather than a tool for thinking. This is a real risk. It reflects a misuse of grammar, not its necessity. Reconciliation lies in proportionality. The same words—prompt, policy, escalation, provenance, trace—can scale with context. A two-person team might record prompts and traces lightly in a shared document, while a bank subjected to regulatory scrutiny must treat them as formal artefacts. The vocabulary is common; the implementation differs.

The quiet motif here is the contract hidden inside the conversation. Every time someone says "the AI suggested this" or "the model decided that", a tacit contract about roles and limits is in play. Without explicit terms, that contract is unstable. People mis-remember what they asked, exaggerate what the system promised, and underestimate their own agency. With a vocabulary for co-intelligence, the contract can be written down: this is the prompt we used; this is the policy it sat within; this is when we escalated; this is where the data came from; this is how we retraced the path.

The unresolved tension, of course, is how far to push this precision. Language can clarify or chill. Too little, and we sleepwalk into opaque dependence. Too much, and we smother experimentation in paperwork. The forward test is deceptively simple: *after a failure or a success, can your team describe, in shared terms, what the system was asked to do, what boundaries constrained it, where the data came from, and how the final decision emerged?* If the answer is no, more vocabulary is not a flourish. It is a prerequisite for trustworthy co-intelligence.

Chapter 2
Minds, Models, and Feedback

The editor noticed it first. A junior reporter at a national newspaper had begun filing drafts that were suspiciously crisp—polished paragraphs, neat transitions, tidy arguments that sounded faintly unlike her. One afternoon, he walked past her desk just as she nudged her cursor above a half-formed sentence. A small window glowed at the edge of her screen: a writing assistant offering a revised version, then another, and another still. Each suggestion was tidy, plausible, and almost frictionless. She clicked, clicked again, and the draft seemed to assemble itself. The editor watched her hesitate, as if torn between gratitude for the speed and discomfort at the ease. When he asked later what she thought of the tool, she gave a laugh that landed somewhere between pride and apology. "It helps," she said, "but I worry I'm forgetting how to write."

That small confession—half-joke, half-warning—captures a quiet shift at the centre of modern cognition. We have always leaned on scaffolds: notebooks, diagrams, teachers, colleagues. Now our scaffolds anticipate, complete, and propose. They are generous, and sometimes too generous. They spare us labour, but they also steal the very struggle through which expertise forms. A draft written without wrestling ideas into order is quicker, but possibly thinner. A student who reads only the summary may miss the texture of the argument. A lawyer who accepts a model's confidently phrased clause may unwittingly import a risk. The paradox grows sharper each year: the more intelligent our tools become, the more careful we must be in deciding what work they should do and what work we must keep for ourselves.

This chapter steps into that tension. It begins with the human mind—with the patterns by which we learn, remember, and offload. Cognitive science tells us that scaffolds accelerate mastery, but it also tells us that overuse breeds dependency. Chunking compresses complexity into graspable units; spaced retrieval strengthens memory by inviting forgetting before restoring it; cognitive offloading frees attention but risks hollowing skill. These processes are not abstract. They shape everyday life: the student who underlines everything because the notes app remembers; the project manager who trusts the assistant's checklist more than her own intuition; the researcher who never sits long enough with a problem before asking a model for an outline. The mind adapts to its environment. Give it a companion that anticipates too much, and it adapts further still.

Yet humans are not alone in this learning dance. The models we now work with also generalise, interpolate, misread, and fail. They excel at the centre of distributions and stumble at the edges. A clause that appears only in a few contracts over a decade is far more difficult to classify than the common terms that flood the training set. One legal team learned this painfully when their document assistant began mislabelling a rare indemnity clause as a termination condition. It took them three weeks to notice. The failure was not malicious; it was statistical. But the silence of that failure—the absence of a raised hand—revealed how brittle collaboration becomes when only one party knows when it is guessing. The promise of hybrid intelligence rests not on avoiding errors, but on making them visible, traceable, and corrigible.

Visibility comes from feedback. Feedback is the engine of hybrid systems, though it is often mistaken for decoration. A rating, an example, a refined prompt, a corrected output—these seem small, but each shapes the next iteration. A newsroom that uses an assistant to summarise breaking stories soon learns that the initial outputs matter less than the adjustments that follow. Editors craft evaluation sets, run comparison drafts, revert to earlier versions when the model drifts, and negotiate with it in a rhythm of refinement. They are not simply using a tool; they are teaching it, and being taught in return. The conversation becomes a loop, not a command.

Yet no loop works without calibrated trust, and trust in hybrid intelligence must be earned, not assumed. Fluency seduces. Polished sentences, neatly structured arguments, or neatly formatted tables can disguise shaky logic or fictional data. Trust must therefore attach not to the surface of the output, but to its provenance, versioning, and verification. Finance teams learned this long ago. Many now operate dual-channel verification systems: one assistant drafts or analyses; another, isolated from the first, performs an independent check. If the two disagree, humans investigate. This small, disciplined friction prevents the single most common hybrid failure: copy-and-paste acceptance of a plausible but incorrect claim.

The wider story is this: cognition—human and machine—is a system of scaffolds, shortcuts, and feedback loops. When these loops align, work becomes richer, faster, more thoughtful. When they diverge, we slide into complacency. The stakes are not trivial. We are not merely optimising workflows; we are shaping habits of mind.

To understand the interplay between minds and models, we will follow several threads through the chapter. The first explores how humans outsource memory and reasoning, often wisely but sometimes too eagerly. The second examines how models behave under uncertainty—how they interpolate, extrapolate, and occasionally hallucinate—and what this means for the humans reading their outputs. The third turns to feedback: how to design signals that improve systems and strengthen human judgement rather than dilute it. And the final thread deals with trust: how to verify, cross-check, and maintain a healthy scepticism without slipping into paranoia or rechecking every line manually.

Threaded through it all is a subtle motif: the scaffold. Scaffolds are temporary by design. They let us reach, build, and understand. But a scaffold becomes dangerous when we mistake it for the structure itself. Hybrid intelligence asks us to notice when the scaffold is helping us grow—and when it is quietly taking our place.

The questions ahead are not purely technical. They are practical, ethical, and psychological. How much struggle is necessary for mastery? When does offloading enrich our thinking, and when does it empty it? How do we design feedback loops that sharpen both sides of the partnership? And how do we keep trust dynamic, conditional, and earned?

If the first chapter of this book introduced the handshake between humans and systems, this one looks closely at the arms behind it—how minds adapt, how models behave, and how the exchange between them strengthens or weakens our capacity to think clearly. The answers will not be simple. But they will be grounding. Because the future of hybrid work will belong not to those who offload the most, but to those who understand what should be shared, what should be checked, and what must still be done by the mind itself.

How Humans Learn with Scaffolds

In October 1885, in Freiburg, Hermann Ebbinghaus sat at his desk reciting lists of nonsense syllables—*ZAK, BAF, LIP*—and charting how quickly he forgot them. He was alone, methodical, and quietly reshaping the study of memory. His experiments produced the now-famous forgetting curve, showing that most information decays within hours unless revisited. Yet Ebbinghaus also discovered something subtler: when he broke material into smaller groups and spaced the reviews, learning accelerated without overwhelming the mind. Chunking and spacing acted as scaffolds—temporary supports that helped him climb a mental structure more efficiently. The notes in his diary record a curious tension. The scaffolds made learning easier. They also made it easier *not* to learn.

That tension now defines much of modern cognition. In June 2022, at the University of Cambridge's Faculty of Education, a small study of undergraduate revision habits found that students who relied heavily on digital note-taking apps reviewed more often but retained less conceptual detail. The apps generated summaries, highlighted key concepts, even produced automated flashcards. But when asked to reconstruct arguments without prompts, these students performed inconsistently. Their devices remembered *for* them, and the act of remembering *by* them weakened. A scaffold had become a substitute.

Scaffolds shape every corner of human learning. Yet not all scaffolds serve us well, and not all dependencies announce themselves. A short prompt from a writing assistant nudges a sentence into shape. A search engine retrieves half-recalled facts. A task manager arranges our day more elegantly than we ever could. These aids are welcome until they are not. The question pressing upon hybrid intelligence is simple: *how far can we lean before we stop building our own strength?* That question will return like a quiet motif, a beam we keep testing for load.

Begin with chunking, the most natural scaffold of all. Show its power and the pattern becomes unmistakable. Chess masters, as Adriaan de Groot demonstrated in Amsterdam in 1946, do not hold the board in individual squares; they store arrangements—attacks, defences, openings—compressed into familiar units. When asked to recall random positions, their advantage evaporates. Chunking is not a superpower; it is structure applied to chaos. Cognitive scientists have replicated this phenomenon across domains: jazz improvisers in New York in the 1950s, medical students analysing chest X-rays in London in the 1990s, even firefighters in Gary Klein's observational studies of emergency crews in the 1980s. When the mind encounters structured complexity, it seeks to compress.

Explain chunking and its implication becomes clear. It is a scaffold that reduces cognitive load, but only when we do the grouping ourselves. If an external system chunks too early—summarising before we struggle—it steals the moment in which comprehension forms. A document assistant that condenses a twenty-page report into ten bullet points may feel efficient; the danger is visible behaviour. The analyst who reads the bullets nods along but cannot later recall the causal links or the exceptions. Efficiency masks erosion.

Spaced retrieval works differently but carries the same motif. Ebbinghaus showed that memory strengthens when the mind moves between forgetting and remembering. Barbara Oakley's teaching experiments in Rochester in the early 2010s confirmed that students who deliberately spaced problem sets retained core techniques months longer than those who practised intensively in a short burst. Retrieval is labour. It requires the learner to reconstruct, not merely re-read. Yet many modern tools soften that labour. A note-taking app that shows yesterday's highlights each morning, or a reading assistant that displays definitions on hover, removes the tiny moment of friction in which a memory is tested. When the test vanishes, the trace fades.

Consider a concrete metric. In 2021, a team at the University of Tokyo studied language learners using apps that automatically surfaced vocabulary before students reached the point of struggle. Review sessions became more pleasant; quiz performance improved after each session; long-term retention, however, fell. The behaviour that mattered was not the number of reviews but the absence of retrieval effort. The scaffold carried too much of the weight.

Cognitive offloading is yet broader. Show it, and you see it everywhere: writing lists to remember tasks; drawing diagrams to clarify thought; bookmarking articles for later; searching instead of recalling. Cognitive offloading has deep historical roots. Socrates worried that writing itself would weaken memory. Medieval monks in scriptoria externalised knowledge into marginalia. But digital scaffolds extend offloading to a degree that would have startled even the most prolific scholastics. The act of remembering shifts from internal reconstruction to external lookup.

Name this tendency clearly. It is not laziness; it is design. Interfaces encourage offloading because friction feels unfriendly. Explain the mechanism: when external supports grow too convenient, we develop *transactive memory*—a term from Daniel Wegner in 1985 describing how people remember who knows things rather than remembering the things themselves. In a team, this is healthy. In an individual, when the "other knower" is a tool, the implication becomes sharper. We become skilled at locating information but less skilled at reconstructing it independently. A manager who relies on a project assistant to recall every dependency may find her situational awareness thinning. A researcher who stores all insights in a common note-taking system may struggle to articulate the argument unaided.

The motif returns here: how far can we lean? Cognitive offloading becomes damaging when the tool replaces the mental manoeuvre rather than supporting it. The risk becomes visible in small decisions. A student sees a long reading and immediately generates a summary. A writer asks a model to brainstorm themes before forming a view. A policy analyst offloads the first draft of a briefing to an assistant and edits rather than creates. These habits accumulate. Over time, the scaffolds stay in place long after the structure should stand on its own.

Historical examples illuminate why scaffolds must be temporary. In 1943, during pilot training in Kansas, the US Army Air Forces introduced a checklists programme after repeated accidents were traced to memory lapses during take-off. The checklist became a *permanent* scaffold because the task—flying a complex aircraft—was too high-stakes to rely on memory alone. Contrast that with the reliance on phrasebooks by novice codebreakers in Bletchley Park in 1940. The books were designed to disappear as fluency emerged. Alan Turing's team explicitly instructed trainees to stop using the guides once they could "hear" patterns internally. The limitation here is important. Some scaffolds must persist because stakes and complexity demand externalisation. Others must fade for mastery to develop. The reconciliation lies in context: scaffolds must match the nature of the task, not the convenience of the moment.

One credible counter-example shows the nuance. In 2018, at the University of Copenhagen, researchers examined whether medical trainees who relied on diagnostic checklists performed worse in subsequent unaided assessments. Surprisingly, they did not. The checklist improved accuracy even when later removed. The behaviour explained the result: trainees used the checklist to deepen attention, not replace it. They paused, compared, and evaluated. The scaffold guided rather than carried. That distinction is the hinge. Offloading that sharpens attention is supportive; offloading that bypasses attention is corrosive.

Digital note-taking apps offer a practical lens for examining this hinge. These apps promise perfect recall. They sync across devices, generate backlinks, surface related notes, and summon summaries instantly. They are, in many ways, marvels of cognitive engineering. Yet they produce a quiet behavioural pattern worth measuring. People take more notes and revisit them less. The volume rises; the digestion falls. In 2020, researchers at the University of Michigan tracked students using popular apps across a semester. They found that the median student created over 1,200 individual notes but re-read fewer than 60 by term's end. The tool became a hoarding mechanism, not a learning one.

A short exercise can help identify when such scaffolds have tipped from support to substitution. Think of a recent insight—something you claim to understand. Open your note-taking app and locate the corresponding entry. Then close the device. Now reconstruct the insight from memory in a paragraph. Not in bullet points. Not with prompts. If the paragraph flows, the scaffold served its purpose. If you struggle, reshuffle ideas, or recall only the structure of your notes rather than the argument itself, the scaffold has remained in place too long. Repeat the test again after a week. If the idea dissolves without your notes, dependency has taken root. The exercise is deceptively simple. It reveals whether the mind has built structure or merely borrowed it.

The danger, however, is not that scaffolds exist. It is that they are invisible. People rarely say, "I offload too much." They say, "It's quicker this way." Efficiency becomes the metric, even when depth is the goal. The editor watching his reporter accept revision after revision saw efficiency, but he also saw a behavioural tell: she stopped pausing between suggestions. No friction, no reflection. Clicking became instinct. Her scaffold had quietly become the structure.

The quiet motif of load-bearing returns. A scaffold should reveal the structure's shape; it should not become the structure itself. To decide how far to lean, we must understand which mental movements form expertise. Chunking requires active grouping; spaced retrieval requires desirable difficulty; offloading requires reflection before delegation. When tools remove the difficulty, they hollow the skill.

Another example sharpens this boundary. In 2023, researchers at ETH Zurich studied programmers using AI coding assistants. The assistants improved completion speed by 15–25% on standard tasks, but when asked to debug unfamiliar code without assistance, heavy users struggled more than light users. The metric was telling: time-to-correct averaged nearly twice as long. The model had scaffolded coding, but it had also displaced the micro-struggles through which debugging intuition develops. The limitation is not that the tool existed; it is that the programmers mistook speed for understanding. The reconciliation lies in intentionality. Use the assistant to explore solutions, not to outsource thought. Use it to test hypotheses, not to generate them wholesale.

Yet scaffolds can also expand possibility. Consider the vocabulary-learning research at MIT in 2022. Students using an app that spaced and varied prompts showed improved retention months later compared to those using manual flashcards. The scaffold worked because it mirrored the mind's natural rhythms—spacing, variation, retrieval. The app did not shortcut retrieval; it engineered it. Here, offloading strengthened rather than softened memory.

So what should guide our use of scaffolds? That question returns us to the motif. *How far can we lean before the structure stops being ours?* That question must remain open. But we can watch behaviours. Do we pause before accepting a suggestion? Do we try to retrieve before we search? Do we condense a text ourselves before asking for a summary? These micro-decisions determine whether scaffolds serve or supplant us.

The unresolved tension is this: as our tools grow more fluent, the temptation grows to offload earlier, more often, and more completely. But learning thrives not in ease but in struggle—just enough struggle to shape understanding, not so much as to overwhelm it. The forward test is quiet and personal: *if the scaffold vanished tomorrow, how much of the structure would remain?*

How Models Generalise and Fail

In March 2022, at a law firm in Frankfurt, a contract review assistant flagged a supplier agreement as routine. The associate skimming the output noticed nothing amiss until a senior partner intervened. Buried in the tenth page sat a rare indemnity clause shifting liability for environmental contamination onto the client. The model had classified it as a standard limitation-of-liability term. When the engineering team reconstructed the event, the reason was painfully simple: across the firm's historical corpus of about 40,000 contracts, that clause appeared only eight times. The model had never really "seen" it. It filled the gap with the nearest familiar pattern. Plausibility replaced precision. The assistant had interpolated—smoothly and wrongly.

That quiet misclassification illustrates a central truth about modern models: they generalise well across the centre of a distribution and fail, often silently, at the edges. The silence matters. Humans tend to catch their own uncertainty; they pause, frown, or reread. Models display confidence as formatting—clean summaries, assertive bullet points, tidy labels—masking the doubts that should give us pause. A brittle model wrapped in fluency is a potent hazard. Yet brittleness is not a flaw to be eliminated; it is a feature to be understood and managed. Hybrid intelligence depends on seeing where generalisation strengthens judgement and where it threatens to dull it.

To see how generalisation works, start with what modern models actually do. They map inputs to outputs by searching for statistical regularities across vast training corpora. They generalise by smoothing those regularities—compressing thousands of similar phrases, structures, or situations into a conceptual neighbourhood. When a clause looks mostly like a limitation term, the model treats it as one. This is interpolation: moving between known points. But edge cases live outside those smooth regions. When confronted with an unfamiliar pattern, the model does not say "I don't know." It guesses. The guess may be elegant. The guess may be wrong.

A named example makes the mechanism concrete. In 2018, Google's medical AI group tested a diabetic retinopathy detection system in clinics across Thailand. The tool performed impressively in controlled trials but faltered in noisy real-world settings. Photographs with low lighting or minor blur triggered rejections; the model had not been trained on such imperfections. Nurses found themselves retaking images repeatedly, delaying care. The system's brittleness—its narrow tolerance for variation—became visible not in its accuracy metrics but in the behaviour it imposed: nurses hovering over equipment, patients waiting, workflow slowing. The model had generalised from pristine data. It failed at the edges of realism.

Explain this brittleness and its implication emerges. Models do not build causal understanding. They approximate patterns. When those patterns shift—even slightly—the cracks appear. A rare phrase in a contract, an unusual medical photograph, a deviation in punctuation, a cultural idiom absent from the training set: each becomes an edge case. Edge cases are not rare to the humans who must live with their consequences. They are the contour of reality itself.

Calibration attempts to express this uncertainty, estimating how confident a model should be. A well-calibrated model expresses lower confidence when it is unfamiliar with a pattern. But calibration, too, struggles at the extremes. In January 2021, researchers at the University of Cambridge evaluated calibration across natural-language inference models and found systematic overconfidence on adversarial examples. The visible behaviour was stark: models rated incorrect inferences as "very likely" with polished explanations. The explanation for this overconfidence lies in training: frequent patterns dominate, and the model assumes that linguistic fluency equates to correctness. The implication is direct. Calibration cannot be assumed; it must be tested and tuned continuously. Without it, humans risk mistaking eloquence for truth.

A second example illustrates the brittleness of generalisation in a different domain. In November 2020, during the pandemic, the UK's National Health Service trialled an automated triage chatbot for COVID-19 symptoms. While the system handled common presentations effectively, it struggled with atypical symptoms in older adults. Internal audits reported a discrepancy: human clinicians escalated such cases at twice the rate of the chatbot. The failure was not catastrophic, but it exposed how models trained on typical symptom clusters misread the elderly's more ambiguous signals. The behaviour mattered: families were advised to seek help later than clinicians would have recommended. The system had interpolated from the centre of the dataset and missed the edges where clinical nuance resides.

A credible limitation complicates this picture. Not all edge-case failures indicate fundamental brittleness. Some tasks genuinely possess stable structures, and models can handle them reliably. Spell-checkers rarely misclassify rare words within English orthography. Optical character recognition systems, when trained well, consistently decode clear printed text. In such domains, edge cases are constrained. The structures are rigid. The reconciliation lies in understanding domain variability. High-variance domains—law, medicine, finance, journalism—contain tails too long and diverse for interpolation alone. Low-variance domains permit automation without undue risk. Hybrid intelligence must treat these categories differently.

Returning to the Frankfurt case, we can see why guardrails matter. After the misclassification, the firm introduced three simple behaviours. First, the assistant displayed a confidence interval beside each label, with colour coding that encouraged scepticism when needed. Second, any clause with fewer than fifty historical examples triggered an automatic human review. Third, the system highlighted deviations from the contract's internal style: sudden shifts in phrasing, unusual legal structures, or changes in tone. These were not abstract safeguards. They were visible actions. Lawyers paused when they saw amber or red confidence indicators; juniors discussed unusual styles with seniors; partners demanded explicit justifications when classifications crossed the rarity threshold.

Guardrails serve two purposes. They prevent silent failure—errors that slip through because no one knows to look. And they create friction intentionally. Friction is often treated as inconvenience; in hybrid work, it is a safety mechanism. A model that requires a human to acknowledge uncertainty before acceptance introduces a moment of reflection. Reflection slows the slide from assistance into overreliance.

The motif of visibility runs through all of this. A well-designed hybrid system makes uncertainty, provenance, and boundary conditions visible. A brittle system hides them. When models mirror human language with ease, they risk convincing us that all problems sit in the centre of the distribution. Edge cases are invisible until they explode.

Two further examples sharpen this motif. In 2016, ProPublica investigated the COMPAS sentencing tool used in Broward County, Florida. Judges were shown risk scores without detailed explanations of the underlying features. The opacity masked structural bias: Black defendants were disproportionately labelled high risk. The behaviour that revealed the flaw was not a single misclassification but a pattern: defendants asking "Why me?" and receiving no meaningful answer. Visibility failed.

Contrast that with a 2022 project at the Financial Times, where editors worked with an automated summarisation assistant. The tool displayed its source sentences beside each summary. When it misinterpreted a statistic or softened a political claim, editors could trace the error immediately. The assistant made its path visible; editors kept agency. Generalisation remained useful because its boundaries were in view.

A counter-example tempers optimism. In 2023, a major tech company experimented with adding longer uncertainty explanations to its internal planning assistant. The feature backfired. Employees skimmed past the explanations and relied more heavily on the system's topline summary. The visible behaviour was troubling: fewer manual checks, more copy-paste decisions, and a decline in cross-team verification. The limitation here is human behaviour itself. Visibility does not guarantee attention. The reconciliation lies in design: guardrails must shape action, not merely present information. Short warnings, forced acknowledgements, or branching paths can help, but the system must nudge users towards scepticism without drowning them in noise.

Generalisation and failure also intersect with drift. As models update or learn from feedback, their interpretations of edge cases can shift. Drift is rarely announced. It appears in the behaviour of users who sense that something feels "off". In 2021, a newsroom in Toronto using an automated headline assistant noticed that political stories received more sensational suggestions after a model update. Editors raised alarms; the system had drifted towards patterns dominant in its latest training data. A rollback corrected it. But what triggered the alert was human intuition detecting a change in style. Drift is not just a technical phenomenon. It is a behavioural signal.

To understand calibration more deeply, consider what it does for hybrid work. Calibration shapes trust. Trust, properly understood, is measured in decisions: how often a user accepts an output without checking; how often they override; how often they escalate. Perfect calibration produces a signature: high confidence aligns with correctness; low confidence produces scrutiny. Miscalibration distorts this signature. People accept confidently wrong outputs or recheck confidently right ones. The quiet motif of calibration is balance: a calibrated system keeps humans in the right cognitive mode—alert where needed, efficient where safe.

Calibration, however, requires constant testing. In July 2022, a team at Stanford measured calibration drift in large language models after fine-tuning. They found that confidence scores became less predictive over time, especially in rare contexts. The implication is straightforward. Calibration is not a property of a model; it is a property of a model *at a particular moment.* It must be monitored like any other operational metric. A calibrated system in January may be miscalibrated by June.

Returning again to hybrid intelligence as a behavioural system, consider the three acts that expose model limits: reading carefully, asking "Does this make sense?", and seeking a second channel. These are not magical behaviours. They are visible, mundane, repeatable. A finance team in Edinburgh using dual assistants—one to generate, one to verify—found that disagreement occurred in approximately 9% of analytical summaries. That 9% was pure gold. It revealed the brittle edges where interpolation failed. Humans focused there.

The final question, then, is where to place the boundary between trust and scepticism. Models will continue to improve. Training corpora will expand. Architectures will become more efficient. But interpolation remains interpolation. Rare cases remain rare. Edge cases remain human.

The unresolved tension is deceptively simple: *when a model produces a fluent answer, what signals tell you whether you should trust it or test it?* That question is not technical. It is cognitive. And every hybrid system must help humans ask it at the right moment.

The Feedback Loop as Engine

In September 2021, at the offices of *The Globe and Mail* in Toronto, an editor watched a political summary tool drift. The assistant had been introduced months earlier to help produce "first-pass" digests of parliamentary debates. At launch, it performed reliably: concise, neutral, occasionally bland but serviceable. Then, after a mid-year model update, something shifted. Summaries of contentious bills grew sharper in tone, sometimes veering towards sensational phrasing. One morning, the assistant described a minor procedural dispute as a "bitter standoff"; another afternoon, it framed a routine parliamentary query as "a scathing rebuke". The newsroom began to feel a subtle unease. Nothing catastrophic had happened. Yet the assistant's voice had changed, and no one could say exactly when.

It was a subeditor, poring over side-by-side comparisons of older and newer summaries, who spotted the pattern. The system had drifted towards the rhetorical style dominant in the most recent tranche of data used for fine-tuning—a set of political blogs with punchier language. The discovery sparked a short, intense meeting. Was the assistant broken? Should it be disabled? Instead, the team reached for something they had quietly been developing for months: an evaluation set of thirty benchmark articles, each paired with an agreed-upon summary produced by senior editors. They ran the assistant against those benchmarks. The gap was visible at once. Fourteen outputs deviated in tone; six introduced emphasis unsupported by the source text. The tool was rolled back to its earlier version by the end of the day.

That scene captures why feedback is not decorative. It is the engine that makes hybrid systems work. And it reveals a deeper truth: without structured, continuous feedback loops—ratings, examples, rubrics, evaluation sets, and rollbacks—models gradually slide away from their intended behaviour. Drift is not an anomaly. Drift is the default. Feedback is how we correct course.

Feedback begins with showing, not telling. A journalist dissatisfied with a summary can simply say "this is wrong," but that conveys little. What moves the system is a concrete example of what *right* looks like. Editors at *The Globe and Mail* gathered exemplar summaries over months, refining tone sentence by sentence. When they provided those examples as reference outputs, the model did not just learn the structure of a good summary; it learned the judgement embedded in each stylistic choice. Naming this process as reinforcement through examples clarifies what is happening. It is not scolding a system. It is *shaping* it.

Explain this shaping and the implication becomes clear. Examples anchor intention more precisely than instructions. A rubric adds structure, turning general preferences into criteria: factual accuracy, faithfulness to the source, neutrality of tone, sufficiency of context. When editors marked outputs against a three-point rubric, the feedback loop strengthened. Metrics emerged: how often the assistant captured key actors, how frequently it omitted critical qualifiers, how consistently it avoided interpretive flourish. Each metric reflected a visible behaviour. Each behaviour could be improved.

But feedback is not only about correction; it is also about protection. In January 2023, editors at *Le Monde* collaborated with a summarisation model and noticed it occasionally imported subtle bias from source materials. They responded not by removing the system, but by introducing an explicit "bias sweep"—a second-level pass in which the assistant produced a neutral paraphrase of its own summary. Editors compared the two and rated divergences. The tool was adjusted in weekly cycles, and the divergence rate dropped from 18% to 6% over the first month. Structured feedback—precise, repeated, measurable—became a safeguard against drift and bias.

To understand the engine more fully, consider the role of evaluation sets. An evaluation set is a standing reference point: a set of tasks that represent what "good" looks like, preserved like a control group in an experiment. Without such sets, improvement becomes guesswork. In software testing,

Goldman Sachs' trading desks in London began using evaluation sets in 2020 to monitor automated compliance alerts. They compared outputs from updated systems against historical benchmarks to detect shifts in sensitivity. The behaviour revealed by this method was telling: small model updates that improved detection in common scenarios sometimes degraded performance in rare but critical ones. The implication is straightforward. Evaluation sets help detect regressions that would otherwise go unnoticed.

This principle extends to hybrid intelligence. When *The Globe and Mail* used its thirty benchmark articles, it did so not out of academic habit but because the set served as a lens. It showed deviations clearly. It turned drift into something measurable. And crucially, it allowed editors to act with confidence. Without that lens, the assistant's shift in tone might have been dismissed as editorial imagination.

Still, feedback loops carry limitations. One credible counter-example comes from a publishing house in Berlin that experimented with reader ratings to improve book-description generators. Instead of converging towards quality, the system drifted towards sentimentality. Readers rated emotionally heightened descriptions more highly, and the model learned to produce them more readily. The feedback loop amplified taste rather than truth. Reconciling this requires recognising that feedback signals must align with the underlying goal. Ratings without rubrics distort. Rubrics without examples remain abstract. Examples without evaluation sets fail to detect drift.

Feedback loops function at multiple layers. The newsroom example uses prompt adjustments—editors refine the instruction itself. It uses example-based feedback—reference summaries. It uses rubrics—criteria for judgement. And it uses evaluation sets—stable comparisons. These layers interact. When the assistant drifted, editors first adjusted prompts, then reviewed examples, and finally compared versions. The rollback was not defeat. It was mastery.

The quiet motif running through these layers is the compass. A compass does not eliminate uncertainty; it provides orientation. Feedback is that compass for hybrid systems. Without it, models wander. With it, they can be steered.

A second example from outside journalism shows how powerful such compasses can be. In 2019, Airbnb's trust and safety team in San Francisco implemented human feedback loops to improve fraud-detection models. They used a curated dataset of confirmed fraud cases, updated monthly. Analysts tagged borderline cases, providing written rationales. Over a six-month period, false positives fell by 27%, while detection of rare fraud patterns improved by 12%. These outcomes were not magic. They were behaviour: analysts marking anomalous features, models incorporating those marks, and evaluation sets confirming improvement. The system did not become perfect. It became *tunable*.

Yet feedback loops can also entrench error when signals are noisy. A content moderation team at a social platform in 2020 attempted to use crowd-sourced ratings to refine an automated hate-speech detector. Reviewers from different regions applied inconsistent cultural standards, introducing confusion rather than clarity. The model's confidence degraded. The visible behaviour became paradoxical: it flagged more benign content and missed more harmful content. The limitation here is that not all feedback is equal. The reconciliation lies in segmentation: feedback must come from evaluators who share the relevant frame of reference, and rubrics must be explicit enough to minimise divergence.

Guardrails play a crucial role within the loop. Returning to the Frankfurt law firm described earlier in this chapter, guardrails prevented silent misclassification. In the newsroom, guardrails took another form: version control. Every update to the assistant required sign-off from a senior editor and a verified benchmark score. When the political summaries drifted, the team reverted to the most recent stable version. The rollback was swift precisely because the guardrail existed. And like all good safeguards, its presence altered behaviour. Editors became more attentive to tone shifts, more willing to compare versions, more sceptical of "improvements" not supported by evidence.

Trust, too, reshapes the loop. Trust is visible not in sentiment but in action: how often editors accept outputs without modification, how often they correct phrasing, how often they escalate ambiguous cases. A newsroom in London tracked acceptance rates in 2022 across its assistant-generated summaries. They observed a pattern: as editors grew more familiar with the assistant's quirks, acceptance rates stabilised at around 60%, with the remainder split between edits and rejections. Trust did not mean blind acceptance. It meant calibrated reliance.

As feedback deepens, the boundary between human and model becomes collaborative rather than supervisory. A senior political editor at *The Globe and Mail* recounted how she began using the assistant's failures as teaching moments. "When it gets something wrong," she said, "I ask why. And nine times out of ten, the error shows me something about the text I hadn't noticed." The feedback loop, then, is not one-way. It shapes human judgement as surely as it shapes model behaviour.

The motif of the compass returns again. A compass ensures orientation; it does not walk the path. Feedback loops ensure alignment; they do not eliminate drift. The work is continuous. Calibration must be maintained. Evaluation sets must evolve. Rubrics must be revisited as contexts change. Ratings must be interpreted judiciously. Examples must expand as style and standards mature.

The tension that remains is fundamental. *How much control should humans retain over the loop, and how much should the system learn autonomously?* Too little human involvement, and drift accelerates unnoticed. Too much, and the assistant becomes a bottleneck rather than a partner. Every hybrid system confronts this decision. And every team must decide where to place its compass—between the promise of automation and the discipline of feedback.

Calibrating Trust and Verification

On 14 March 2020, as markets convulsed in the first shock of the pandemic, a risk analyst at a London investment firm noticed something strange. The firm's forecasting assistant—a language-model tool fine-tuned on years of internal commentary—began issuing daily summaries that sounded confident yet subtly wrong. One morning, it attributed a bond-spread spike to "renewed optimism" rather than fear; another afternoon, it described a central bank announcement as an "aggressive tightening" when the bank had, in fact, held rates steady. Nothing in the wording seemed implausible. Everything was wrong. The analyst printed the summaries and laid them beside older ones from February. A drift had occurred, quiet but consequential. When he checked the model logs, he found the reason: a version update three days earlier had altered the assistant's priors. The assistant had not malfunctioned. It had evolved. The human had to catch it.

That moment, a simple printout on a desk in the City, illustrates why trust in hybrid systems must be earned and then monitored. Trust is not a feeling. It is a series of behaviours: when a user accepts an output without checking; when they pause to compare sources; when they escalate uncertainty. And trust can fail in both directions. Blind trust invites errors to compound. Chronic distrust suffocates the benefits of collaboration. Calibration sits between the two—a discipline, not an instinct.

Calibration begins with provenance. Show where an output comes from, and trust becomes inspectable. At the London investment firm, the analyst noticed drift only because he habitually checked the assistant's version number in the corner of its interface. He had been trained to do so after a 2018 scare at another bank, JPMorgan Chase, where a machine-learning volatility model misfired due to an unannounced data-ingestion glitch. That event triggered the creation of a provenance checklist: every automated analysis had to display its data sources, timestamps, and model version. Naming provenance as a requirement formalised what humans often rely on implicitly: the right to ask "Where did this come from?" and to expect a clear answer.

Explain provenance and its implication becomes clear. Without it, trust collapses into impression. With it, verification becomes a workflow. A trader seeing that a summary was generated from stale pricing data behaves differently from one who sees it built from live feeds. Trust, here, is visible in the decision: accept, adjust, or challenge.

But provenance alone is insufficient. Versioning matters just as much. Models shift. Fine-tuning changes tone and emphasis. Retrieval pipelines alter the evidence they surface. A system that behaves reliably in April may drift by June. Calibration therefore demands that version histories be legible. Morgan Stanley's wealth-management division implemented this in 2023 when it released a client-advice assistant. Every suggestion included a version tag that linked to a changelog written in plain language. Advisers could read what had changed: new retrieval filters, altered weighting of risk factors, updated citations policy. The behaviour this enabled was simple but powerful. Advisers paused when version numbers changed. They compared outputs with last week's. They asked questions. And when discrepancies emerged, they could escalate with specificity: "Version 2.3.7 mishandles inflation-adjusted projections; revert or patch."

Implication: version transparency is not administrative neatness; it is a stabiliser. It prevents humans from mistaking model evolution for model reliability. It turns drift into something legible before it becomes harmful.

Cross-checks form the third pillar. They translate calibration into action. The London risk analyst belonged to a team that practised dual-channel verification: one assistant generated a summary, and a second assistant—trained on different data and parameters—performed an independent check. Humans compared divergences. The metric mattered. Across ninety days, the disagreement rate averaged 11%. Each disagreement triggered human review. In calm markets, the discrepancy rate fell to around 4%; in volatile weeks, it climbed above 20%. Those spikes were not noise. They were signals that the underlying models had entered unfamiliar territory. Trust was calibrated not by sentiment but by divergence.

A second named example shows this pattern in a different field. In 2021, the US Consumer Financial Protection Bureau reviewed mortgage-risk models used by several lenders. One institution employed dual-model cross-checking: a legacy statistical model alongside a newer deep-learning system. When the two disagreed on applicant risk scores, loan officers were required to document the decision path—sources consulted, anomalies noted, thresholds applied. The behaviour this produced was discipline. Officers hesitated before accepting a model's confident score when the companion model flagged uncertainty. The implication is practical. Cross-checks do not slow workflow; they sharpen judgement.

The quiet motif running through these practices is the hinge. At what point does trust tip from vigilance into complacency? The hinge is small—no larger than the pause before acceptance, the glance at a version number, the scan of a provenance tag. Hybrid intelligence depends on this hinge being strong.

Yet verification is not without limitations. One credible counter-example comes from a bank in Singapore that attempted to automate cross-checking entirely. Engineers built a meta-model to adjudicate disputes between two forecasting systems. Instead of improving reliability, the meta-model amplified noise. It weighted one model's confidence too heavily and learned the other's quirks. The visible behaviour was unsettling: human analysts trusted the meta-model simply because it sat "above" the others. When its errors surfaced—incorrect probabilities on credit-event scenarios—the team had to unwind layers of misplaced reliance. The reconciliation lies in recognising that cross-checking must include humans. Machines can disagree usefully; only humans can interpret the disagreement.

Verification checklists help bring humans back into the loop. One finance team in Edinburgh introduced a three-step checklist after a series of embarrassing copy-paste errors in 2022: verify provenance, verify version, verify divergence. Each step required a tangible action. Analysts clicked a source link, compared numbers with the primary data feed, and noted discrepancies in a shared log. The checklist took less than a minute. Yet over six months, audit reports showed a 35% decline in acceptance of spurious outputs. The behaviour had changed. Calibration had become a habit.

Checklists also surface assumptions. When a model suggests that two numbers "match," the human must ask, *match to what?* When a forecast describes a trend as "strong," the human must ask, *relative to which baseline?* These are not philosophical questions. They are operational. And they shape the line between trust and verification.

Calibration also requires awareness of context. During the volatility of March 2023, a New York hedge fund observed an unusual pattern: their macro-analysis assistant provided marginally more accurate summaries than human analysts on rapidly shifting headlines. But when conditions stabilised, the pattern reversed. The divergence metric guided behaviour. Analysts trusted the assistant more in high-velocity contexts and leaned on human synthesis in calmer periods. Calibration shifted with the environment. Trust was dynamic, not fixed.

The motif of the hinge returns. Trust must be adjustable. Verification must be routine. Systems that encourage passive acceptance—through polished formatting, authoritative tone, or frictionless UX—push the hinge in the wrong direction. Systems that require small but meaningful acts of verification keep the hinge steady.

Looking across domains, three forces shape trust: transparency, variability, and friction. Transparency shows the path. Variability reveals uncertainty. Friction invites scrutiny. Each force is behavioural. When a version number stands out, people pause. When two assistants disagree, people look closer. When a provenance link shows stale data, people challenge. Trust is not blind; it is enacted.

A reporter in Toronto once described her rule of thumb when working with a model: "If I can't explain why I trust it today, I don't." Her rule captures the essence of calibrated reliance. Trust must be articulable, not assumed. Verification must be lightweight, not suffocating. And the hinge between them must remain visible.

The unresolved tension is simple to pose and hard to live with: *when an assistant produces a fluent, convincing answer, how will you know whether to accept it, question it, or seek a second view?* Every hybrid organisation must decide where to place that hinge—and how to keep it from rusting.

Chapter 3
Interfaces to the Brain

The room was silent except for the soft hum of the amplifier. A young woman sat at a desk in a laboratory at the University of Tübingen, her hands resting motionless beside a keyboard that she would never touch. A cap threaded with sensors clung to her scalp, each electrode picking up the faint electrical murmurs beneath. "Think of the letter you want," the researcher said. A grid flickered on the screen. A second later, an *S* appeared—hesitant, a little delayed, but unmistakably hers. She smiled, half amazed, half suspicious of her own mind. For a moment, intention had travelled from cortex to cursor without the mediation of muscle. Then, on the next attempt, the system hesitated and misfired. Noise drowned signal. The cursor jittered. The research team exchanged glances. The promise was visible; so were the limits.

That modest demonstration—just a letter on a screen—captures the fragile wonder of brain-computer interfaces. They begin in biological turbulence, translating spikes, rhythms, and oscillations into legible patterns. They promise forms of communication and control that bypass the body yet rely on its most delicate machinery. And they sit atop a tension that cannot be resolved by engineering alone: the desire to understand the brain more deeply colliding with the instinct to shield our inner life from intrusion. We want access and anonymity, power and protection. The line between them shifts every year.

The broader story is older than the technology itself. In 1924, Hans Berger recorded the first human electroencephalogram in Jena, meticulously tracing the rhythms of his son's brain. He believed these signals revealed an interior life previously inaccessible to science. A century later, that belief still lingers. The dream of a direct interface—reading intention, aiding movement, restoring communication—sits alongside a growing unease. If thought can be captured, can it be misread?

If intention can be inferred, can it be manipulated? Brain–computer interfaces pull the future closer, but they also press fundamental questions to the surface.

Like all powerful tools, BCIs live in gradients, not absolutes. On one end sit invasive implants that record neural patterns with exquisite detail, restoring movement to people with paralysis or enabling a faster form of communication than eye tracking. On the other end sit non-invasive headsets, lightweight and commercially available, whose resolutions are coarse but whose reach is expanding. In between lies a broad spectrum: clinical electrodes for rehabilitation, research-grade EEG systems for cognitive studies, and emerging consumer devices that promise focus training, stress monitoring, or adaptive interfaces. The engineering is advancing, but the governing question persists: *what should be done through the brain, for the brain, and to the brain?*

To appreciate the stakes, we must first understand the noise. BCIs do not read thoughts; they read patterns—messy, overlapping, ever-shifting. A typing-by-thought demonstration, like the one in Tübingen, works because algorithms learn to distinguish intention from interference, the slow drift of electrodes, and the unpredictable fluctuations of biological rhythms. Noise management becomes the beating heart of the interface. Error correction models refine guesses. Latency stretches and contracts depending on electrode quality and the user's fatigue. A demonstration may look effortless, but behind every letter lies a chain of probabilities stitched together, each vulnerable to disruption. Systems promise fluency; physiology answers back with static.

Yet the technical challenges pale in comparison with the ethical frontier emerging around readout and stimulation. Reading from the brain raises familiar concerns—privacy, consent, inference—but with a heightened intensity. A neurofeedback headset used in a classroom, for instance, may track broad patterns of attention, but the boundary between "attention support" and "behaviour monitoring" is thin. A pilot programme in Copenhagen in 2023 confronted exactly this tension when students and parents were asked to sign consent forms outlining what data would be collected, how it would be stored, who could access it, and for what pedagogical purpose. The most important moment of the process was not the data capture but the briefing beforehand. Students had the right to refuse. Teachers had limits on what they were allowed to infer. The system was designed not only to measure attention but to respect the dignity of those whose attention was being measured.

Writing to the brain—neural stimulation—raises a different set of questions. Deep brain stimulation has, for decades, offered relief to patients with severe Parkinson's disease, tremor, or depression. Yet its effects can ripple into personality, mood, and identity. When interfaces extend beyond readout into modulation, the stakes rise. Consumer BCIs remain far from this domain, but the boundary must be articulated early. Not every innovation is destined for everyday use. Some belong firmly in the clinic, under regulated protocols and professional oversight.

If the ethics are complex, the practical horizon is more grounded. Hype obscures the near-term reality. Most gains in the next decade will come not from high-bandwidth neural typing or mind-controlled robotics, but from modest, targeted applications: assistive communication for individuals with severe paralysis; rehabilitation support for stroke patients; early detection of cognitive fatigue in environments where lapses carry risk. A factory in Osaka demonstrated the subtle power of this approach when a pilot programme used non-invasive EEG to track indicators of fatigue in shift workers. Rather than monitoring productivity, the system advised micro-breaks before errors accumulated. Workers reported feeling less pressured, not more. The technology succeeded because it stayed close to human needs, not corporate fantasy.

This principle—human needs over technological spectacle—animates the emerging field of neuro-UX. Designing interfaces to the brain is not merely a technical challenge; it is a psychological and ethical one. A headset that demands intense concentration becomes exhausting. A calibration routine that leaves a user uncertain corrodes confidence. A neurofeedback visualization that shames rather than guides undermines dignity. Humane design acknowledges these fragilities. In a rehabilitation clinic in Lyon, therapists introduced a subtle innovation during BCI calibration: gentle haptic pulses delivered through a wristband whenever the system correctly interpreted the user's intention. Patients reported feeling reassured; the confirmation helped rebuild trust after each misfire. The clinic learned a simple lesson. Feedback must be timely and tactful. Interfaces must soothe, not startle.

Throughout this chapter, the quiet motif to watch is thickness—the thickness of the boundary between mind and machine. That boundary is porous in places, firm in others, and always negotiated. Signals pass through it. Intentions cross it. But values must anchor it.

We will move carefully between engineering realities and human consequences. We will explore how signals become interpretations, how error correction becomes a form of translation, how privacy frameworks must evolve, how regulation lags behind but cannot be allowed to sleep. And we will examine what it means to design interfaces that extend capacity without erasing autonomy.

As brain–computer interfaces move from laboratory curiosities to mainstream tools, the central question grows sharper: *how much of ourselves are we willing to expose in exchange for new forms of capability?* The answer will not be uniform. But it will define the next boundary of hybrid intelligence.

Signals, Sensors, and Noise

In May 2021, at the Stanford Neural Prosthetics Translational Laboratory, a man paralysed from the neck down typed the sentence *"Hello world"* using only imagined handwriting. A tiny array of electrodes, implanted in his motor cortex, captured neural patterns associated with the memory of writing letters by hand. Algorithms translated those spikes into strokes on a screen. The result astonished even the research team: a sustained output of roughly 90 characters per minute, close to the handwriting speed of an able-bodied adult. Yet alongside the triumph sat an instructive truth. The system faltered each time the participant grew tired; the signal drifted; the decoder misclassified a curve as a straight line; noise crept in. The most intimate interface in the room was also the most fragile.

That scene, celebrated across laboratories from Palo Alto to Geneva, captures the essential paradox of brain–computer interfaces. They hold the promise of restoring communication, movement, and autonomy. They also confront the stubborn physics of biological signals. The brain does not speak in words or icons. It speaks in rhythms, spikes, bursts, and silences—patterns born of chemistry and electricity, modulated by mood, fatigue, and even the humidity of the room. To translate intention into action, BCIs must make legibility out of turbulence. The work is delicate. The errors are revealing. Noise is not the obstacle; it is the medium.

This subchapter enters that space where engineering meets physiology, and where the signal-to-noise ratio decides what becomes possible. The motif to watch—threaded quietly throughout—is the tension between clarity and distortion. Every interface to the brain lives inside that tension.

Begin with the basic question: what counts as a "signal"? In non-invasive systems, the signal is a composite. Electroencephalography (EEG) caps measure voltage fluctuations produced by millions of neurons firing in synchrony. Infrared-based functional near-infrared spectroscopy (fNIRS) measures haemodynamic changes, inferring neural activity indirectly through oxygenated blood flow. Magnetoencephalography (MEG) tracks faint magnetic fields, though its bulk and cost confine it largely to research facilities. Each method captures a coarse shadow of neural activity. Information spreads across centimetres of tissue, skull, scalp, and gel. Electrode placement changes quality. Sweat, hair, and movement distort readings. The resolution is global rather than granular—useful for broad intention, less so for the nuance of complex thought.

Show this in a concrete case. In 2022, researchers at Imperial College London tested an EEG-based spelling interface intended for home use. Participants wore a lightweight cap and focused attention on flashing letters. The system correctly identified targets roughly 78% of the time under controlled lighting. But when the ambient environment changed—sunlight from a window, slight muscle tension, a shifting chair—the accuracy dropped sharply. The explanation was banal but profound: the electrical noise of everyday life drowned the subtle neural rhythms the system relied on. The implication follows immediately. Non-invasive BCIs are exquisitely sensitive not only to brain activity but to the environment wrapped around it.

Invasive systems face a different landscape. They bypass the skull entirely, recording directly from cortical tissue. Depth electrodes and microelectrode arrays can isolate the firing of individual neurons or small populations. The resolution is extraordinary. But the signal still drifts. Electrodes degrade. Tissue responds. Immune reactions alter impedance. In a landmark study at Brown University's BrainGate project in 2012, participants could control robotic arms with impressive precision. Yet the engineering team reported needing to recalibrate decoders frequently as electrodes shifted or lost sensitivity. The visible behaviour was subtle: slower cursor movement, occasional misfires, emergent lag. Explanation: the biological environment changed around the implant. Implication: even inside the skull, the signal is never static.

Nowhere is this clearer than in typing-by-thought demonstrations. The Stanford case from 2021 remains the most compelling. But a quiet detail in the team's paper reveals the deeper lesson: error correction algorithms contributed heavily to the perceived fluency. When the participant imagined writing an *m*, the decoder produced probabilities over possible letters; language models smoothed ambiguities; autocorrect mechanisms snapped uncertain strokes into contextually likely shapes. The system was not reading letters from the cortex. It was inferring them through statistical reconstruction, blending neural intent with linguistic expectation. The motif returns—clarity emerging from distortion.

Latency tells a related story. A non-invasive BCI may take hundreds of milliseconds to classify intention because it relies on time-locked responses. Invasive systems can respond more quickly but still require computational smoothing. The lag is small—ten to fifty milliseconds—but perceptible. Users describe it as "thinking into mud" or "pushing through syrup". In 2020, at the École Polytechnique Fédérale de Lausanne, researchers exploring motor imagery noted that even elite users needed months of training to internalise the delay. Their behaviour changed. They thought in anticipatory rhythms, aligning intention with expected system timing. The machine adjusted to the brain; the brain adjusted back.

Noise, too, comes in flavours. Electrical noise from equipment. Physiological noise from blinking or jaw tension. Cognitive noise from distraction or stress. Emotional noise from anxiety. Show this multiplicity through a real event. During a 2019 trial at the Wyss Center in Geneva, a participant controlling a cursor via a subdural grid experienced repeated classification errors whenever a family member entered the room. The neural signature of emotional arousal modulated the signal enough to confuse the decoder. The system could not distinguish intention from emotion. The implication is stark. BCIs not only read the brain; they read everything that stirs it.

Two examples outside the laboratory broaden the picture. In 2015, the University of Minnesota demonstrated drone control using non-invasive EEG. Participants steered a quadcopter through a hoop by imagining specific movements. The success rate was impressive for its time, but the system struggled in outdoor environments where wind noise and sunlight affected sensors. In 2020, Neuralink showcased a pig with an implant that recorded neural activity associated with sniffing. The implant worked flawlessly under controlled conditions. But translating that into reliable consumer-grade devices remains uncertain. The limitation is not ambition. It is noise.

A counter-example tempers the narrative. In 2016, Japanese researchers at the ATR Computational Neuroscience Laboratories used fMRI to decode simple visual patterns with high fidelity. When subjects viewed black-and-white shapes, the system reconstructed them nearly pixel for pixel. The catch was monumental machinery: an fMRI scanner costing millions, requiring the participant to lie perfectly still. This level of signal clarity will not scale to everyday life. The reconciliation lies in constraints. High fidelity is possible, but not yet portable.

Noise management, therefore, becomes the defining craft of BCI engineering. Algorithms filter artefacts, track signal drift, and correct errors based on context. Designers reduce electrical interference through shielded cables, improve electrode contact, and stabilise temperature effects. But the most important technique remains behavioural: calibration. Users perform intentional tasks, and the system learns their neural signatures. Calibration must be repeated often because neural states shift. This repetition is not failure. It is maintenance.

A quiet motif returns: the line between intention and noise is thin. And every interface must decide where to draw it.

The typing-by-thought demonstration returns to illuminate this boundary. The Stanford participant occasionally produced erroneous letters when fatigue peaked. Engineers implemented a rejection threshold: if the system's confidence fell below a boundary, it produced nothing. Silence became a feature, not a failure. Users preferred a blank space to an incorrect symbol. The rejection behaviour restored trust. The system did not pretend certainty. It paused. Humans do the same.

The implications extend beyond research. As non-invasive BCIs reach consumers—from concentration headsets to adaptive gaming rigs—noise becomes a human-factor problem. A headset that loses signal when hair shifts creates frustration. A feedback algorithm that mistakes stress for distraction erodes credibility. In 2023, a gaming BCI start-up in Seoul discovered that users wearing over-ear headphones experienced frequent signal dropouts. The electromagnetic fields from the audio drivers interfered with the EEG. Their "fix" required redesigning the headset frame entirely. Technical noise became a product-design constraint.

The demands grow sharper in clinical contexts. In 2022, a stroke rehabilitation clinic in Lyon reported that their BCI therapy sessions produced the highest motor gains when sessions were quiet, predictable, and emotionally neutral. Even subtle interruptions—a door opening, a therapist speaking—altered patient performance. The therapist noted a simple behaviour: patients who had slept poorly produced noisier signals. The clinic adapted by adjusting training intensity. The interface became responsive not only to neural signals but to context.

We return to the motif once more: clarity emerging through turbulence.

This brings us back to the central tension. BCIs promise directness—intent translated into action without the delays and distortions of muscle. Yet they depend on interpreting noisy, probabilistic patterns. The promise of immediacy sits atop layers of inference. The risk is that users mistake fluency for fidelity.

A forward test, therefore, lingers at the threshold of every deployment: *when an interface claims to detect intention, how will we know whether we are seeing a signal, an artefact, or a guess?* That question defines the boundary of trust in brain–computer communication, and it will determine which systems feel like extensions of ourselves—and which remain fascinating, fallible machines.

The Ethics of Reading and Writing Minds

In August 2023, at a secondary school in Aarhus, Denmark, a group of fifteen-year-olds lined up to collect lightweight neurofeedback headsets for a month-long pilot funded by the municipal education department. The device, produced by the Copenhagen start-up NeuraLight, measured broad EEG rhythms associated with sustained attention. Teachers hoped it would help students identify when their focus dipped during long reading blocks. Before any pupil touched the headset, however, the school assembled parents, teachers, and students in the auditorium. A lawyer from the city's data-protection office walked them through a twenty-two-point consent flow: what signals would be collected, what would *not* be inferred, how long the data would be stored, and who—precisely—would have access. One slide, displayed in bold type, read: "This device cannot read thoughts. It will never guess your emotions. You may refuse at any time." The outcome was subtle but telling. Roughly a third of students opted out, some because they disliked head-mounted devices, others because they felt uneasy about any form of monitoring. Those who opted in reported that the tool helped them notice restlessness earlier, but they also insisted on weekly briefings about data deletion. The system's success, if it can be called that, hinged less on neural signal quality than on the transparency that framed its use.

This scene captures the emerging ethical terrain of brain-computer interfaces: a terrain shaped not only by technology but by norms, consent rituals, and cultural expectations about what should remain private inside the skull. Reading neural activity is no longer confined to research labs in Zürich or Boston; it is trickling into classrooms, gyms, and consumer products. Writing to the brain—through electrical or magnetic stimulation—remains more regulated, but even there boundaries are shifting as experimental therapies begin to cross into commercial wellness markets. The central motif that threads through this chapter is the *threshold*: the line between acceptable insight and intrusive inference, between empowerment and surveillance, between restoration and manipulation. The threshold is narrow. It moves.

Reading neural activity has long been framed as a clinical act. Electroencephalography entered medicine through the careful work of Hans Berger in 1924; his earliest recordings in Jena captured rhythmic oscillations associated with drowsiness and wakefulness. For decades, EEG, MEG, and invasive recordings sat firmly within hospitals and research centres. The ethical scaffolding around them was built correspondingly: specialised protocols, trained technicians, and informed consent procedures overseen by institutional review boards. Those rituals created an implicit social contract. The brain could be measured, but only within a protected space where risks were controlled and interpretations mediated by professionals.

Show how that contract is now being stressed. Consumer EEG headsets—marketed for focus training or meditation—

encourage users to treat neural data as casually as step counts. In 2022, the US company Muse released a model that generated moment-by-moment "calm scores" during meditation sessions. The system provided real value for some users, giving them a metric to anchor their practice. Yet the privacy policy, updated in May 2022, noted that anonymised data could be used for product research. The visible behaviour was entirely ordinary: users uploaded sessions automatically. But the implication was profound. Neural rhythms, once confined to clinics, became data flows.

Name the concern precisely. It is not that such devices "read minds"—a phrase that obscures more than it clarifies—but that they infer internal states from patterns users may not realise they are sharing. Explain this clearly. A person's breathing pattern or step count reveals something about behaviour. A person's neural oscillations may reveal something about cognitive effort or fatigue. The distinction matters because the brain carries traces of identity in ways no other organ does. The body may betray habits; the brain betrays tendencies. That raises the stakes.

The Aarhus example illuminates how educators can mitigate this. The school required a dual-consent process: parental consent paired with explicit pupil assent. Data flowed only to the research team, not to teachers. The headset displayed raw scores to students but refused to surface trend lines to staff. The school's behaviour communicated the ethical principle: reading neural data requires not just permission but understanding. Consent is not a checkbox; it is an ongoing relationship with the data subject, especially when the subject is a child.

Contrast this with an instructive counter-example. In 2019, a technology firm in Hangzhou supplied "engagement monitoring" headsets to several local primary schools. The devices claimed to classify students' attention levels in real time. Teachers saw colour-coded dashboards: green for "focused", yellow for "distracted". Parents were not consulted, and pupils could not opt out. Follow-up reporting by *The South China Morning Post* documented discomfort among families and scepticism among neuroscientists. The limitation was stark: consumer-grade EEG could not meaningfully infer individual attention, and the dashboards' apparent authority masked low signal fidelity. But the ethical failure ran deeper. The threshold was ignored entirely. No consent, no transparency, no acknowledgment of uncertainty. To reconcile this with the Aarhus example is to see the line clearly: ethics begin not with capability but with boundaries.

Writing to the brain raises a different set of questions. Deep brain stimulation, used clinically since the late 1990s for Parkinson's disease, has offered profound relief to thousands. Here, the boundary is carefully patrolled: implanted electrodes stimulate precise neural circuits under medical supervision. Patients are screened, informed, and supported. Yet stimulation is expanding beyond disease treatment into nebulous territories like "cognitive enhancement" or "mood optimisation". In 2021, a wellness company in California launched a transcranial direct current stimulation (tDCS) headset marketed for "creative flow". Regulatory oversight was minimal. Some neuroscientists warned that repeated stimulation—even at low intensities—could produce unpredictable effects on neural plasticity. The visible behaviour in early adopters ranged from heightened alertness to headaches. The implication is plain. Writing to the brain without clinical justification risks eroding the norms that protect identity and agency.

Another named example clarifies the stakes. The Human Brain Project's ethics unit in Geneva published a 2020 report urging that any commercial stimulation device include three features: explicit disclosures about functional limits, clear warnings about unknown effects, and a friction-based user interface that requires deliberate activation. The report argued that the ease of stimulation must never outpace understanding of its consequences. That recommendation stems from a philosophical intuition as old as medical ethics itself: interventions on the brain touch not only function but selfhood.

The motif of the threshold recurs here with force. Reading neural activity risks over-interpretation. Writing to the brain risks over-intervention. The boundary between them is not fixed; it shifts with technology, context, and cultural norms.

Bring the discussion into a more grounded domain. A neurofeedback programme introduced in Helsinki in 2022 attempted to train adults with ADHD to regulate beta rhythms associated with sustained focus. The system included a robust consent flow: participants reviewed plain-language explanations of what the EEG could detect, what it could not, and how feedback loops worked. Sessions were monitored by clinicians, and data was stored locally rather than in the cloud. The visible behaviour of clinicians—explaining limitations, adjusting thresholds, emphasising agency—embodied a core ethical principle: neurotechnology must not impose narratives upon users; it must give them tools they can interpret and control.

Yet even well-designed consent flows confront a limitation: comprehension. Neuroscience is complex. Interfaces can mislead simply by appearing authoritative. A quiet risk surfaces when users believe that a device reveals truths about their mind that it cannot possibly measure. This risk is not imaginary. In 2018, the University of Essex conducted a study on "neuroessentialism" and found that people were more likely to accept personality feedback labelled as "brain-based" even when it was randomly generated. Behaviour changed accordingly: participants altered study patterns, sleep routines, even dietary choices in response to fabricated neurofeedback. The implication is uncomfortable. The mere presence of brain-related language can shift a person's self-understanding, regardless of accuracy.

The threshold motif sharpens: the ethical danger lies not only in misuse of data but in misplaced belief in what the data signifies.

This leads to a deeper philosophical question. Does neural data possess a special moral status? One argument says yes: the brain is uniquely tied to identity, consciousness, and autonomy. Another argues no: data is data, and the moral weight lies in its use, not its origin. The behaviour of institutions, not the biology of the organ, determines harm. Yet a middle position dominates current scholarship. Neural data may not be uniquely sacred, but it is uniquely revealing—and uniquely easy to misinterpret. That blend demands heightened safeguards.

Two named cases illustrate these diverging views. In 2021, Chile amended its constitution to include "neurorights"—protections against the commercial exploitation of neural data. The move was hailed by some ethicists as visionary. Others worried it would stifle research by muddying distinctions between invasive clinical signals and benign EEG noise. Meanwhile, in 2023, the UK's Ada Lovelace Institute published a report urging "contextual integrity": BCI data should be governed not by a special legal category but by rules tied to purpose, risk, and vulnerability. The implication is pragmatic. Ethics cannot depend on metaphysical views of the mind; they must depend on concrete harms and benefits.

The Aarhus classroom offers a grounded path forward. Its consent flow included three simple rituals that doubled as ethical signals: a briefing, a refusal option, and a deletion schedule. Each ritual produced observable behaviours: parents asked sharper questions; teachers reframed expectations; students felt empowered to disconnect without explanation. These behaviours reveal the heart of ethical neurotechnology. Safeguards are not philosophical abstractions. They are practices that reshape relationships.

The threshold motif leads us to a final uncertainty—one that every researcher, designer, educator, and policymaker must confront. *When reading neural signals becomes effortless, and when writing to the brain becomes safer and more precise, who will decide where the boundary lies between assistance and intrusion?* That question is not theoretical. It is coming. And it will test not just our technologies but our commitments to autonomy, dignity, and the delicate privacy of thought.

Practical Horizons for BCI

In October 2022, at a rehabilitation centre in Utrecht, a former cyclist who had suffered a brainstem stroke began steering a cursor across a tablet using a non-invasive brain–computer interface. The system, developed by the Dutch research consortium INTENSE, translated slow cortical potentials into directional commands. The outcome was modest in absolute terms—a message composed over five patient minutes—but transformative for him. He could select icons, confirm choices, and write short notes to his family without relying on eye tracking, which exhausted him. The clinicians kept a timer beside the screen. Whenever his performance dipped below a threshold—latency rising above 600 milliseconds, error rate exceeding 20 per cent—they paused the session. The system's utility depended not only on decoding accuracy but on fatigue curves, comfort, and the patient's willingness to continue. That pattern, observable in dozens of clinical trials across Europe, shows where brain–computer interfaces genuinely help today: in narrow, high-need contexts where even slow communication can restore agency.

That is the quiet truth beneath the noise of commercial hype. The near-term future of BCI is not full telepathy, thought-to-text at conversational speeds, or mass adoption of cognitive wearables. It is a cluster of constrained but meaningful applications—assistive communication for people with severe paralysis, motor rehabilitation following stroke or spinal injury, and fatigue or attention monitoring in high-risk environments. These horizons are grounded not in speculation but in what physiology, ergonomics, and regulation currently permit. The motif running through this landscape is *fit*: how tightly a technology matches the biology, context, and comfort of the person using it. Fit determines success.

Consider assistive communication. Few developments have matched the progress of intracortical BCIs for people with locked-in syndrome. In 2021, the Stanford group led by Jaimie Henderson and Krishna Shenoy reported, in *Nature*, that a participant could "handwrite in the mind" at around 90 characters per minute using a microelectrode array implanted in the motor cortex. The behaviour was astonishing: imagined strokes produced real letters. Yet even this breakthrough came with boundary conditions. The implant required neurosurgery, signal quality drifted over weeks, and error correction algorithms carried significant weight. The patient visited the lab regularly for recalibration. The implication is clear. High-bandwidth invasive BCIs are clinically promising but technically demanding, requiring a level of support and risk tolerance that constrains widespread use.

Non-invasive systems invert that trade-off. They are safe and portable but less precise. Yet they can still deliver practical wins in carefully chosen settings. A 2020 study at the University of Padua showed that stroke survivors using EEG-based motor imagery systems during therapy achieved measurable improvements in wrist extension compared with conventional physiotherapy alone. The mechanism was not magic. By engaging motor networks through repeated imagined movements, users strengthened the neural pathways needed for voluntary control. Therapists adjusted session length not by guesswork but by monitoring behavioural signs: slower responses, rising frustration, increased artefacts. Rehabilitation gains emerged from aligning neural workload with patient endurance—a direct expression of the motif of fit.

Fatigue detection offers another near-term horizon, though the ethical stakes shift when BCIs enter workplaces rather than clinics. In 2023, a manufacturing plant outside Osaka piloted a non-invasive EEG headset to identify when operators showed early signs of cognitive fatigue. Rather than monitoring productivity, the system flagged periods when sustained-attention metrics dipped below a predefined baseline. Supervisors used these signals to schedule micro-breaks of two to three minutes. The result was a small but meaningful reduction in minor assembly errors during late shifts. Workers reported feeling supported rather than monitored, in part because the firm set strict boundaries: the data was processed locally, stored for 24 hours only, and could not be used for performance evaluation. The behaviour that mattered was not the detection of fatigue but the organisational commitment to use the signal in service of safety rather than surveillance.

Such use cases reveal a broader pattern. Successful BCIs today operate as *adjuncts* rather than replacements. They augment therapies, reinforce routines, or offer subtle cues. They do not dominate workflows. Their quiet strength lies in incrementalism. But incrementalism also exposes constraints—technical, ergonomic, and regulatory—that shape the practical horizon.

Power is the first constraint. Most portable BCIs rely on low-power wireless chips and must balance sampling frequency with battery life. Higher sampling improves accuracy but drains power faster, creating a trade-off users feel physically. In 2022, a Paris-based start-up developing an fNIRS headband for cognitive-load monitoring discovered that doubling sampling rates reduced battery life from eight hours to three. Users complained. The engineers compromised, introducing adaptive sampling that increased frequency during detected workload peaks. This adjustment exemplifies the motif: fit is not static; it must be tuned.

Comfort is the second constraint, particularly for long-term or consumer use. EEG caps with wet electrodes offer better signal quality but are impractical for daily wear. Dry electrodes improve usability but introduce motion artefacts. One research team at Carnegie Mellon University noted in 2021 that even slight shifts—caused by hair compression, sweat, or head movement—corrupted signal stability over time. Participants touching the headset inadvertently altered electrode impedance, revealing how fragile "everyday BCI" remains. Comfort is not superficial; it is structural. It shapes whether a device becomes part of a routine or sits discarded in a drawer.

Regulation forms the third constraint. Medical-grade BCIs must undergo rigorous safety assessments and clinical validation. Consumer-grade BCIs, by contrast, often slip through regulatory cracks because they claim to "enhance wellness" rather than diagnose or treat. This distinction matters. When a Russian manufacturer released a focus-training headset in 2019, its marketing suggested it could "improve academic performance." Regulators intervened only after independent researchers showed that its attention metric correlated poorly with validated psychological measures. The behaviour that triggered oversight was not a malfunction but misleading inference. The implication is that regulation will shape which BCIs gain public trust—and which become cautionary tales.

Two further examples sharpen the limits and the promise. In 2016, DARPA's "Restoring Active Memory" project demonstrated that direct cortical stimulation could modestly improve recall in patients with brain injuries. The gains were statistically significant but not spectacular. More importantly, responses varied widely across individuals. This variability underscores the central truth: neural modulation works only when tuned delicately, and tuning remains labour-intensive. Meanwhile, in 2022, Meta's Reality Labs halted work on invasive BCIs for augmented reality, citing ethical, technical, and commercial challenges. Their public statement emphasised ergonomics and consent. A device worn for hours must be comfortable, private, and transparent about what it measures. The threshold was not technological limitation alone; it was the mismatch between ambition and context.

Through these examples, the motif of fit returns. What works in a clinic may fail in a classroom; what succeeds in a rehabilitation ward may falter on a factory floor. The practical horizon is not a single point but a band—narrow, concrete, and shaped by constraints designers must respect.

Still, possibility glimmers. Hybrid systems that combine neural signals with behavioural or contextual data often outperform pure BCI approaches. In 2021, researchers at the University of Queensland integrated EEG-based fatigue metrics with keystroke patterns and eye-tracking signals, creating a multi-signal model that predicted lapses more reliably than EEG alone. The behaviour was modest but promising. Workers received a gentle prompt—an icon glowing amber—when patterns suggested deteriorating focus. Many described it as a "nudge to breathe." The implication is forward-looking: BCIs may succeed best not by replacing other sensors but by complementing them.

This leads to a deeper insight. The near-term horizon of BCI is not defined by decoding thought. It is defined by scaffolding effort. Whether helping a stroke survivor regain fine motor control or prompting a factory worker to rest, BCIs function as adaptive mirrors—reflecting internal states back to users in ways they can act upon. The signal is not the story; the behaviour it prompts is.

And yet a forward test lingers—pointed, unresolved, and essential. *As BCIs become more portable and more persuasive, who decides when measurement turns into monitoring, and when support turns into subtle coercion?* The practical horizon may be narrow, but it is ethically charged. Those boundaries, not bandwidth, will determine which systems become trusted companions—and which fade under the weight of their own ambition.

Designing Humane Neuro-UX

In February 2024, at the Centre Hospitalier Universitaire de Lyon, a sixty-two-year-old patient named Mariette sat in a motor-rehabilitation suite wearing a non-invasive brain–computer interface. Her task was simple: imagine lifting her left hand so the system could calibrate its classifier. But each time she focused, the cursor on the screen faltered. She stiffened. Her breathing quickened. The physiotherapist, sensing her rising anxiety, activated a feature added only weeks earlier—a small haptic wristband that pulsed gently whenever the system confidently recognised her intention. The pulse arrived: soft, warm, affirmative. Mariette exhaled. Her shoulders loosened. Within minutes, the calibration curve steadied. The session's outcome—a 40 per cent reduction in classification error compared with her previous visit—did not stem from better algorithms. It stemmed from better design. The interface had learned not just how to read her brain, but how not to intimidate her.

That scene captures the central premise of humane neuro-UX. Brain–computer interfaces operate at the most intimate boundary between person and machine. They can unlock communication for those with paralysis, scaffold recovery for stroke survivors, and support workers in demanding environments. Yet they also impose cognitive load, provoke self-consciousness, and magnify small failures into moments of doubt. The system may be technical, but the burden sits with the human. The motif threading through this subchapter is the *gesture*: the small, deliberate acts—timely feedback, optional pauses, clear recoveries—that preserve dignity when the interface falters.

Humane neuro-UX begins with calibration, the moment when the user teaches the machine how to listen. Calibration is cognitively expensive. It demands concentration, patience, and confidence that errors reflect the machine's learning, not the user's inadequacy. The Lyon clinic discovered this the hard way. In 2023, their logs showed that new patients abandoned EEG-based exercises at nearly twice the rate of established users. Behaviourally, the pattern was unmistakable: first-session dropouts coincided with uncorrected misfires. The team responded by adding multi-modal feedback—auditory chimes for system errors, haptic pulses for correct decoding, and a visible progress bar showing how much calibration remained. Naming this strategy "progressive reassurance," they treated calibration as a shared activity rather than a technical hurdle. The implication was immediate. Dropout rates fell from 31 per cent to 14 per cent over six months. Dignity had become a metric.

The importance of timing cannot be overstated. Too little feedback, and users feel lost. Too much, and they feel overwhelmed. A research group at ETH Zürich demonstrated this tension in 2021 when testing a motor-imagery BCI for upper-limb rehabilitation. They trialled three feedback intervals: continuous updates, periodic updates every four seconds, and sparse updates every eight. Continuous feedback produced the highest stress markers—measured via galvanic skin response—because users felt under constant evaluation. Sparse feedback produced confusion. The sweet spot lay with the four-second interval, which gave users breathing room without depriving them of orientation. The behaviour that mattered was subtle: users leaned forward slightly during long gaps, signalling cognitive strain. The system learned to pace itself. The motif of the gesture returned—timing as a humane design choice.

Opt-outs form another pillar of neuro-UX. BCIs, especially non-invasive ones, are often marketed as passive or effortless, but the cognitive reality is very different. Sustained attention is work. The ability to pause, reset, or refuse must be effortless. In 2022, the University of Helsinki piloted a neurofeedback protocol for adults with ADHD. Participants could stop sessions instantly via a blink-pattern command detected by the headset. The feature was designed for convenience but became something more consequential. Users reported a greater sense of agency and less performance anxiety simply because they knew they could end a session without explanation. The opt-out was rarely triggered—less than 3 per cent of trials—but its psychological effect was significant. The implication is profound. Agency is measured not by how often it is exercised but by whether it is structurally honoured.

This emphasis on recovery also extends to error handling. BCIs misfire. They misclassify intention. They drift. Humane neuro-UX acknowledges this openly, not defensively. In 2020, Boston University researchers testing a spelling interface found that users interpreted silent misclassifications—cases where the system output nothing—as personal failure. They revised the interface. Instead of silence, users saw a subtle grey flash indicating that the system was uncertain. The behaviour shift was immediate. Users stopped apologising for errors. They became collaborators rather than performers. The system, simply by revealing its uncertainty, restored parity.

Contrast these examples with a credible counter-example. In 2019, a start-up in Beijing launched a BCI-driven productivity tool for open-plan offices. The device delivered real-time "focus scores" to managers but provided no feedback to employees themselves. Workers described the experience as "being watched by a ghost"—unseen sensors, unexplained judgements, and no means to contest or pause measurement. A subsequent academic review by Tsinghua University revealed significant inaccuracies in the device's attention classification, especially during emotionally charged conversations. Here, the interface failed not because its algorithms were weak but because its UX was extractive. It treated neural signals as managerial data rather than personal information. The reconciliation with humane design is sharp. BCIs succeed when users feel respected; they fail when users feel inspected.

Recoverability closes the loop. Neuro-UX must assume that users will lose signal, drift mentally, or become frustrated. Systems must offer graceful re-entry. At the Lyon clinic, recoverability took the form of a "re-centering ritual": a two-second breathing cue displayed after any prolonged misclassification streak. At home, consumer neurofeedback apps often deploy visual softening—screens dim slightly when signal quality drops—to nudge users to adjust posture or electrode placement without shame. The behaviour these cues support is self-compassion. The technology admits imperfection; the user responds with patience rather than panic.

Two further examples anchor the principle. In 2017, the BrainGate consortium observed that participants using invasive BCIs to control robotic limbs often experienced "mental fatigue collapse"—a sudden drop in performance after prolonged concentration. Early interfaces reacted by tightening thresholds, which only worsened frustration. When designers reversed course and introduced recovery windows—short periods during which errors were ignored and the interface reset—performance stabilised. In 2023, Oculus Research tested an experimental fNIRS system for VR interaction. They found that users regained control more quickly when the system displayed an explicit countdown during recalibration rather than leaving them waiting in ambiguity. The gesture, again, mattered.

The motif threading through these stories—the gesture—reveals a deeper principle. Humane neuro-UX is not decoration. It is not branding. It is a moral and cognitive necessity. BCIs touch the nervous system directly or indirectly; their effects are embodied. A poorly timed alert raises heart rate. A confusing misfire triggers embarrassment. A rigid calibration protocol that assumes perfection induces shame. Conversely, a gentle pulse, a clear pause, a dignified opt-out can restore calm, trust, and willingness to continue. Gesture becomes governance.

This leads to a sharper question, one that sits at the frontier of neuro-UX research. *As BCIs enter homes, clinics, and workplaces, how will designers decide which gestures preserve dignity and which inadvertently manipulate mood or behaviour?* The answer cannot rest on engineering alone. It requires sensitivity to vulnerability, context, and the fragile boundary between assistance and coercion. That boundary—the one governing humane design—will be the next arena where neurotechnology proves its wisdom or betrays its ambition.

Chapter 4
Augmenting Core Capacities

The first sign that something had shifted came in a cramped meeting room at a mid-size law firm in Bristol. A junior associate, preparing a response to a complex breach-of-contract case, asked the firm's retrieval assistant to surface relevant precedents. Within seconds, a cascade of candidates appeared—cases from 1987, 2003, 2015—each linked to the specific contractual phrasing buried deep in hundreds of pages of discovery. The senior partner, who had once spent nights trawling archives to achieve the same result, stared at the screen with a mixture of admiration and unease. "The trick," she finally said, "is not finding the precedent. It's deciding which one actually matters." The room fell quiet. The machine had accelerated perception. But judgement still rested with her.

That scene—unremarkable, almost banal—captures the threshold we now stand on. Our tools no longer merely store documents or automate routines; they expand our cognitive field. They extend what we can notice, remember, and combine. Yet each extension carries a paradox. When perception widens, selection becomes harder. When reasoning accelerates, errors accelerate with it. When memory is outsourced, recall grows brittle. When creativity is amplified, taste becomes the last defence against homogenisation. Augmenting core capacities is not a one-way climb towards greater capability; it is a delicate navigation of gains and losses, clarity and distortion, power and responsibility.

The broader pattern has historical roots. In 1962, the psychologist Jerome Bruner wrote that "a scaffold is not merely a support; it is a transformation." He was describing how children learn, but the principle applies far beyond childhood. Every cognitive scaffold changes the shape of the mind that uses it. The printing press broadened memory beyond the skull. Statistical tables changed how scientists reasoned about uncertainty. Digital search reconfigured what counts as "knowing" something. And now, hybrid intelligence—our partnership with models that retrieve, infer, organise, and synthesise—extends this lineage into new terrain. Tools do not simply add to our capacities. They reshape them.

Augmentation begins with perception: the ability to see patterns, retrieve information, and scan the world more quickly than our biological senses allow. Models can trawl corpora, audio transcripts, images, and structured data simultaneously, tracing connections the human eye would miss. But extended perception can overwhelm as easily as it enlightens. Retrieval-augmented workflows promise speed, yet speed without discrimination can swamp judgement. The legal associate in Bristol found herself navigating abundance rather than scarcity—a challenge as old as knowledge itself, yet newly sharpened by scale.

From perception, the chapter moves to reasoning and planning: the orchestrating capacities that decide what to do with what we notice. Structured prompting has become the lingua franca of hybrid reasoning—decomposing tasks, constraining scope, specifying roles, toggling tools. But structure alone does not guarantee sound reasoning. A project manager who blindly follows model-generated chains of thought can find herself shepherded down elegant but unfalsifiable paths. A checklist, by contrast, demands verifiable steps. This distinction—between plausible reasoning and verifiable reasoning—anchors the coming section. It marks the line between collaboration and abdication.

Memory and attention form the quiet heart of the chapter. These are the capacities most at risk of erosion when support systems become too comfortable. External memory aids—from notes apps to AI-generated summaries—promise liberation from cognitive clutter. Yet the more perfectly something is stored outside us, the less obliged we feel to store any trace inside. A student in Edinburgh, preparing for final exams, discovered this the hard way. Her assistant generated immaculate flashcards for every topic, but when she tested herself without them, the scaffolding collapsed. The gap revealed a truth that cognitive science has long known: memory strengthens not through exposure but through retrieval. Attention, likewise, is not restored by eliminating effort but by training discipline. Hybrid memory systems must therefore follow rotation rules, ensure periodic friction, and honour the difference between help and displacement.

Creativity and synthesis round out the chapter's arc. Models can remix styles, propose variations, and surface combinations no human would generate alone. But creativity is not variety; it is selection under constraint. A designer in Shoreditch learned this when her model, asked for logo concepts, produced dozens of dazzling but derivative iterations. Only when she imposed a storyboard—a sequence of constraints capturing tone, risk appetite, cultural references, and negative space—did the collaboration yield something coherent. Augmentation thrives when human taste governs machine abundance.

Across these domains, a subtle motif returns again and again: **extension without erosion**. The promise of hybrid intelligence is not merely to do more, faster. It is to expand our capacities while preserving the qualities that make those capacities human—our discernment, our curiosity, our sense of proportion, our tolerance for uncertainty, our appetite for the slow, stubborn parts of thinking that no model can automate without cost.

Yet the story is not one of triumph alone. Every augmentation introduces a pressure: to see more than we can interpret, to plan more than we can supervise, to remember less because machines remember more, to create faster because variations proliferate effortlessly. The real challenge is not adopting these tools but absorbing them without hollowing ourselves.

This chapter invites the reader into that tension. It traces how perception becomes selection, how reasoning becomes accountability, how memory becomes discipline, and how creativity becomes authorship. It shows how hybrid systems can refine our capacities without replacing them, strengthen our attention without commandeering it, and broaden our imagination without diluting our judgement.

And beneath every section lies an unanswered question—one that will follow you into the pages ahead: *when our tools stretch the boundaries of what we can do, how do we decide which boundaries must not stretch with them?*

Perception and Search

At 9:14 a.m. on 6 June 2023, in a conference room overlooking Bristol's harbourside, the litigation team at Harcourt Wells LLP faced a deadline that had shrunk from difficult to impossible. They needed to locate any precedent in English contract law where a supplier's *implied notification duty* had been tested under conditions resembling their client's dispute. Traditionally, this meant days of combing through scanned archives and annotations inherited from partners long retired. Instead, the team ran a query through their retrieval workspace. Within eight seconds, the system surfaced three cases—*Reynolds v Norwood Engineering* (High Court, 1987), *Thompson v Calder Systems* (Court of Appeal, 2003), and *Markham v Asterion Logistics* (Queen's Bench, 2015)—each ranked by conceptual similarity rather than keyword overlap. The junior solicitor who triggered the search stared at the list in near disbelief. "It's like it read the question backwards," she muttered. The senior partner corrected her gently: "No—it read the documents sideways." The result was impressive, but the deeper shift lay elsewhere. Perception had changed form. The machine had widened the perceptual field so quickly that the team's task flipped from *finding* to *judging*. The bottleneck was no longer retrieval. It was meaning.

The scene in Bristol captures the central ambition of augmented perception: to extend the human capacity to notice, correlate, and retrieve across far more sensory and informational channels than biology permits. Retrieval systems process text, audio, images, transcripts, logs, and numerical streams as if they belonged to a single semantic landscape. They treat the world not as a filing cabinet but as a topology of relations. Yet this extension creates its own demands. When every relevant scrap can be surfaced in seconds, the quality of human attention—not the sophistication of the algorithm—determines whether the result becomes insight or noise.

A retrieval system begins with a simple idea: *mapping meaning into distance.* Show this with the Bristol example. Document embeddings transformed each precedent into a vector in a high-dimensional space; proximity signalled conceptual kinship. Name the method plainly: dense embeddings, popularised after 2018, allowed queries to match ideas rather than strings. Explain the effect: a clause about "timely disclosure of shipment risk" could retrieve a precedent about "prompt notification of service hazards" even if no phrasing overlapped. The implication is profound. The search space becomes semantic rather than lexical. The solicitor's question is interpreted as *conceptual intent.*

Two more cases underline this transformation. In 2021, the New York Times digitised its entire analog photo archive—nearly five million images stored beneath its headquarters—then embedded the collection to enable conceptual retrieval. Editors could search for "solitude in winter" and surface images from 1949, 1973, and 1998 without relying on captions. The visible behaviour in the newsroom changed. Photo editors began exploratory querying rather than hunting through curated folders. Meanwhile in 2020, radiologists at the University of Toronto built an embedding index of anonymised CT scans, allowing clinicians to retrieve visually similar cases when confronting ambiguous lung lesions. The system offered comparisons in under ten seconds, enabling consultations that previously required senior specialists. Yet each system revealed the same boundary. Retrieval could offer candidates. Diagnosis and narrative required humans.

A counter-example helps temper the narrative. In 2019, a major UK retailer deployed an embedding-based retrieval tool to interpret customer feedback across text, call transcripts, and survey data. Early tests dazzled executives, who believed they could now "hear the voice of the customer at scale." But a later audit showed the system repeatedly clustered sarcasm with genuine praise and mistook regional dialect complaints for jokes. Retrieval was accurate on paper but brittle in context. The limitation was not technical. It was perceptual. The embeddings collapsed nuance that mattered. The reconciliation lies in purpose. Extending perception works best when the underlying domain tolerates abstraction—legal precedent, medical imaging—not when human tone shapes meaning.

Perception, when extended, requires constraint. Humans evolved to scan narrow sensory windows: the few objects we can hold in working memory, the sliver of sound we can attend to at once. Retrieval-augmented workflows rupture that window. They deliver abundance—sometimes too much. And abundance demands choreography. The motif that threads through this chapter is the *beam*: the directed cone of attention that determines what the flood reveals. Without the beam, extended perception becomes glare.

To show the importance of the beam, return briefly to Bristol. After the retrieval assistant surfaced the three cases, the team did not treat them as answers but as hypotheses. They read the passages the model flagged as maximally analogous. They checked the procedural posture of each case. They asked whether the judges' reasoning hinged on industry norms absent from their client's sector. The retrieval system widened the view; the lawyers narrowed it deliberately. Behaviourally, this looked like scepticism. But scepticism is a form of perceptual discipline.

The same pattern appears in other domains. In 2017, the National Institute of Standards and Technology (NIST) analysed forensic examiners' use of pattern-recognition systems for latent fingerprints. The examiners who performed best did not accept algorithmic rankings at face value. Instead, they treated machine outputs as prompts to examine overlooked minutiae—ridge endings, bifurcations, rotational distortions. Retrieval expanded the perceptual field; expert review concentrated it. The beam sharpened. The outcome was not automation but augmentation.

Perception can also be extended across modalities. Retrieval systems can accept text, images, and audio as equivalent query types. A lawyer might highlight a paragraph; an investigative journalist might upload a photograph; a compliance officer might paste part of a transcript. The system maps them to a shared space. Show the effect through another named case. In 2022, the BBC's investigative unit used multimodal retrieval to cross-reference leaked WhatsApp voice notes with satellite images, matching background audio cues—traffic hum, construction noises—to specific neighbourhoods in eastern Khartoum. The behaviour was ingenious but grounded: retrieval acted as a perceptual prosthetic, allowing reporters to triangulate context that human senses alone could not parse.

Yet the limitation persists. Extended perception risks overreach. When a system retrieves everything that *might* be relevant, humans must decide what is relevant *enough*. The risk is not simply noise but misplaced confidence. A well-ranked retrieval result may feel authoritative, even when its connection to the query is tenuous. That risk surfaced in a 2021 audit at a Sydney-based corporate firm, where junior associates increasingly cited the top-ranked retrieved documents without cross-checking their procedural relevance. Senior partners intervened by instituting a "two-source rule": any retrieval result required verification through either manual search or citation cross-links. Behaviour changed. Confidence was earned, not inherited.

Recovering the motif of the *beam*, we can state the principle directly: retrieval systems widen the perceptual field; humans must narrow it deliberately. This narrowing is not a constraint on intelligence; it is an act of interpretation.

Another dimension of extended perception lies in patterning: the ability to detect structural similarity at scales impossible for unaided cognition. In 2020, researchers at MIT built a system that compared millions of scientific papers through embeddings, identifying—months ahead of publication—latent links between coronavirus spike-protein mechanisms and earlier SARS research. The system did not predict the pandemic. It provided accelerants for researchers testing hypotheses about viral binding. The behaviour that mattered was not retrieval alone but serendipity—an engineered form of noticing.

A second example—the European Court of Human Rights' 2023 pilot of a retrieval assistant—shows similar effects. Judges used the system to surface prior judgments involving "constructive removal" even when the term was never mentioned explicitly. This allowed clerks to examine reasoning rather than keywords. Yet the tool was constrained by design: it displayed confidence bands, uncertainty notes, and links to full judgments. The system extended perception; the interface preserved context. The implication is that humane retrieval design requires friction—small reminders that meaning lies beyond the embedding.

The counter-example returns here with force. Multimodal retrieval systems can misclassify edge cases where subtle human distinctions matter. In 2019, a California appellate court review found that automated precedent suggestions incorrectly grouped several negligence cases with intentional tort cases simply because plaintiffs described harm with similar verbs. The limitation is structural. Semantics is not jurisprudence. Retrieval can suggest; it cannot interpret legal thresholds.

Across all these cases, one truth becomes impossible to ignore: extended perception demands extended responsibility. A wider field of view expands opportunity *and* risk. The person directing the beam must learn to switch between exploratory and discriminating modes, treating retrieval as a companion rather than a crutch.

This brings us to the unresolved tension that closes this subchapter. *As retrieval systems grow more fluent, and as perception stretches beyond human scale, how will professionals decide which signals deserve attention and which only imitate relevance?* The beam cannot widen indefinitely. Someone must choose where to point it—and why.

Reasoning and Planning

At 8:03 a.m. on 12 January 2022, in a project room above Liverpool Street Station, the delivery manager at Strathwell Infrastructure, Amelia Kerr, stared at two timelines for the same £14.2 million rail-maintenance programme. One came from her team's new planning assistant—a model fine-tuned on five years of project logs. The other came from her most experienced engineer, handwritten in pencil, annotated with circles, arrows, and hard-earned scepticism. The model estimated twelve weeks to completion; the engineer insisted on eighteen. The difference turned on a single judgement: a drainage diversion near Mile End that had a 30 per cent likelihood of requiring night-time closures. The software treated it as a routine dependency. The engineer treated it as risk incarnate. Kerr made her decision with a simple test. She asked each to justify its estimate in steps. The model produced an elegant chain of thought. The engineer produced a checklist of verifiable conditions that needed to be confirmed on-site. The checklist won. "The model reasons," she later said, "but the checklist *stands accountable*."

The scene exposed a quiet truth about hybrid reasoning: coherence is cheap, verification is dear. A multi-step explanation from a model can sound disarmingly plausible even when built on sand. Human reasoning, by contrast, is slow, error-prone, but anchored in lived contingencies—muddy pits, late deliveries, crews that fall ill. The project room became a microcosm of a broader shift. As models grow capable of structuring tasks, summarising dependencies, and refining goals, the question is no longer whether they can think *with* us. They can. The question is when their reasoning deserves to guide action.

Structured reasoning in hybrid systems begins with the simplest act: showing, naming, and explaining each step. Show it through Kerr's dilemma. A seemingly minor clause—"shift diversion readiness"—produced divergent schedules because the planner lacked context about local permitting delays from 2019. Name the concept plainly: *contextual blind spots*. Explain the mechanism: models interpolate from training patterns but struggle with site-specific irregularities unless explicitly grounded. The implication is immediate. Multi-step planning requires evidence-aware steps, not generative eloquence. Reasoning must pass from fluency to accountability.

Two further cases make this concrete. In 2020, the Danish Tax Authority deployed an AI-assisted audit tool with structured prompting for complex investigations. Analysts input high-level hypotheses—undeclared overseas income, fraudulent deduction patterns—then received chain-of-thought walkthroughs proposing document sequences to review. The system accelerated early triage, but the decisive gains came when analysts converted the model's suggestions into checklists: bank statements to cross-check, asset transfers to timestamp, anomalies to rule out manually. Behaviour changed. Analysts used the model for breadth, then switched to evidence-led steps for depth.

A second example emerged from Tesla's manufacturing engineering team in Fremont, California, in 2021. Planners used a model-driven troubleshooting assistant to diagnose bottlenecks in the battery module line. The assistant excelled at enumerating plausible failure sequences—misaligned robotics, thermal drift in bonding, supply volatility. Yet engineers quickly realised that elegant reasoning hid a shortcoming. The assistant lacked the ability to tie each step to *measurable indicators* such as torque deviation, sensor latency, or cycle time variance. Engineers added a verification layer: each proposed step required a corresponding metric and tolerance band. With this rule, spurious reasoning collapsed immediately. Choices hardened around measurable reality.

These cases reveal the motif that guides this subchapter: the *rail*. Good reasoning is not a meandering story. It is a rail—firm, inspectable, and aligned with physical or organisational constraints. Models generate potential rails; humans decide which can bear weight.

Structured prompting makes these rails explicit. Rather than asking a model to "draft a delivery plan," teams now prompt it to lay out goals, sub-goals, success criteria, dependencies, and risk gates. When done well, the prompt resembles a brief from a seasoned planner: identify the task; define success with measurable indicators; break the work into phases; highlight where human oversight is mandatory. Show this through a named example. In 2023, the UK's National Audit Office tested a structured-prompts workflow for reviewing procurement irregularities. By asking the system to specify its assumptions at each step—cost baselines, vendor solvency, legal thresholds—auditors could check reasoning against statute. The system did not remove human labour; it organised it.

But structured prompts are not a panacea. They impose form without guaranteeing truth. A limitation is visible in 2022 trials at the University of Pennsylvania's Wharton School, where MBA students evaluated model-generated business plans. Chains of thought could appear impeccable while missing market constraints buried in public filings. The counter-example matters. Reasoning models excel at internal coherence, not external grounding. Yet the limitation dissolves when the rails return. Students who added a mandatory cross-link step—checking at least three factual assertions against filings or analyst reports—dramatically reduced false confidence. Verification restored the boundary between narrative and evidence.

Planning gains real strength when models shift from storytelling to constraint solving. Humans break tasks to manage uncertainty; models break tasks to optimise search. Show this through an engineering case. In 2022, Siemens Mobility used a planning assistant for tunnel inspection rotas in Munich. The assistant generated candidate schedules optimised for fatigue limits, equipment rotation, and rainfall forecasts. Engineers adjusted them based on local knowledge: union rules, contractor reliability, seasonal disruptions. The behaviour that mattered was not which agent produced which step but the *handover* between them. The rail passed back and forth.

Breaking tasks is not just a structural action—it is cognitive hygiene. Humans misjudge the complexity of problems when lumped into wholes. Planning assistants counter this by decomposing tasks into units small enough to inspect. Yet decomposition must do more than reduce labour; it must reveal assumptions. Explain it through the motif. The rail is only as strong as its joints. Each task boundary is a joint, a point where hidden assumptions hide. Exposing joints forces clarity: who signs off, what counts as success, what evidence is required to move on.

Goal-setting follows the same rhythm. When a model proposes a plan, it implicitly defines a target. But hybrid work demands explicit targets. In 2021, the Mayor's Office of Data Analytics in New York piloted a model-assisted workflow for housing inspections. The assistant suggested optimal ordering of checks based on risk estimates. Inspectors added a goal-setting step: each suggested ordering required a rationale linked to safety outcomes, not convenience. This visible behaviour—forcing goal alignment—reduced false positives by 18 per cent, as later audits confirmed. The rail remained tied to public purpose rather than algorithmic neatness.

Yet no discussion of reasoning and planning would be complete without addressing sign-off: who approves the plan and under what conditions. The sign-off question became central to Kerr's rail-maintenance dilemma in London. Her engineer's checklist held firm because it tied each step to an observable condition—permits received, equipment available, inspection reports complete. The model's chain of thought could not provide that grounding. Sign-off became the decisive boundary where human judgement remained sovereign.

Planning assistants can support sign-off by maintaining traces—logs that record which assumptions, prompts, and intermediate outputs led to a recommendation. This provenance trail turns reasoning into an auditable artefact rather than a black box. In 2023, the European Medicines Agency tested such traceable planning for pharmacovigilance workflows. Regulators needed to know why a flagged safety signal was prioritised over others. The planning engine provided not just the reasoning but the sources. Auditors could follow the rail from end to origin. Responsibility became transparent.

But traceability alone cannot solve a deeper tension: models can overfit to patterns, humans can overfit to stories. The failure modes differ, yet both distort the rail. A counter-example makes this honest. In late 2020, a leading consultancy used a reasoning assistant to plan a transformation project for a Swiss insurance firm. The assistant produced a precise work breakdown. The human team accepted it with minimal challenge because it matched their expectations. The plan failed. The model had overfit to its training distribution; the humans had overfit to familiarity. The reconciliation? Introduce deliberate disruptors—steps where the assistant is required to generate *alternative plans,* and humans are required to articulate why they reject them. This behaviour—structured dissent—strengthens the rail.

The final movement brings the motif into sharp relief. Hybrid reasoning promises speed, structure, and breadth. Human reasoning contributes judgement, accountability, and context. Together, they can produce rails strong enough to carry real work. Yet the tension persists. *When the model offers a plan so coherent that it feels inevitable, who pauses to test whether the rail rests on solid ground or vanishes into fog?*

Memory and Attention

At 7:52 p.m. on 19 October 2021, in a cramped study bedroom at the University of Leeds, second-year medical student Priya Malhotra stared at a stack of digital flashcards that had ballooned past 4,000. Her revision assistant—fine-tuned on past exam papers—generated perfect prompts on cranial nerves, enzyme deficiencies, and the nuances of heart murmurs. It even predicted which items would likely appear in January's finals. Yet after a fortnight of high-speed drilling, Priya realised she could answer vast numbers of questions while barely remembering how she knew the answers. "It feels like the knowledge is stored *elsewhere*," she wrote that night in her notebook, "and I'm just acting as an access point." The discomfort surprised her. The system had made her faster, calmer, and ostensibly better prepared. But it had also dulled something she relied on: the friction that forces concepts to stick. When she shifted to self-testing—no generation, no hints—her accuracy plummeted. That drop was unpleasant. It was also a sign of learning.

The scene in Leeds captures a tension that permeates hybrid cognition. External memory aids expand our capacity to store, recall, and reconfigure information. They can turn scattered knowledge into ordered structures and flatten the emotional cost of revision. Yet they can also hollow out our internal scaffolds. When the path to recall becomes too smooth, the underlying representation remains thin. Memory thrives on effort, not ease. Attention thrives on limits, not abundance. The difficulty lies in designing workflows that respect both truths.

Show this tension through the Leeds example. Priya's assistant created flashcards with impeccable phrasing and frequency estimates derived from past papers. Name the mechanism: algorithmic spacing. Explain its effect: the model spaced items based on predicted exam relevance rather than her personal forgetting curve. The implication was subtle but significant. She rehearsed what the system deemed important, not what *she* struggled with. Effective memory work demands the opposite. Spacing should follow forgetting, not prediction.

Hybrid memory makes this clearer when we examine its cognitive architecture. Working memory—the narrow mental workspace—handles roughly four chunks at a time, a constraint demonstrated repeatedly since Miller's classic research in 1956 and refined in later studies by Cowan (2001). External aids free that workspace. They compress readings into highlights; they transform complex topics into digestible prompts; they capture insights the moment they surface. But the externalisation comes with a trade-off. If too much is offloaded, the internal structure withers. The pianist who never rehearses hands separately may play fluently yet carry no deep motor map. The student who drills flashcards without generating answers may recognise terms without understanding mechanisms.

Concrete cases show the spectrum. In 2019, researchers at the University of Tokyo tracked engineering students who used AI-generated summaries during problem-solving sessions. Behaviour shifted. Students who relied heavily on the summaries solved routine problems more quickly but struggled with transfer tasks—questions that required adapting a principle to a new setting. The metric was stark: transfer accuracy dropped by 22 per cent (Yamada et al., 2019). The summaries gave them speed, not structure. A second example arrives from workplace training. In 2022, Airbus experimented with an instruction assistant for maintenance technicians in Hamburg. The assistant provided component diagrams, torque specs, and procedural steps. Technicians completed tasks faster, yet supervisors noticed a change. Failures during simulations increased when the assistant was removed. Deeper inquiry revealed that technicians had followed instructions accurately but had not formed internal models of why each step mattered. Offloading had become dependence.

A counter-example tempers this pattern. In 2020, the Royal College of Nursing piloted AI-assisted knowledge reinforcement modules. Instead of generating answers, the assistant asked nurses to summarise clinical guidelines in their own words, then compared the summaries with source documents and highlighted gaps. The behaviour was different from the Tokyo or Hamburg cases. The system forced *effortful recall*, preserving the cognitive demands of memory formation. The difference suggests a principle: augmentation strengthens memory only when it preserves desirable difficulty.

To frame this systematically, introduce the motif that threads through this subchapter: the *rotation*. Memory thrives when attention rotates between supported and unsupported modes—between external scaffolds and bare, unaided recall. Rotation acts as a safeguard against cognitive atrophy. It also ensures that offloading does not become outsourcing.

Show the rotation through Priya's eventual adaptation. After noticing her overreliance on generated flashcards, she instituted a rule: for every ten AI-generated cards reviewed, she created three manual ones drawn from her weakest domains. She spaced these manually created cards using the Leitner system—a box-based rotation method dating back to 1972—placing difficult cards in frequent boxes, easier ones in slower cycles. The behaviour mattered. She reclaimed ownership of the forgetting curve. When she sat her January exams, her recall comfort felt markedly different. She remembered not just the facts but the paths she had taken to retrieve them.

To understand why rotation works, consider cognitive offloading more broadly. Offloading comes in many forms: jotting down a reminder; using autocomplete for citations; letting a system highlight essential lines in a research article. Offloading helps attention by reducing the clutter that overwhelms working memory. But there is a threshold beyond which offloading dilutes the attentional muscle. Behaviourally, this shows up as shallower concentration, quicker distraction, and a reduced ability to hold complex problems in mind.

Two examples illustrate productive offloading. In 2018, Google's People Analytics team experimented with summarisation assistants for performance reviews. Employees who used AI-generated summaries for their *first pass* but then rewrote them manually produced reviews that were judged clearer and more evidence-driven by independent raters. The offloading created a scaffold; the manual rewrite created ownership. Similarly, in 2021, Imperial College London's MSc Data Science cohort used structured note-templates generated by an assistant. Students who alternated between AI-generated outlines and personal annotations demonstrated stronger exam performance than those who relied on either approach alone. Rotation grounded the learning.

A challenge arises when offloading becomes continuous rather than intermittent. Consider a limitation case. In 2022, a tech start-up in Berlin trialled a meeting assistant that generated live summaries and action points. Employees grew adept at glancing at prompts instead of listening fully. When the assistant malfunctioned for three days, meeting productivity collapsed. Participants could not recall discussion points without the summary feed. The problem was not the tool. It was the absence of rotation. Offloading had become the default state rather than a strategic choice.

Spaced review—another central mechanism—benefits from rotation as well. Spacing relies on the finding that information strengthens when revisited just before it is forgotten. But spacing becomes skewed when external systems schedule revisits based solely on generic difficulty rather than personal struggle. The Leeds case shows this directly. Priya needed spacing aligned to her errors, not predicted frequency patterns. Spaced review becomes powerful only when it respects the learner's forgetting curve.

A named example deepens the point. In 2019, King's College London trialled adaptive revision platforms for medical students. The platforms used personalised difficulty ratings derived from past answers. When combined with student-generated questions, performance improved significantly; when students relied exclusively on system-generated prompts, performance gains plateaued. The visible behaviour differed in a single respect: agency. Students who authored some questions engaged deeper cognitive processing. Rotation protected attention.

The motif returns. Rotation is not merely a technique; it is an attentional ethic. It reminds learners that cognitive tools are allies, not proxies. It also helps professionals resist the automation of attention. In hybrid environments—where assistants summarise, annotate, retrieve, and cue—attention must remain selectively applied. Without deliberate rotation, attention dissolves into passivity.

The relationship between memory and attention is recursive. Memory anchors attention; attention consolidates memory. Hybrid systems complicate this relationship by smoothing cognitive effort. External aids can make tasks feel easier than they should. But desirable friction is a teacher. It signals where understanding is shallow or where recall is fading. When tools remove that friction entirely, they risk hiding the thresholds where learning must occur.

A final example shows rotation in the workplace. In 2023, a major UK law firm introduced retrieval-augmented drafting for junior associates. The system suggested summaries, clauses, and citations. Associates who alternated between AI-assisted drafts and independent drafting retained legal structures better than those who relied fully on automation. Supervisors saw it plainly: the associates using rotation asked sharper questions and made fewer conceptual errors during review meetings. The behaviour indicated deeper mental models, not just smoother surface performance.

The unresolved tension closes the subchapter: *As external memory grows more powerful, how will individuals decide which parts of their cognitive labour must remain internal to preserve expertise—and which can safely be rotated outward?*

Creativity and Synthesis

On 4 May 2023, in a compact studio in Shoreditch lit by a single skylight, graphic designer Lila Fernández confronted a problem she had never quite faced before. She had fed a model

forty of her previous poster designs—bold geometry, saturated reds, delicate serif annotations—and asked it to propose variations for a commission from the Barbican Centre. Within minutes, the model produced dozens of drafts. They looked coherent. They looked professional. They looked, to her alarm, *generic*. The compositions blended into one another, the palette drifted toward fashionable gradients she never used, and the line weights softened into a style she would never sign her name to. "It's me," she murmured, "but sanded down."
The experience forced a reckoning. The model had not misunderstood her. It had understood her **too** well, averaging her work into a statistical essence. Her personal taste—the micro-choices she made instinctively—had dissolved into a central tendency. To recover her voice, she began building a storyboard, pinning her sources of constraint and refusal: what colours she would never use, what typographic tensions defined her, what risks she welcomed, and what lines she would not cross. Only after fixing these human rails did she ask the model for variations again. This time, the results surprised her in the right way. The machine offered possibilities. She chose.

The scene is not an anomaly. Creative domains across design, writing, architecture, and research are discovering the same pattern: models excel at remixing, but they do not care about taste. They respect correlations, not commitments. Creativity requires the courage to commit. The orbit of hybrid creativity therefore turns not on novelty alone, but on *direction*—the steady human pull that says, "This, not that."

Show the dynamic through Lila's case. The model trained on her portfolio distilled her visual language into latent dimensions: curvature, density, palette, symmetry. Name this process plainly: representational compression. Explain the consequence: when the compressor dominates, individual quirks flatten. The implication is unavoidable. Without guardrails, creativity collapses into style drift—the kind that earns likes on social media but fails to move a discerning eye.

Two contrasting examples illuminate the stakes. In 2022, the New Yorker's art department experimented with model-assisted concept sketches for upcoming features. Editors provided thematic descriptions; the model returned rough visuals. Artists integrated fragments—an unexpected colour echo, a bold silhouette—but rejected the model's default symmetry. The practice freed time without diluting voice. A year earlier, in 2021, film director Chloé Zhao used a visual reference engine to explore lighting moods for *Eternals*, generating iterated palettes inspired by thousands of cinematographic stills. The engine's suggestions were treated as study material, not final frames. Zhao's choices—her appetite for dusk blues, her insistence on long-shadow contrast—shaped the final aesthetic. In both cases, human taste remained sovereign.

A counter-example sharpens the lesson. In 2020, an advertising agency in Sydney deployed an ideation model to produce campaign slogans. The team grew enamoured with the speed of concept generation and stopped grounding their decisions in audience insight. The slogans tested poorly: consumers described them as "algorithmically smooth" and "lacking bite." The model had produced syntactic creativity but semantic emptiness. The limitation was not the technology but the abdication of taste. The reconciliation came when strategists reinstated a hard rule: no concept proceeded unless justified with a human-derived constraint—tone, demographic relevance, or cultural signal.

This subchapter's motif—the *frame*—emerges naturally here. Creative synthesis begins not with infinite variation but with a frame that defines intention. A frame is not a cage. It is a promise. It says: these are the edges within which the play will unfold.

To understand why the frame matters, consider the model's fundamental operation. It recombines patterns across vast corpora, sampling the statistically plausible. It can interpolate between Baroque and brutalist, between Bauhaus grid and psychedelic swirl. But the model does not know what is at stake. A poster is not merely colour and form; it is a message, a mood, a position. The human contribution enters here. Taste is a filtration system—a refusal engine—that filters thousands of plausible options through the sieve of identity and purpose.

Show → Name → Explain → Implication becomes our analytic rhythm.
Show: Lila rejects the model's drift toward gradient-heavy backdrops.
Name: aesthetic boundary.
Explain: gradients, though popular, blunted the tension she prized between hard geometry and empty space.
Implication: without boundaries, the model tends toward the statistically fashionable, collapsing distinctive style.

The frame also protects against something subtler: aesthetic contagion. When humans review dozens of model-generated variations, they risk adopting patterns they never consciously chose. Behaviourally, this shows up as incremental drift—slightly rounder shapes, slightly brighter hues—that accumulate until the final work feels unlike its author. Creative integrity requires active filtration, not passive acceptance.

A second example emphasises the value of structured constraints. In 2023, the architecture firm BIG (Bjarke Ingels Group) experimented with an AI-assisted massing generator. Rather than asking for unconstrained forms, designers began with strict parameters: maximum height, sunlight envelopes, circulation paths. When the system generated dozens of options, the team selected only those that aligned with their philosophical stance on "hedonistic sustainability"—the idea that environmental responsibility should feel joyful, not punitive. The frame ensured that the outputs remained aligned with institutional taste.

And yet another dimension emerges: risk appetite. Humans possess a capacity that models lack—the willingness to stake identity on a choice. This willingness often distinguishes memorable creativity from technical competence. In the 1970s, designer Paula Scher pushed typographic scales to provocative extremes; in 2010, choreographer Crystal Pite inverted traditional narrative arcs in contemporary dance. Models cannot replicate risk appetite because risk is not statistical. It is reputational and emotional. It carries consequence.

Human risk appetite complements model abundance. Consider a 2022 experiment at the Royal College of Art, where students used AI to generate dozens of textile prints. Most model outputs clustered around safe, symmetrical motifs. One student, determined to push against convention, used a storyboard to specify constraints—"broken symmetry," "visible repair marks," "frayed continuity"—and had the model iterate within these edges. The work that emerged was raw, evocative, and recognisably hers. The model provided the raw ore; she selected the metal.

A limitation shows the necessity of the frame. In 2021, a Los Angeles animation studio tested generative tools for character design. The system produced hundreds of variations, yet studio leads reported "style collapse"—characters drifted toward a homogenous aesthetic reminiscent of widely shared online art. The human tendency to select the most polished-looking outputs amplified the collapse. The reconciliation arrived when the studio enforced a storyboard method: before any generation, artists documented three non-negotiables (motion posture, emotional register, narrative role). With these in place, the system's outputs diversified rather than converged. The frame protected originality.

Synthesis—the act of combining elements into new wholes—thrives under these conditions. Systems can propose improbable juxtapositions; humans judge which tensions produce meaning. The frame operates quietly, like a doorway. It invites variation but rejects dilution. It ensures that the creative act retains its moral dimension: the willingness to choose, not merely to accept.

To deepen the motif, observe how professional workflows evolve. In 2023, Penguin Random House's design division piloted a hybrid cover-design process. Designers began by sketching a storyboard of thematic anchors—"melancholy but not defeat," "brushstroke texture," "resistance through stillness." They then prompted the model with these anchors to explore variations. Successful designs emerged not from model spontaneity but from the designers' disciplined framing. The visible behaviours were telling: designers spent more time articulating constraints and less time cleaning up generic outputs. Creativity shifted upstream.

Meanwhile, in scientific research, synthesis appears differently. In 2022, neuroscientists at ETH Zurich used a literature-embedding engine to surface conceptual links across subfields. But the creative step—deciding which link was meaningful—remained human. The system could show that a paper on hippocampal oscillations from 2013 shared conceptual DNA with a 2017 robotics paper on navigation algorithms. But only the researchers could decide whether this juxtaposition mattered enough to become a hypothesis. The frame was intellectual rather than aesthetic, but the principle was identical: constraints precede insight.

Still, the allure of unlimited variation brings risk. Abundance can seduce. When options proliferate without judgement, attention scatters, and synthesis weakens. This mirrors findings from consumer psychology. Iyengar and Lepper's 2000 study demonstrated that too much choice can impair decision-making. In creative work, the effect is amplified. Without a frame, the model's prolific variation becomes a fog.

The storyboard method intervenes here. It demands that creators distil intention before generation. A storyboard articulates four anchors: the emotional tone, the structural constraints, the material references, and the risk posture. Once these are set, the model becomes an instrument, not a director. The behaviour changes. Creators stop asking, "What can the model produce?" and begin asking, "What direction am *I* insisting on?"

Returning to Lila's Shoreditch studio, we see this shift clearly. After building her storyboard, she prompted the model with narrow constraints: *maintain hard geometry; avoid gradients; emphasise negative space; explore asymmetry in colour blocks.* The variations that followed startled her with their freshness precisely because they respected her identity. The frame guided the remix. The output expanded her horizon without erasing her fingerprint.

The unresolved tension remains: *As models grow more fluent and generative abundance becomes the baseline, how will creators decide which elements of their voice must be protected by a frame—and which can be surrendered to the wild play of machine variation?*

Chapter 5
Workflows, Roles, and Handovers

The first sign that something had shifted came not from a model's failure, but from a human shrug. At 10:47 a.m. on a damp Tuesday in March, a customer-support team in Manchester watched their escalation dashboard light up—a dozen queries routed from the assistant in under a minute, each tagged "ambiguous sentiment: human review required". The queries were trivial: refund eligibility, password resets, an oddly polite complaint about a missing kettle lid. Yet the assistant had refused to decide. When asked why, its trace showed a pattern: conflicting cues, low confidence, and no stable precedent in its supervised corpus. The team lead leaned back in her chair and said, almost to herself, "It knows *exactly* where it shouldn't tread."

What followed was even more revealing. The agents did not simply take over; they commented, corrected, and fed back their rationales. Edge cases—once the bane of queue times—became data points for refining the shared playbook. And gradually, a new shape emerged. The line between human and machine ceased to be a wall. It became a membrane, flexing with context and judgement.

The Manchester example captures the spirit of this chapter: hybrid workflows are not merely pipelines. They are *agreements*—about responsibility, attention, timing, and truth. They rely on craft, not just computation. And they expose an uncomfortable fact: as models grow more capable, the riskiest point in any workflow is not the model's output, but the space between agents. Handovers can compress or distort intent; roles can blur or calcify; metrics can seduce teams into chasing the wrong victories. The work is no longer about automating tasks. It is about choreographing people and systems through sequences of decisions with clarity, humility, and shared purpose.

To grasp this choreography, we must begin by accepting that no hybrid workflow survives without a designed human-in-the-loop. The phrase has been repeated so often in policy documents that it risks losing its meaning. But when examined closely, it reveals a deeper logic. Human-in-the-loop is not a safety valve to bolt on afterwards. It is a philosophy of operation: define who decides, when escalation occurs, and how rollback is triggered. Without explicit decision points, responsibility diffuses. Without escalation criteria, uncertainty festers. Without rollback paths, attempts at automation gradually ossify into brittle routines. The Manchester team learned this instinctively. They formalised their intuition into a repeatable pattern: if the assistant hesitated, a specialist intervened; if the specialist disagreed, they documented why; if the same edge case repeated, the workflow evolved. Improvement became a continuous loop, not an afterthought.

But defining roles and decisions is only part of the puzzle. We must measure whether the workflow actually works. And here the modern obsession with output volume becomes a trap. Models can produce more, faster, and more fluently than any team in history. Yet volume masquerading as value is one of the signature illusions of hybrid work. A marketing team in Copenhagen discovered this during a blind review. When evaluators compared content produced under the hybrid workflow with the team's traditional output, ratings diverged sharply depending on what was measured. Timeliness improved dramatically, accuracy improved modestly, but emotional resonance—what readers actually cared about—declined. The assistant was excellent at generating options, yet subtly flattened the team's tone into something "polite but forgettable". The blind review forced a reckoning. Quality had become multidimensional, and only metrics tied to *intent* revealed the truth.

This tension recurs across nearly every profession adopting hybrid systems. Lawyers gain speed in research but grapple with the erosion of narrative coherence in argumentation. Product teams accelerate documentation but struggle to maintain conceptual integrity across versions. Medical administrators use models to triage forms more efficiently yet find that patients perceive the process as colder, even when outcomes improve. The question becomes urgent: *Who defines quality in a workflow where human and machine share authorship?* If the metric favours quantity, the assistant wins. If the metric favours nuance, the human does. A mature workflow demands both.

As the workflows mature, new roles appear—roles that would have sounded faintly comical a decade ago but now feel essential. Prompt librarians who curate organisational knowledge. Policy stewards who safeguard permissible boundaries. Evaluators who audit behaviour drift and ensure consistency. These roles exist not because models are weak, but because hybrid systems amplify organisational behaviour. Left unattended, a model will absorb every inconsistency a team exhibits: every half-written rule, every ambiguous exception, every undocumented preference. A small firm in Edinburgh discovered this when their design assistant began producing layouts that drifted away from brand identity. The underlying cause was mundane: three designers had each updated the prompts in different ways. Drift accumulated invisibly. A rotating steward solved the problem—not through technology, but through governance. The model was not improved; the *team* was.

At the centre of all this lies the most fragile point of hybrid work: the handover. Clarity dies here, quietly. A procurement assistant may recommend a supplier, but unless the handover contains an input specification, confidence level, evidence pack, and next action, the recommendation floats free of accountability. The danger is not malicious error; it is silent slippage. A misunderstood constraint. A missing assumption. A half-seen ambiguity that multiplies across steps. A London procurement team avoided this fate by redesigning their handovers entirely. Every model recommendation had to travel with an "evidence pack"—citations, traces, and a statement of uncertainty. Reviewers did not simply accept or reject; they confirmed or corrected. Responsibility became a sequence, not a destination.

This chapter explores these tensions not as abstract principles but as operational realities. How do teams design workflows that bend without breaking? How do they create roles that reduce drift rather than multiply bureaucracy? How do they measure quality with eyes clear enough to resist the illusion of fluency? And most critically: how do they craft handovers that preserve meaning, even when intelligence is distributed across agents?

As hybrid work deepens across industries—from support desks to policy teams, from creative studios to regulatory bodies—the stakes sharpen. The future will not belong to organisations that automate the most. It will belong to those that choreograph the clearest sequences of responsibility, evidence, and judgement.

And so a final question hangs over this chapter like a quiet metronome: *When both humans and systems participate in every task, who ensures that the thread of intention survives the handoff?*

Designing the human-in-the-loop

At 9:12 a.m. on 14 February 2023, a support agent at Horizon Utilities in Leeds watched an automated triage system stall on what should have been an effortless refund request. The customer's email was calm, the account history straightforward, and the policy clear. Yet the assistant assigned a confidence score of 0.42 and pushed the case to the human queue marked *"semantic inconsistency detected: review required"*. When the agent opened the file, the anomaly was obvious: a single contradictory timestamp buried in a thread of nineteen messages. The machine had not failed; it had hesitated. And because Horizon had designed an explicit escalation rule—low-confidence outputs must pause for human review—the hesitation became a feature, not a flaw. The agent resolved the case in under four minutes, documented the rationale, and fed the edge case into the team's improvement log. One ambiguous timestamp had revealed the beating heart of hybrid systems: the choreography of intervention.

This vignette hints at a broader shift. As organisations intertwine human judgement with model-driven automation, the question is no longer whether the human should be "in the loop", but *how precisely* that loop should be constructed. The Leeds example makes the stakes visible. A missing rule would have allowed the assistant to guess. A lax policy would have let the guess slip through unchallenged. A silent handover would have concealed the root cause. Instead, a crisp decision point, a named escalation path, and a documented rollback transformed uncertainty into learning. The motif flickers: a loop is only trustworthy when its boundaries are deliberate.

The first claim follows: hybrid workflows are fragile without explicit decision points. Show this through the Horizon case; name the principle; explain its contours; draw the implication. Decision points are the architecture of responsibility. When the moment of choice is unmarked, accountability dilutes. A system that does not specify when to pause, ask, or defer grants uncertainty the chance to masquerade as certainty. In 2021, the Dutch Tax Administration faced public criticism when automated risk flags for benefits claims were found to have proceeded without structured human decision points. Reviewers intervened late and inconsistently. The absence of a clear moment for human judgement allowed opaque heuristics to dominate outcomes. The implication is stark: decision points are not merely operational conveniences; they are ethical infrastructure.

Escalation rules form the second pillar. They govern how uncertainty travels. Consider the case of the Metropolitan Police's 2019 live facial recognition pilot in London. When the system flagged a potential match, officers were expected to verify the identification visually. But internal audits later revealed that escalation criteria were unevenly applied: some officers deferred quickly to the system, others disregarded it entirely. The inconsistency reduced the reliability of the pilot's findings and eroded public trust. Here the visible behaviour—hesitation, overreliance, or scepticism—exposed a deeper truth: escalation rules must define not only what uncertainty *looks like*, but *where* it goes. Without this, hybrid systems drift into a pattern of silent divergence, where operational practice fragments across individuals. The implication is practical: escalation must be codified, trained, and continuously stress-tested.

A credible limitation appears in systems that handle high-volume, low-risk tasks. In such environments, exhaustive escalation may introduce friction disproportionate to the potential error. Retail fulfilment workflows at Amazon (Seattle, 2020) showed that over-escalation slowed throughput and produced reviewer fatigue. Human reviewers became desensitised to alerts, sometimes approving outputs without scrutiny. Yet reconciliation lies in nuance: escalation need not be binary. It can be weighted. Metrics can route only anomalous, high-variance, or irreversible cases to humans. Light-touch interventions, such as sanity checks or batched reviews, preserve speed without sacrificing oversight. The principle is not maximal escalation; it is *targeted escalation*.

Rollback procedures complete the triad. Rollback is rarely glamorous, but it distinguishes mature hybrid systems from experimental ones. A rollback procedure answers a simple question: *What happens when the model drifts?* In 2022, Reuters implemented a semi-automated summarisation tool for financial briefings. When analysts noticed subtle distortions in two consecutive summaries—omissions that softened risks—they invoked a rollback, reverting to an earlier configuration. The decision was grounded in evidence: comparison of summaries, timestamped discrepancies, and cross-checks with source transcripts. The implication is reassuring: a rollback pathway does not signal failure; it signals control.

If decision points, escalation, and rollback create the scaffolding, then hybrid Standard Operating Procedures (SOPs) give the structure its lived form. An SOP for a human-in-the-loop system differs from conventional process documents. It must choreograph two agents—one human, one non-human—through a sequence of interpretations. The SOP becomes a contract defining: the input the system may accept; the cues it must surface; the thresholds that trigger human intervention; the evidence required for overrides; and the timeline for learning updates. The Horizon Utilities team built such a template by observing behaviour patterns: when the assistant hesitated, when it guessed, and when it misread contextual cues such as long email chains. Their SOP grew not from theory, but from accumulated rationale logs. Every edge case annotated. Every judgement justified. Gradually, the SOP became a living artefact of organisational memory.

Rationale logging sits at the centre of this chapter's motif: clarity. A rationale converts a decision from an intuition into a traceable, teachable object. It shows what was considered, why an interpretation prevailed, and what uncertainty remained. In 2020, the Mayo Clinic's dermatology triage tool required clinicians to record a short justification whenever they overrode an AI-driven severity ranking. This behaviour—just a sentence or two—generated a dataset of expert heuristics that later helped calibrate the model and expose systematic blind spots. The implication extends beyond healthcare: rationale logs strengthen institutional reasoning. They make tacit knowledge explicit.

Yet rationale logging encounters a familiar limitation: cognitive load. Humans tire. Documentation grows unwieldy. The paradox is that too much logging can undermine clarity by producing a mass of undifferentiated explanation. The reconciliation lies in selectivity. Not every action needs a rationale—only decisions with ambiguity, reversibility, or impact. This tiered approach preserves human attention while enriching the dataset that guides improvement. It honours the motif: clarity articulated, not drowned.

Two further named examples sharpen the contours of the human-in-the-loop design. First, consider the French National Library's digitisation project in 2018. OCR systems were paired with human reviewers to correct transcription errors in rare manuscripts. Escalation thresholds were finely tuned: highly degraded pages or unusual typefaces triggered mandatory human review, while clean scans flowed automatically. The result was a measurable reduction in post-correction workload without compromising accuracy. Visible behaviour—fewer corrections per page—anchored abstractions like quality and trust.

Second, recall how in 2016 the U.S. Federal Aviation Administration deployed a hybrid weather classification system for air-traffic controllers. When the model flagged severe weather patterns with low confidence, alerts escalated automatically. Controllers verified, annotated, and fed back their decisions. The process revealed a limitation: during peak workload, human reviewers could not provide timely feedback. Here, hybrid design met operational constraint. The reconciliation involved time-bounded escalation: if a reviewer did not respond within a specified window, the system defaulted to a conservative recommendation. This decision preserved safety while recognising human limits.

These historical cases illustrate a convergence: hybrid systems demand not simply technical oversight, but organisational acuity. They compel teams to confront foundational questions. What constitutes a decision? When is uncertainty constructive? Who owns the consequences of ambiguity? And how should knowledge move across agents—neither bottlenecked by humans nor flattened by machines?

The closing movement now gathers itself around a final motif: the hand on the threshold. In every hybrid workflow, there comes a moment when a model pauses and a human must step in. Not mechanically. Not reflexively. But with clarity about what is at stake and why they are there. As teams refine their SOPs, they will face a question that cannot be automated: *Where exactly should human judgement be placed so that the system becomes wiser, not merely faster?*

No hybrid design is complete until that question is answered—and answered again, each time the system learns.

Measuring quality without illusions

In November 2022, a marketing team at Orchard Media in Manchester faced an awkward revelation. They had spent six weeks testing an AI-assisted workflow for campaign copy. Output volume soared—triple the usual number of variants per brief—but conversions on the pilot campaigns fell by 11%. The team assumed the model was "creative"; the data told another story. A blind review, run by an external agency, placed the AI-assisted outputs below the human-only baselines on clarity, tone alignment, and factual precision. The problem was not speed. It was the illusion that more text meant more value. That morning, Orchard's head of strategy pinned a line to the meeting-room wall: *"Quality is not an opinion; it is an outcome tied to intent."* It became the motif of the redesign that followed.

The scene captures a recurring pattern in hybrid work. As systems accelerate production, organisations risk mistaking volume for value, fluency for accuracy, and engagement for satisfaction. The Manchester review exposed a truth others were learning too. The Associated Press, during its 2020 experiment with automated earnings reports in New York, produced thousands more summaries than its reporters ever could. Yet editors discovered that a subset contained subtle distortions—incorrect revenue comparisons, misplaced qualifiers—that required time-consuming human correction. More reports existed; fewer were publishable. Speed had outpaced scrutiny. The motif returns: intent defines quality, not volume.

The first claim emerges naturally: quality measurement begins with accuracy, not activity. Show the behaviour; name the principle; explain its force; draw the implication. Accuracy is observable alignment with reality—facts checked, numbers consistent, claims traceable. At Orchard Media, the blind review revealed that 27% of AI-generated lines contained factual references to non-existent promotions. The team had assumed the model would only remix provided inputs. The outputs showed a different tendency: pattern completion masquerading as truth. Accuracy became a metric, not an assumption. And once defined, it reshaped the workflow. Prompts were tightened. Fact sources were specified. Reviewers compared outputs to briefs, not instincts. The implication is clear: accuracy measurement disciplines imagination without suffocating it.

A second metric anchors quality to time: timeliness. Not raw speed, but *fit-for-context delivery*. In 2018, the Japanese weather agency JMA deployed a machine-learning model to produce rapid storm advisories. Their measure of success was not "faster advisories", but *precise advisories issued within critical windows*. Analysts tracked whether warnings arrived at least 20 minutes before threshold wind speeds. Timeliness expressed itself in visible behaviour: earlier evacuations, fewer false alarms. In commercial settings, timeliness may show up as fewer last-minute edits before publication, quicker client approvals, or reduced rework cycles. The Orchard team began measuring "time to usable draft", not "time to first draft".

The redefinition captured value that speed-only metrics concealed.

A credible counter-example tempers the story. Some teams report that speed alone transforms output value: contact centres that resolve queries in half the time or compliance teams that process reports days earlier. Yet when auditors investigate, they often discover a missing variable—*the denominator changed*. Queries became shorter because the model rewrote them. Reports were "processed" earlier because they were routed differently, not evaluated more deeply. Here the limitation is genuine: speed metrics can improve without value improving. Reconciliation lies in composite measurement. Speed counts, but only when accuracy and satisfaction remain stable.

This introduces the third essential metric: satisfaction. Not a nebulous sentiment, but a measured response tied to *intent*. If the goal is persuasion, satisfaction might be the reader's likelihood to act. If the goal is clarity, it might be comprehension scores. In 2019, the BBC ran a usability study on automated news digests in London. Participants rated human-written and machine-written summaries blind. Machine versions scored well for conciseness but poorly for narrative coherence. Researchers quantified this gap using a simple behaviour: the rate at which readers requested the "full article" after reading a digest. Satisfaction became a traceable signal of unmet needs.

For Orchard Media, satisfaction manifested in client approval latency. Before the hybrid workflow, clients typically approved copy after one or two rounds. During the pilot, the median increased to four. The metric exposed a dissonance: the system produced more variants, but fewer resonated. The implication was immediate. The team narrowed ideation prompts, introduced brand-specific guardrails, and required reviewers to mark which outputs matched the brief's emotional intent. Satisfaction measurement aligned production with purpose.

The article now threads its quiet motif again: illusions collapse under measurement. In hybrid systems, illusions often arise from two sources—misaligned baselines and unexamined assumptions. Baselines first. When teams compare hybrid outputs to existing outputs, they must compare like with like. In 2021, a European consultancy piloted an automated slide generator for pitch decks. Leaders judged the pilot a failure because slides "looked worse than the old way". But analysts later discovered they had compared automated drafts to *final polished slides*, not earlier drafts. When measured properly—draft vs draft—the hybrid workflow cut early-stage preparation time by 60% without lowering quality. The baseline error, not the automation, created the illusion.

Unexamined assumptions form the second source. Teams often believe hybrid systems will improve everything: accuracy, speed, creativity, and coherence. But hybrid systems are uneven. They improve some variables while degrading others. In 2020, the U.S. Government Accountability Office tested AI-assisted contract review systems across several agencies. Findings were consistent: models excelled at detecting common clauses, but misclassified rare ones. Overall processing time improved, but human reviewers spent more time correcting edge-case errors. The system was "faster on average" but "slower on anomalies". Only by measuring anomaly resolution time did the team perceive the mixed effect. The implication resonates: without granular metrics, hybrid performance feels better while becoming worse in the places that matter most.

Two further named examples deepen the analysis. First, the Financial Conduct Authority in London ran a 2022 experiment to classify consumer complaints. Accuracy was measured not at the category level, but at the *regulatory consequence level*: did misclassifications change the required response? This reframing revealed that 94% of apparent model errors had no regulatory impact, while the remaining 6% carried significant risk. Quality measurement pivoted from correctness in the abstract to correctness with consequence. Second, at the University of Copenhagen in 2017, researchers evaluating automated essay scoring found that while model–human agreement looked strong, closer inspection showed divergence on essays with unconventional structures. The visible behaviour—grading outliers poorly—exposed the brittleness that global accuracy scores concealed. The reconciliation in both cases required slicing metrics by intent and context, not aggregates.

The blind-review method used at Orchard Media embodies these principles elegantly. Reviewers saw only anonymised outputs. They judged clarity, truthfulness, tone, and intent alignment using a rubric designed before any model was tested. The results were uncomfortable but clarifying. Hybrid drafts were shorter, punchier, and structurally tidy. Yet they hesitated around nuance: qualifiers were flattened; caveats softened; rare product details misrepresented. The team responded by creating a *quality triad*: accuracy (correct facts), timeliness (usable by deadline), and satisfaction (resonant with purpose). Every output was scored against the triad. Illusions evaporated.

A tension now surfaces—the tension every hybrid team must face. Metrics can discipline, but they can also narrow. If timeliness dominates, creativity shrinks. If accuracy dominates, experimentation freezes. If satisfaction dominates, novelty declines. So the unresolved question becomes a forward test: *Which metric deserves primacy for this task, at this moment, in this context—and what trade-offs will we accept to honour it?*

Team roles in hybrid teams

In April 2021, at a ten-person consultancy in Bristol named Latchmere Insights, a quiet crisis unfolded. Their analysts had integrated three different language models into their research workflow, each adopted enthusiastically by a different consultant. Within months, briefs splintered into incompatible formats, prompts multiplied across hidden folders, and client reports showed subtle tone drift. One client asked why their "evidence-led summary" now read like a product brochure. Another queried why citations were inconsistently formatted. The firm finally traced the chaos to a simple fact: no one owned the system. Tasks were delegated to automation, but responsibility for the automation itself belonged to no one. That week, Latchmere introduced a rotating role—the *steward*—a person appointed every fortnight to standardise prompts, enforce policies, and prune unused tools. Drift fell sharply. Response quality recovered. The firm discovered what many others would soon learn: hybrid teams require new roles, or entropy wins.

The small Bristol office illustrates a broad structural shift. When software behaves predictably, teams need operators. When software behaves generatively, teams need custodians—people who define boundaries, curate patterns, and intervene when behaviour deviates from intent. Hybrid systems are not static assets; they are active participants whose outputs depend on inputs, context, and accumulated adjustments. Without deliberate governance, they sprawl. And without clear roles, governance dissolves into guesswork. The Latchmere case shows this visibly: three analysts produced incompatible outputs not out of negligence but because no one measured consistency. The motif will return—*alignment emerges from ownership*.

The first major claim follows naturally: hybrid teams need someone who curates the language of interaction. Show the behaviour; name the role; explain its purpose; draw the implication. The *prompt librarian* emerges as a foundational figure. At Latchmere, the librarian consolidated over 120 ad hoc prompts into 17 audited templates. Each template mapped to a specific type of deliverable—market overview, executive summary, risk register—and included examples, evidence requirements, and red-flag phrasing to avoid. The role is not about writing clever prompts. It is about maintaining a living corpus of interaction patterns that reduce variance and encode institutional judgement. The implication is straightforward: without this curation, individuals rely on memory and improvisation, and the system inherits their inconsistencies.

A second role defines the boundaries within which hybrid work operates: the *policy steward*. The steward at Latchmere reviewed every model integration weekly, ensuring that none exceeded the firm's data-handling commitments or client confidentiality agreements. This mirrors more mature examples. The Information Commissioner's Office in London, during a 2020 audit of automated decision tools, insisted that organisations maintain a designated owner who can explain how a model uses personal data, what limits apply, and how those limits are enforced. The steward performs this function internally. They trace where data travels, how long outputs persist, and who may access logs. They articulate rules in human terms. The implication is not merely compliance: clarity about limits improves creativity. When teams know where the edges lie, they innovate confidently inside them.

A third role focuses on outcomes: the *evaluator*. This person measures whether hybrid work improves accuracy, timeliness, and satisfaction—as defined earlier in the chapter. The evaluator at Latchmere ran monthly quality reviews using blind scoring. They compared hybrid outputs to pre-hybrid baselines and isolated regression patterns—over-long summaries, weakened qualifiers, vanishing caveats. The role resembles the independent assessment methods used by the UK's Behavioural Insights Team in its 2019 experiments with text-generation tools: evaluators judged outputs without knowing their origin, exposing weaknesses humans would overlook. The evaluator ensures that illusions—speed as value, fluency as truth—never accumulate unchecked.

A credible counter-example grounds the analysis. In 2022, a mid-sized legal firm in Toronto attempted a hybrid workflow without formal roles. Their belief was principled: *professionals should govern their own tools*. Lawyers drafted their own prompts, defined their own standards, and edited their own outputs. For a few months, productivity rose. But quality audits later revealed inconsistencies. Footnote conventions varied. Risk language drifted. Some teams used the model for scenario summarisation; others banned it entirely. The firm eventually appointed an AI governance committee, then discovered that committees with diffuse responsibility simply dilute responsibility. Their fix echoed Latchmere: assign named individuals with rotating authority. The counter-example reconciles cleanly: autonomy without shared structure creates fragmentation, and committees without ownership create inertia.

This leads to the deeper explanation: hybrid teams differ from traditional teams because generative systems amplify small behavioural differences. A prompt phrased casually by one analyst can reshape the tone of an entire department's outputs if others copy it. A neglected policy file can lead to silent data exposure. A misaligned evaluation rubric can reward the wrong behaviours. Every system accumulates human decisions; every decision accumulates consequences. Team roles therefore become the scaffolding of consistency.

Another named example sharpens the point. In 2020, the Danish Tax Agency introduced a machine-learning assistant to support caseworkers in Copenhagen. Within six months, investigators observed that classification models had drifted, partly because individual caseworkers modified prompts locally without documenting changes. The agency appointed a model steward to review prompts weekly, verify parameter settings, and roll back drifted versions. Classification accuracy stabilised. A visible behaviour marked the shift: caseworkers stopped maintaining their own shadow versions and instead submitted update requests to the steward. The motif returns—alignment emerges from ownership.

A second checkable example comes from the charity Shelter in London, which piloted an AI-supported triage tool in 2021 to categorise housing queries. Early results looked promising, but a later audit revealed inconsistent application of escalation rules—some advisers accepted model suggestions blindly while others ignored them. The charity introduced a lightweight role rotation: each week, one adviser served as the "triage lead", reviewing edge cases, annotating anomalies, and updating a shared decision log. Within two months, the accuracy of escalations improved by 18%, measured through follow-up case reviews. The principle shows itself: when someone owns the exceptions, others trust the system.

These roles—librarian, steward, evaluator—interact. The librarian curates patterns. The steward defines limits. The evaluator checks outcomes. If one fails, the others inherit the burden. In practice, the most dangerous failure mode is *role collapse*, where teams blur distinctions and assume one person can perform all three functions. That pattern appeared at a design studio in Brighton where the head of research became the de facto owner of prompts, policies, and evaluations. Over time, staff deferred to her instinct. When she went on leave, no one knew the current policy or the latest approved prompt templates. Model sprawl re-emerged. The studio responded by distributing duties: librarianship rotated monthly; stewardship remained stable; evaluation alternated every quarter. Each role produced visible artefacts: updated templates, policy diffs, quality dashboards. The system gained resilience.

Anti-patterns now surface. One is the "prompt hoarder"—the person who treats prompt design as personal intellectual property. They keep private libraries, resist sharing techniques, and undermine collective learning. Another is the "policy absolutist"—the steward who treats every deviation as a violation rather than a signal to improve the policy. A third is the "evaluation minimalist"—someone who reduces quality measurement to a single metric, usually speed, and ignores nuance. Each anti-pattern erodes trust not through malice but through misalignment. The remedy is structural, not moral: clarify responsibilities so that individuals cannot distort the workflow inadvertently.

A quiet motif threads again: ownership. Hybrid teams thrive when ownership is distributed, time-bounded, and visible. The Latchmere steward's rotation exemplifies this. Every two weeks, a different consultant steps into the role. They prune prompt libraries, archive outdated tools, check policy compliance, and run a light audit of outputs. The rotation prevents expertise from becoming bottleneck and responsibility from becoming invisible. It also generates a behaviour that metrics can track: drift events decline when stewards rotate consistently. The firm measured drift by counting how many prompts deviated from the approved template library. Before the rotation, divergence occurred in 41% of outputs; after, it fell below 10%. Ownership, embodied in named individuals, produced measurable stability.

A limitation deserves acknowledgement. Smaller teams sometimes struggle to maintain multiple roles, especially when staff are stretched thin. They fear that formal roles introduce bureaucracy. Yet evidence from the Bristol and Shelter cases shows that role rotation, not role proliferation, is the mechanism that matters. A single person can serve as librarian one month and evaluator the next, so long as the functions remain distinct. Reconciliation here is pragmatic: keep roles minimal, but responsibilities explicit.

As hybrid systems become core infrastructure, teams face a growing tension that cannot be resolved once and for all. Who decides when a role changes hands? Who updates the templates as models evolve? Who verifies that policy constraints still reflect organisational ethics rather than outdated fears? The forward test asks a sharper version of the stewardship question: *In your team, who owns the system this week—and how will you know when ownership has quietly shifted to no one?*

Handovers between humans and AI

In September 2022, at the procurement office of Leeds Teaching Hospitals NHS Trust, a quiet misalignment nearly cost the organisation £240,000. A language-model assistant had been trialled to accelerate supplier assessments. It generated a polished summary recommending a medical-equipment vendor, praising delivery history and contract compliance. Yet it omitted a critical detail: the vendor's pending regulatory warning, buried in an annex the model had not processed. The procurement officer, Ravi Shah, caught the omission only because he habitually cross-checked supplier IDs against the Medicines and Healthcare products Regulatory Agency database. The system had produced fluent output without evidence, confidence, or clear scope boundaries. A flawless handover had been replaced by a stylish guess. The Trust halted the pilot for a week, then rewrote its workflow: every model output had to arrive with an *evidence pack*, a structured declaration of what the system saw, what it ignored, and how sure it believed itself to be. Clarity had to be rebuilt from first principles.

The Leeds case captures the essential danger. Handovers fail not because humans or systems malfunction in spectacular ways, but because each assumes the other knows what came before. People expect the system to flag uncertainty. Systems expect people to interrogate them. Between these expectations lies the classic failure mode of hybrid work:

ambiguity. And ambiguity spreads quietly. It lives in skipped fields, unspoken assumptions, silent defaults, and the seductive brevity of an AI-generated summary. Teams underestimate how quickly ambiguity accumulates. It is the gravity that pulls workflows apart unless countered by explicit handover contracts—agreements about input, confidence, evidence, and next action.

A first principle becomes visible through demonstration: clarity must be *constructed*, not assumed. Leeds formalised a contract with four parts. First, the *input specification*: the system receives structured instructions defining data scope, recency limits, and mandatory sources. Show the behaviour: the procurement tool now logs the IDs of every document it processes, and the officer can verify that the annex containing the regulatory warning is included. Name the component: explicit input spec. Explain the purpose: it prevents invisible omissions by making data boundaries inspectable. Implication: every downstream decision inherits transparency rather than surprise.

A second part of the contract addresses epistemic uncertainty: the *confidence declaration*. At the European Centre for Disease Prevention and Control in Stockholm, a 2021 pilot used machine-learning tools to summarise emerging research during respiratory outbreaks. Summaries were delivered with a numerical confidence range based on calibration with historical data. When staff saw a summary reading "0.42 confidence: insufficient signal", they understood instantly that human review was mandatory. Pair the abstraction—confidence—with visible behaviour: analysts decided whether to escalate based on the threshold alone. The implication is straightforward: when confidence is declared, trust becomes calibrated, not instinctive.

A third component exists to anchor claims: the *evidence pack*. The Centre included the citations the model used, the passages extracted, and a short rationale linking them. Leeds followed the same pattern. This pack made the model's reasoning visible without requiring it to mimic human thought. A limitation surfaced as well. Evidence packs can be voluminous, overwhelming staff already time-constrained. The reconciliation was procedural: Leeds introduced a two-tier structure, with a human-readable summary at the top and machine-readable logs beneath. The motif begins to appear—*trace before trust.*

A fourth component organises responsibility: the *next-action declaration*. The output specifies exactly who must act, by when, and with what conditions. In the procurement pilot, model recommendations now end with a directive such as "Human verification required: cross-check regulatory warnings; reject if unresolved." The behaviour shows its value: officers know the boundary between model suggestion and human decision. Ambiguity shrinks.

Two further named examples reinforce the structural pattern. In 2020, the Dutch Council for the Judiciary tested automated summarisation tools for court judgments in The Hague. Early trials produced concise summaries but failed to flag which parts derived from precedents rather than the primary text. Judges introduced a handover contract requiring the system to highlight every interpretive leap it made. Outputs changed visibly: sections derived from precedent appeared in blue; verbatim extracts appeared in black. This separation allowed judges to assess how conservative or adventurous the summary was. The implication extends beyond law: handovers must reveal the system's epistemic posture, not merely its surface content.

Another example comes from 2023 at the Singapore Land Authority, which trialled an AI assistant to review land-use proposals. The assistant initially returned binary recommendations—approve or decline. But planners discovered that binary outputs masked the assistant's uncertainty. They replaced the binary with graded recommendations mapped to explicit actions: "Approve with caveats," "Flag for environmental review," "Insufficient data—request surveys." Each grade corresponded to a defined workflow. The behaviour metric that validated the redesign was turnaround time: reviews with graded outputs cut escalation delays by 19%, as planners no longer wasted time decoding opaque suggestions. Again the motif appears: *trace before trust.*

A credible counter-example exposes the limits. At a media company in New York, editors introduced a newsroom assistant to generate interview briefs. They relied on the model's summaries without evidence packs or confidence declarations. Occasionally, the system misattributed quotes or drew unsupported causal links. Editors corrected errors manually but did not formalise contracts. Weeks later, when a high-profile feature mischaracterised a source's past statements, the correction required was substantial. The organisation concluded that human review alone cannot guarantee safety without structured handovers. The reconciliation is not to distrust systems but to make their cognitive boundaries inspectable.

A deeper explanation now emerges. Handovers succeed when they transform invisible internal states into visible commitments. Because models interpolate patterns from training data rather than retrieve certainty, their outputs contain gradients of plausibility. Humans, by contrast, operate with sparse but high-stakes reasoning. When a human takes the baton from a system, they need to know where the baton came from, whether it is intact, and whether the track ahead is clear. The contract—input spec, confidence, evidence, next action—does not mimic human cognition. It *compensates* for it.

Metrics provide grounding. Leeds measured the rate at which officers requested clarification from the system before and after the introduction of evidence packs. Before: 37% of summaries triggered follow-up queries. After: 8%. They also recorded the proportion of recommendations overridden on review. Before: 28%. After: 13%. These concrete shifts show how structural clarity improves decision quality, not by automating judgement but by illuminating its preconditions.

The motif can now be extended. *Trace before trust* also means preserving the lineage of each handover. When a human edits a model output—by adding a caveat, removing an unsupported claim, or adjusting a recommendation—the system should embed that correction into the next cycle. Leeds introduced a correction log, capturing human overrides and tagging them as rule updates, outlier fixes, or input failures. This allowed the procurement lead to identify recurring causes of misclassification, such as supplier IDs formatted inconsistently across documents. The visible behaviour changed: staff annotated corrections systematically rather than editing silently. Clarity stopped evaporating at the human boundary.

Yet limitations persist. Handovers cannot eliminate the need for judgement. Even with perfect evidence packs, model confidence declarations may mislead if calibration is poor. A procurement officer might overweight a high confidence score even when the input spec is incomplete. A planner in Singapore might trust a graded recommendation too readily in a politically sensitive case. The tension is irreducible: clarity enables good judgement but never replaces it.

A final grounded example consolidates the argument. In 2021, the Scottish Government Digital Directorate ran a pilot to evaluate AI-assisted procurement scoring. Their workflow introduced a strict requirement: every automated recommendation had to be accompanied by a traceable chain linking evidence to scoring criteria. When the model suggested awarding higher weight to environmental credentials, the evidence pack disclosed exactly which lines in supplier documents justified the recommendation.

Procurement officers said the process felt slower at first, but more defensible. The key behaviour: officers could articulate why a recommendation was upheld or rejected. The implication: accountability stems from explanation, not automation.

Handovers between humans and AI therefore become the hinge on which hybrid competence turns. Without explicit contracts, teams inherit guesswork. With them, they inherit clarity, traceability, and stable decision paths. Yet a final unresolved question remains. As systems become more fluent and humans more accustomed to their support, how will teams prevent the contract itself from becoming a ritual—recited, clicked through, but no longer *read*?

Chapter 6
Guardrails, Safety, and Accountability

The warning surfaced quietly, almost politely. In early 2022, a midsized charity in Manchester testing a research assistant for fundraising discovered that the system had begun generating persuasive but fabricated summaries of donor histories. No alarms sounded. No error messages flashed. The assistant merely wrote with a little too much confidence about people it did not truly know. A junior analyst spotted the drift only because she kept a habit of cross-checking sources manually. The charity paused the pilot and reran its entire workflow within a sandbox, restricting the assistant to verifiable databases and logging every query it made. What emerged was sobering: the assistant had not malfunctioned; the boundary around its permissible information had never been drawn clearly enough for either humans or machines to recognise a breach. The episode marked a turning point for the organisation. They realised they needed guardrails not as constraints on innovation but as the conditions that make innovation trustworthy.

That moment of discomfort, shared quietly around the office, captures the emotional core of this chapter. Hybrid intelligence places us inside systems that behave competently most of the time, occasionally brilliantly, and sometimes deceptively—without intent, but with consequence. The risk does not lie in dramatic failure; it lies in mundane ambiguity. A harmless autocomplete here, a sloppy assumption there, a misinterpreted data source that no one notices until a mistake has already been acted upon. The more fluent the tools become, the harder it is to see where the seams are. And when seams disappear, accountability can vanish with them. The enduring question surfaces early and refuses to leave: how do we build systems that remain safe *because of* their flexibility, not despite it?

The need for guardrails is not new. Every technology that extends human decision-making produces its own shadow of risk—printing presses with censorship, telegraphs with intercepted wires, aircraft with cockpit checklists. But hybrid intelligence introduces a distinctive inversion. In earlier technologies, constraints protected humans from external hazards: faulty circuits, physical dangers, corrupted files. Now the constraints must often protect humans from *false confidence*—the ease with which a machine's poise can lull us into quiet acceptance. A language model that infers the wrong demographic trend. A vision system that misclassifies a boundary condition. A document assistant that removes nuance in the name of clarity. The safety problem becomes epistemic before it becomes operational. We must govern what the system *claims to know* before we can govern what it does.

This chapter turns toward the structures that make such governance possible. It is about the systems around the system: the policies, permissions, permissions-within-permissions, and auditable traces that bind together humans, models, and institutions into a coherent whole. It is a chapter about clarity, but also about humility—the recognition that safety is rarely achieved through one decisive rule, but through many small, steady decisions that accumulate into reliability.

The first thread concerns boundaries that must move yet remain legible. A charity's restricted-browsing pilot offers a concrete picture. They allowed the assistant to query a tightly curated set of data sources and required each query to be logged. When fundraising staff reviewed the logs, they could see precisely how a claim had been assembled. They soon learned that guardrails would need regular revision as their fundraising landscape changed—new donor categories, new compliance obligations, new reputational sensitivities. A boundary drawn once is a boundary that will eventually fail. But a boundary revised openly and auditable becomes a shared anchor between humans and systems. The underlying tension surfaces: a fixed policy is safe but brittle; a fluid policy is adaptive but risky. How we navigate that tension will return throughout the chapter.

The second thread is fairness. Hybrid systems learn from data that encode the world's patterns—and therefore its distortions. A hiring assistant trained on a decade of historical applications may inherit the subtle biases embedded in earlier decisions. When a recruitment team uses counterfactual prompts to simulate how candidates would score under different demographic attributes, they confront a difficult question: is the model reflecting the past, or perpetuating it? Fairness requires structural attention, not wishful thinking. It requires sampling checks, narrative reviews grounded in lived experience, and systems that show their reasoning pathways rather than hiding inside probabilities. Fairness is a methodological practice, not a sentiment. And like boundaries, it must be renewed repeatedly.

Security and provenance form the third thread. These topics can feel procedural, even dry, but in hybrid intelligence they become intimate. Data minimisation dictates what the system sees at all; key management dictates who may alter its parameters; content credentials dictate whether you can reconstruct a document's origin from its final form. Imagine a newsroom that signs every edit cryptographically from collection to publication. A journalist can review the lineage of a paragraph the same way a historian might trace a footnote. Security, in this sense, is not mere protection against threat; it is a defence of interpretability—a way to preserve the story of how a decision was made.

And then comes the most human thread of all: responsibility. Who answers for an error when the system suggested the step but a human clicked "approve"? A municipal chatbot offers a cautionary example. Deployed to help residents navigate housing services, it began giving incorrect guidance about eligibility criteria. The city avoided public harm because escalation rules were in place: whenever the system detected uncertain conditions, queries were routed to trained staff who could intervene. But the moment raised a sharper question: is responsibility located in the team that built the model, the team that deployed it, the team that monitored it, or the individual who last touched the case? Our argument in this chapter is simple to state and complex to apply: systems may advise, but humans decide—unless the organisation has explicitly delegated a decision to automation under tightly defined oversight.

Throughout the chapter, a quiet motif will recur: *the trace.* A boundary without trace cannot be checked. A fairness audit without trace becomes performance. A secure system without trace may be fortified yet opaque. Accountability without trace collapses into blame. Traceability—of decisions, of data paths, of human overrides—forms the connective tissue of safe hybrid intelligence. It lets us rewind a workflow not to assign fault but to recover understanding.

Yet the chapter will not pretend that guardrails solve everything. They do not eliminate complexity; they organise our relationship with it. They do not remove uncertainty; they make it legible and shareable. They do not ensure fairness; they give teams the tools to recognise when fairness is drifting. They do not eliminate risk; they prevent risk from being silently compounded.

The final paragraphs here must open, not close. As hybrid intelligence becomes woven into public institutions, private workplaces, and informal everyday practices, a pressing question emerges: how do we sustain safety not as a one-time engineering effort but as a culture? How do we ensure that guardrails do not become stale constraints or ceremonial checkboxes? How do we uphold accountability when system boundaries evolve faster than job descriptions?

The chapter that follows invites you to treat guardrails not as barriers but as the architecture of shared judgement. It asks what must be protected, who must be empowered, and how clarity can be designed rather than assumed. And it leaves us with a tension that cannot be smoothed away: in a world where intelligence is increasingly distributed between humans and machines, how do we build systems that remain safe without becoming timid—and remain bold without becoming careless?

Setting Boundaries That Move

At 10:17 a.m. on 9 March 2022, in a modest office off Oxford Road in Manchester, a fundraising analyst at St Helier Children's Charity noticed something odd in the activity log of their experimental research assistant. The assistant had produced a persuasive profile of a potential donor, complete with inferred interests and past affiliations, yet the source list showed only three legitimate databases. The rest of the references—neatly formatted URLs pointing to non-existent pages—were hallucinated. The anomaly triggered the charity's first full audit of its hybrid workflow. Within a week, they reconfigured the system into a sandboxed environment, restricting browsing to a pre-approved set of sources and recording every outbound request. The outcome was immediate: false inference rates fell, and the fundraising team regained confidence in data they could verify. That single morning's discovery became a quiet proof of a larger principle: boundaries must move as systems evolve, but they must remain legible enough for humans to see the shift.

The tension at the heart of boundary-setting emerges sharply in such moments. A fixed rule risks irrelevance the moment data changes; an unfixed rule risks drifting into incoherence. Hybrid intelligence systems amplify this tension because they operate across domains—legal, financial, clinical, creative—where context matters as much as capability. Boundaries are not only constraints; they are commitments. They determine what a system may touch, what it may generate, and what it must never assume. And as the St Helier pilot showed, they only function when they can be inspected, queried, and revised in shared daylight.

The idea of a *trace* threads through this subchapter. A boundary without a trace becomes a rumour; a boundary with a trace becomes an understanding. In Manchester, the charity's logs revealed not merely what the assistant accessed but how it behaved when encountering ambiguous prompts. The team observed that ambiguous donor names triggered speculative leaps, while structured queries kept responses tight. This behavioural detail—tiny yet telling—helped them redraw permissions with clarity. They introduced tiered access: surface-level data for general staff, deeper behavioural insights for senior analysts, and external browsing only for a small, trained group. The trace made the boundary enforceable.

Historical moments remind us that boundaries have always had to shift with technology. The BBC's adoption of editorial checklists in 1927, for example, evolved rapidly as radio expanded from news bulletins to live debates. Procedures written for slow, linear scripts no longer made sense once programmes turned spontaneous. The organisation had to refine rules while keeping them transparent to the journalists who used them daily. The lesson echoes here: adaptation must remain visible. When rules change invisibly, people stumble. When rules change visibly, systems cohere.

Yet boundary-setting does not always land cleanly. Consider the contrasting case of a software consultancy in Cambridge that, in 2021, restricted its internal coding assistant from touching any external repositories. The rule was meant to protect intellectual property, but the ban throttled legitimate use. Developers received bland, context-poor suggestions because the assistant could not reference open-source idioms. Productivity dropped, and the boundary—though safe—

became a drag on human judgement. The firm revised its policy months later, allowing curated open-source contexts with attribution. This counter-example highlights an important truth: a boundary that is too narrow can be as damaging as one that is too loose. The craft lies in proportion, not paranoia.

To work at all, boundaries must map cleanly to behaviour. A fundraising researcher interacts with systems differently from a compliance officer or a data scientist. Tiered permissions recognise this variation by embedding a question into the workflow: *who should be allowed to ask what, and why?* A well-designed hybrid environment separates actions by confidence level: low-risk retrieval for all users; moderate-risk enrichment for trained staff; high-risk inferential tasks for supervised zones only. What matters is not the exact categories but the clarity with which they are communicated. A system that whispers its boundaries through error codes fails; a system that speaks them plainly enables good decisions.

Sandboxing provides a second structural tool—one that pairs with tiered permissions like a brace. A sandbox isolates the system to a controlled, observable environment where unexpected behaviours cannot spill into operational tasks. St Helier's team used their sandbox not simply as a firewall but as a diagnostic chamber. They tested how the assistant behaved when intentionally fed ambiguous donor profiles. They measured its latency under restricted bandwidth conditions. They observed which prompts caused it to generate unverified connective tissue. These observations allowed them to redesign their standard operating procedure: each fundraising query would generate an accompanying evidence pack detailing the sources used, confidence levels, and any instance where the model deferred due to insufficient data.

The quiet motif of *the trace* returns here. Sandboxing without a trace becomes mere isolation; sandboxing with a trace becomes insight. Logs, when intelligible, are not bureaucratic artefacts—they are cognitive scaffolds for teams operating with systems smarter than their audit trails. A log that reveals which database the assistant queried, at what timestamp, with what filter, provides more than transparency; it provides accountability with granularity.

A second named example deepens the picture. In 2023, the Dutch National Library (Koninklijke Bibliotheek) piloted a document-analysis system for historical newspapers. The system used embeddings to cluster articles by theme, but early tests surfaced a subtle failure. The assistant began grouping politically sensitive stories too aggressively, pulling together unrelated material under the guise of thematic similarity. Librarians tightened rules, restricting the assistant's clustering to metadata only unless an authorised curator unlocked semantic search for a controlled set of archives. They added a requirement for curators to annotate ambiguous clusters manually. The result was not only safer categorisation but richer historical insight. Moving boundaries improved accuracy because the movement was deliberate and documented.

Boundary-setting, however, encounters an unavoidable limitation: some contexts evolve faster than policies can track. Fundraising landscapes shift with economic cycles; legal obligations change with new regulations; public expectations change even faster. A boundary drawn in January can be outdated by September. Recognising this is not defeatism; it is the premise for adaptive governance. The implication is clear: boundaries require scheduled revision cycles—quarterly audits, exception reviews, controlled experiments—so that movement does not become drift.

The counterpoint must also be addressed. Rapid policy revision risks

Bias, Representation, and Fairness

In February 2019, a medium-sized tech firm in Leeds noticed an anomaly in its internal hiring assistant. The system, designed to shortlist candidates for engineering apprenticeships, returned recommendations that skewed heavily male. The team had fed it years of historical hiring data, assuming this would provide a solid foundation. It did, but at a cost: the model reproduced the very imbalance they sought to correct. When their HR director, Claire Dalton, compared the assistant's shortlist with a blind human review, the disparity was stark. The discovery forced the firm to halt automation for technical roles and begin a systematic audit. That audit, slow but deliberate, revealed the quiet pressure that historical data exerts on hybrid systems. Bias hides in patterns that look like facts.

The Leeds incident captures a fundamental tension: hybrid systems extend our reach, yet they inherit our blind spots. A hiring model trained on skewed inputs signals competence while quietly narrowing opportunity. The surface looks smooth. The underlying currents pull hard. Fairness becomes not an abstract virtue but a practical question: who gets shown the path, and who does not? And that question gains urgency as more organisations integrate assistants into early screening, research, and triage. A system that misrepresents reality can redirect lives with a single, silent inference.

A motif recurs throughout this subchapter: *the shadow in the sample*. Every dataset, no matter how large, casts a shadow where some groups appear dimmer, rarer, or mislabelled. That shadow shapes predictions unless actively confronted. The Leeds team learned this through granular analysis. They reran their hiring assistant with balanced synthetic data created to neutralise historical imbalances. The shortlist shifted dramatically: more women, more applicants from vocational colleges, more diversity in experience. The shift showed that nothing in their job requirements inherently favoured one profile; the bias lived in the sample, not the role.

From this scene emerges the first major claim: sampling checks determine whether a hybrid system sees the world as it is or only as it once was. Show it through the Leeds case. Name the principle—sampling bias is the distortion caused when the distribution of training data does not match the distribution of reality. Explain it simply: if most examples of "successful engineer" in a dataset correspond to men aged 25–40 with certain credentials, a model will naturally treat that pattern as predictive. Implication: any domain with entrenched inequalities—finance, housing, recruitment, healthcare—demands deliberate correction before automation enters the workflow.

A second example reinforces the pattern. In 2020, the New York City Automated Decision Systems Task Force reviewed a predictive policing tool used in Brooklyn between 2012 and 2016. The tool disproportionately flagged neighbourhoods already subject to heavier police presence, creating a feedback loop. More patrols meant more recorded incidents; more recorded incidents meant more predicted risk. The system did not "intend" bias, but its behaviour reproduced it. When the task force applied a counterfactual audit—asking how the model would behave if demographic variables were neutralised—the hotspots shifted significantly. The test exposed the shadow in the sample and demonstrated the power of counterfactual prompts: structured nudges that force a model to reveal how much its output depends on sensitive attributes or their proxies.

Counterexamples matter, and one must be addressed: some argue that with large enough datasets, bias washes out. Scale becomes a talisman. But this hope collapses in practice. Even vast datasets repeat structural skews. If millions of images underrepresent disabled people, or if millions of documents frame leadership through a narrow lens, then a larger dataset only amplifies the missing. The limitation is real. To reconcile it, one must treat scale as a multiplier of whatever is already present, not a solvent. The implication is clear: fairness does not emerge from size; it emerges from scrutiny.

To make scrutiny operational, hybrid teams use three techniques: sampling checks, counterfactual prompts, and lived-experience reviews. Each converts abstraction into visible behaviour. Sampling checks begin with distributional measures: does the dataset reflect the populations affected by its outputs? Does it overrepresent certain groups or practices? These checks rely on measurable gaps—percentage differences, representation counts, missing categories. They move the discussion from general worry to concrete imbalance. A dataset that includes 40 per cent women in early-career engineering roles but a hiring model that suggests only 10 per cent female candidates has a measurable distortion that cannot be hand-waved away.

Counterfactual prompts probe deeper. They ask the model to produce outputs given hypothetical shifts in input attributes: *Generate the same recommendation assuming the candidate's gender is unspecified. Classify this CV assuming the education history is reordered.* These prompts expose whether a model's reasoning hinges on irrelevant or sensitive factors. When the Leeds team used counterfactual prompts, they found the model ranked one applicant significantly higher when the university name was omitted. A superficial reading suggested prestige mattered. A closer reading showed the model overweighted institution-specific phrasing patterns. The counterfactual trace made the flaw visible.

Lived-experience reviews add a complementary dimension. Technical audits capture patterns; human reviewers capture meaning. When the BBC launched its 2022 internal content-classification assistant, they invited experienced journalists to review outputs from perspectives not present in the engineering team. Journalists flagged subtle issues:

mislabelling stories involving regional dialects, confusing satire with straight reporting, underrepresenting culturally specific references. These reviewers did not rely on statistical gaps alone; they relied on lived familiarity with nuance. Their feedback reshaped annotation guidelines and improved the assistant's calibration. When hybrid systems confront the shadow in the sample, lived-experience reviewers illuminate what metrics alone miss.

A hiring assistant example brings the techniques together. In 2023, a logistics firm in Rotterdam deployed a shortlisting tool to accelerate screening for warehouse supervisors. After initial trials, the firm ran demographic parity checks—comparing the proportion of shortlisted candidates across demographic groups with the proportion in the applicant pool. They discovered mild but persistent under-shortlisting of older applicants. Instead of discarding the system wholesale, they paired quantitative checks with narrative feedback. Reviewers described how the assistant misinterpreted career gaps and undervalued supervisory experience gained in small family businesses. These narratives, combined with metrics, drove specific revisions: adjusting weighting for non-traditional experience, revising feature extraction rules, and adding prompts requiring the assistant to justify decisions with evidence rather than impressionistic phrasing. The model, after retraining, returned shortlists that aligned far more closely with human review.

The shadow motif returns again: the shadow is not only in the dataset; it is in the interpretation of outputs. A system that hides its reasoning casts a longer shadow. Transparent evidence packs—summaries of which features or patterns influenced an output—shorten it. A hiring assistant that states, *"Ranked lower due to missing supervisory keywords,"* invites correction. A system that simply returns a score invites unexamined trust.

Yet fairness audits face a practical limitation. If teams overcorrect, they risk distorting valid distinctions. Not every disparity is discrimination; some reflect genuine differences in experience, training, or role requirements. The task is not to engineer identical outcomes but to ensure that differences arise from relevant factors, not historical prejudice or data artefacts. Reconciling this requires a discipline of justification: every disparity must have a reason traceable to job-related criteria. The moment that reason evaporates, the shadow grows.

The broader implication emerges: fairness in hybrid systems is not a static attribute but a practice. It is sustained by recurring cycles of measurement, review, and refinement. It requires more than dashboards; it demands curiosity about the origins of patterns and humility about one's assumptions. Sampling checks ask, *Is the sample complete?* Counterfactual prompts ask, *Does the model rely on what it should not?* Lived-experience reviews ask, *Does this output make sense to those it affects?* Together, they create a boundary of scrutiny that moves with the system rather than lagging behind it.

The subchapter ends with an unresolved tension that no audit fully settles. As hybrid systems integrate deeper into hiring, healthcare triage, support escalation, and academic selection, one question sharpens: how do we decide what counts as fair when every metric reveals a different facet of reality? Bias hides in silence, but fairness hides in overconfidence. The next step demands judgement. What balance will your organisation strike between statistical parity, individual explanation, and cultural nuance—and how will you justify that balance when the shadow shifts again?

Security, provenance, and trace

In August 2022, the Associated Press newsroom in New York trialled a new workflow for documenting the life of a photograph. Each image—whether shot on assignment in Kyiv or pulled from a wire desk in London—was embedded with content credentials: signed metadata recording who captured it, when, and what edits followed. The shift was prompted by a specific incident earlier that year, when a misattributed photo circulated widely before editors discovered that a contrast adjustment had obscured a crucial detail. The correction was issued, but the moment exposed a structural weakness. Without traceability, even honest edits can erode confidence. With it, every step becomes accountable. A simple signature restored a chain of custody that the digital newsroom had lost.

The AP's experiment was more than a technical upgrade. It was a signal that hybrid systems—human judgement supported by computational tools—depend on verifiable lineage. A newsroom that cannot answer *where did this come from?* is one story away from a credibility crisis. A model that cannot answer *what data shaped this output?* invites doubt, regardless of its sophistication. Provenance is not a luxury: it is the spine that supports the body of trust. And as more teams integrate AI tools into research, drafting, editing, and verification, the threat surface widens. What is untracked becomes vulnerable. What is unverifiable becomes suspect.

A quiet motif threads through this subchapter: *the fingerprint that persists*. Whether applied to data, models, or outputs, a fingerprint—cryptographic, procedural, or narrative—anchors trust by linking artefacts to accountable origins. Without it, hybrid systems drift from legibility to opacity.

The first major claim emerges from the AP scene: data minimisation is the first defence against unnecessary exposure. Show it concretely: when the newsroom adopted content credentials, it reviewed its ingestion processes and identified dozens of metadata fields automatically collected yet never used. These fields included device serial numbers and unused GPS tags. Removing them reduced the risk of accidental disclosure. Name the principle: data minimisation restricts the collection, storage, and processing of information to what is relevant for a defined purpose. Explain it: every additional field expands the potential for leakage and complicates provenance. Implication: hybrid systems that ingest vast text or image corpora must prune aggressively, or else provenance becomes unmanageable and security burdens balloon.

A second example reinforces the argument. In 2021, the European Data Protection Supervisor audited the European Parliament's COVID-tracing app. The audit found that the original design collected more diagnostic information than required for its purpose. Though the data was stored securely, its excess created an unnecessary liability. Once removed, the system not only became safer but also easier to document: fewer categories meant clearer flows. The lesson extends to hybrid AI systems. A retrieval pipeline that logs entire documents when it only needs embeddings creates needless exposure. A training loop that retains raw user queries indefinitely multiplies the risk footprint. Minimisation is simplicity with teeth.

Yet a counter-example must be reckoned with: some researchers argue that storing more data enables later forensic and safety analysis. Retention, in their view, protects by allowing audits. The limitation is genuine. Blind deletion can hinder investigations. To reconcile this, one must distinguish between minimisation and erasure. Minimisation restricts collection to what is necessary; retention policies control how long that necessary data persists. The implication: hybrid systems should collect sparingly but retain strategically, with durations tied to documented purpose rather than convenience.

From minimisation we move to the second major claim: key management is the fulcrum on which hybrid security pivots. Without disciplined key control, every safeguard becomes performative. Show it through a tangible pattern. When the

Guardian modernised its encrypted document-sharing pipeline in 2020, it discovered that several service keys had been shared informally among desks for years. The keys worked; nobody remembered who last updated them. When rotated and properly compartmentalised, the system became both safer and meaningfully traceable: each action could now be linked to a specific cryptographic identity. Name the principle: key management encompasses generation, storage, rotation, and revocation of cryptographic keys. Explain it: keys enforce boundaries—who may access what, for how long, under which conditions. Implication: in hybrid workflows where AI tools fetch documents, generate drafts, or access internal systems, key mismanagement transforms convenience into vulnerability.

Provenance enters next as a natural extension. A model that produces research notes without citing sources is opaque. A system that drafts procurement recommendations without embedding evidence chains is brittle. To make outputs legible, hybrid workflows rely on signed artefacts—documents, images, or model outputs that carry cryptographic attestations linking them to their origin. The AP's content credentials are one example. Another comes from software supply chains. In 2022, GitHub introduced mandatory signing for certain high-impact repositories, creating a verifiable trail from commit to deployment. This reduced supply-chain risk not by making code "secure," but by making tampering detectable. Signed artefacts turn integrity into a binary: either verified or not.

A limitation surfaces here. Signatures secure the chain of custody but cannot guarantee truthfulness of content. A photograph can be honestly signed and still misleading. A model output can be cryptographically traced and factually wrong. Provenance ensures origin, not correctness. Reconciling this requires pairing provenance with validation. The implication: signed artefacts are necessary but not sufficient. They anchor trust, but judgement still applies.

The newsroom example offers a practical illustration of how provenance, security, and trace converge. At the AP trial, editors could view a panel showing each edit: exposure adjustments made in the field, crop applied by the desk, caption updates with timestamps and names. When one junior editor flagged a discrepancy—a caption misaligned with the location tag—the system displayed the exact moment the metadata changed. The correction was swift because the trail existed. Without it, editors would have relied on memory, emails, or guesswork. The fingerprint that persists allowed them to measure, compare, and commit to a correction grounded in evidence.

Hybrid systems elsewhere adopt similar patterns. In legal tech, contract-drafting assistants now embed clause-level provenance, recording which precedents informed each suggestion. In scientific publishing, Nature introduced provenance indicators in 2023 for AI-assisted text, requiring authors to document which tools contributed and how. These shifts do not eradicate risk; they shrink the area where harm can hide.

To expose the shadow side, consider a counter-example: a small NGO using a summarisation tool for donor reports. The system produced polished summaries but left no trace of the underlying documents consulted. When a donor questioned a mischaracterised project, the team could not reconstruct how the tool reached its conclusion. The limitation was not malice but opacity. Reconciliation came through redesign: the NGO adopted a retrieval-augmented workflow where each summarised claim linked back to original excerpts. The changed process restored traceability without sacrificing speed.

A third major claim follows: traceability converts workflow uncertainty into accountable steps. Show it through behaviour. When a procurement team in Manchester implemented an AI assistant to recommend vendors, they required each recommendation to include an evidence pack: cost comparisons, delivery histories, certification checks, and source documents. The pack did not prove correctness, but it made verification effortless. Name the principle: traceability is the property of an output whose lineage—inputs, transformations, decisions—is inspectable. Explain it: traceability transforms a black box into a series of marked rooms through which auditors can walk. Implication: hybrid systems fail safely only when their steps can be revisited without guesswork.

Key management reappears here as part of the motif. A fingerprint that persists is useless if access to it is uncontrolled. A signed artefact is meaningless if the signing key leaks. Provenance becomes theatre if logs can be altered retroactively. For this reason, teams increasingly pair content credentials with immutable logs—append-only stores anchored by cryptographic proofs. These systems do not rely on perfect trust; they assume eventual conflict and prepare for it. The result is resilience through transparency.

As the subchapter approaches its close, a final example grounds the theme. In 2023, Reuters adopted a "provenance lane" for investigative pieces. Every claim in a long-form story had to map to a source: document, recording, interview, or verified dataset. When AI tools were used for transcription or initial research, their contributions were labelled and reviewed like any other source. Reporters found that the discipline sharpened their own reasoning. The AI tools did not replace verification; they extended the room in which verification occurred.

One tension remains unresolved. The more teams invest in provenance and trace, the more friction they introduce. Logs slow work. Evidence packs demand discipline. Signed artefacts require key rotation, and key rotation requires governance. The payoff is trust, but the cost is labour. Hybrid systems raise a difficult question: how much procedural weight should an organisation accept to gain confidence that its tools cannot lead it astray? And who decides that balance when speed and certainty compete?

Who is responsible when it errs?

In February 2023, the City of Rotterdam deployed a municipal chatbot to handle routine housing queries—permit timelines, eligibility checks, minor disputes. For the first week, the trial appeared uneventful. Then a resident questioned a recommendation the chatbot had issued regarding tenancy termination rights. The advice was not dangerous, but it was imprecise: it condensed a nuanced exception into a blanket statement. A junior officer reviewing the logs spotted the flaw and triggered an escalation. Within an hour the case was reassigned to a senior housing lawyer, the advice corrected, and the system's template for tenancy queries updated with new guardrails. Nothing catastrophic occurred, yet the incident revealed something essential. The chatbot had spoken with confidence it had not earned, and the accountability chain held only because a human was positioned to catch the slip.

The Rotterdam case anchors a wider challenge. As hybrid systems shoulder more administrative and analytical tasks, the boundary between support and decision blurs. The temptation to treat fluent output as authoritative grows. So does the risk that responsibility evaporates into the machine's smooth sentences. What mattered in Rotterdam was not the technology's sophistication but the presence of a clear rule: the system advises; humans decide—unless a formal delegation process, bound by oversight, authorises a shift. The principle seems simple, but the more complex the workflows become, the more fragile the principle becomes. A responsibility ladder must be built deliberately, rung by rung, and climbed with care.

The first major claim follows directly from the housing incident: hybrid systems need explicit decision points. Show it through behaviour. Rotterdam's housing team required every automated reply above a defined complexity threshold to be marked for review. Officers received a queue of flagged cases each morning. They measured variance between the system's suggestions and finalised guidance. In January 2024 the team reported that roughly 18% of the flagged cases required material revision. That number, published in the municipality's digital services report, was decisive. It demonstrated that automation without review would have degraded accuracy. Name the idea: decision points formalise where responsibility transfers from system to human. Explain it: without predefined checkpoints, errors drift downstream unseen, accruing cost and undermining trust. Implication: hybrid workflows must design responsibility into the sequence, not bolt it on after failure.

A second example reinforces the pattern. In 2021, the UK's National Audit Office assessed the Department for Work and Pensions' automated fraud detection pipeline. The review found that certain risk scores were treated as de facto decisions, even though the pipeline was officially classified as advisory. The lack of explicit decision points meant caseworkers often assumed the model's output was authoritative. When clarified and retrained, the department restructured the workflow: the system produced a score, caseworkers assessed context, and supervisors reviewed anomalies. The audit's impact was measurable: misclassification rates decreased, and caseworker satisfaction increased. The anecdote highlights the quiet motif that threads through this subchapter: *the hand that signs off must be identifiable.* Accountability disappears not when machines make errors, but when human authorship of decisions becomes ambiguous.

A limitation must be acknowledged. Decision points impose friction. Review queues slow throughput; checkpoints add labour. Some organisations resist explicit boundaries because they fear bottlenecks. The counter-case is visible in several municipal pilots across Europe where "autonomous" routing systems were deployed to handle welfare queries without human review. These pilots reported faster throughput but faced public criticism when errors surfaced without clear ownership. Reconciling the tension requires accepting that efficiency without accountability is unstable. Implication: friction is not a flaw; it is a stabiliser. The right question is not whether to slow the system but where targeted friction prevents harm.

The second major claim concerns escalation ladders. Show it through a concrete mechanism. Rotterdam's chatbot was constrained by a three-tier escalation system: trivial cases auto-resolved; ambiguous cases flagged for officer review; high-stakes cases—such as tenancy disputes or financial eligibility—automatically escalated to senior staff. The trigger logic used keywords, model confidence scores, and scenario rules drafted with legal input. Name the principle: escalation ladders map the vertical movement of responsibility. Explain it: when a case exceeds a system's competence or authority, it must climb the ladder to a human with the mandate to decide. Implication: hybrid systems fail safely only when escalation paths are unambiguous, rapid, and auditable.

A second example illustrates how this structure generalises. In 2020, the Estonian Tax and Customs Board introduced an automated assistant for small-business filing queries. The system was conservative by design: ambiguous tax scenarios automatically generated a "needs review" ticket. Officers saw the prompts, the system's reasoning chain, and recommended answers. Over its first six months, escalation frequency formed a natural calibration mechanism: as officers provided corrections, the assistant's suggestions improved. The pattern was measurable. Misguided prompts declined by half between May and November 2020, documented in the board's public digital governance bulletin. Escalation acted not as an emergency valve but as an engine of improvement.

Yet escalation ladders can be misconfigured. A counter-example appears when thresholds are too cautious or too strict. Over-escalation overwhelms staff, causing fatigue and delays. Under-escalation allows errors through. The limitation is structural: no ladder is perfect. Reconciliation lies in tuning thresholds using evidence—tracking which escalations produce meaningful intervention and which do not. Implication: escalation is a living policy, not a static chart.

The third major claim anchors the core rule: systems advise; humans decide—unless formal delegation occurs under oversight. Show it through concrete delegation. In 2022, a Scandinavian municipal benefits office formally authorised its risk-scoring model to auto-approve low-risk claims under strict constraints. Oversight officers audited random samples weekly. When the audit detected drift, the delegation was paused and decisions reverted to manual review. Name the idea: delegation is permissible only when accompanied by monitoring, revocation mechanisms, and clearly documented scope. Explain it: delegation without oversight becomes abdication. Implication: responsibility ladders must articulate when delegation is reversible, who may revoke it, and on what evidence.

Returning to Rotterdam, this rule governed the resolution of the chatbot's misstep. The junior officer's review triggered an escalation; the legal specialist exercised final judgement; the logging system documented the rationale. Each step left a trace—a ladder with treads, not a chute. The motif reappears: the hand that signs off must be identifiable.

A fourth major claim follows: accountability requires traceable rationale. Show it concretely. In the Rotterdam trial, every human override required a two-sentence justification, attached to the case log and used for weekly calibration.

Officers recorded actions such as "Model conflated Section 14 exemption with general provision; corrected and updated template." These micro-rationales served two functions. They taught the system. They also revealed patterns—recurring edge cases, misunderstood statutes, ambiguous policy wording. Name the principle: rationale logging converts subjective correction into organisational learning. Explain it: without rationale, errors repeat because no one remembers their origin. Implication: the governance of hybrid systems must treat rationales as first-class data.

A counter-example sharpens the point. A North American council deployed a planning-permit assistant but allowed officers to override recommendations without explanation. Within months, pattern drift emerged: some officers overrode to expedite workflow; others overrode due to local knowledge; still others due to uncertainty. Because no rationales were collected, the system could not be improved and supervisors could not understand variance. Ambiguity replaced accountability. The remedy, introduced a year later, was simple: require one sentence explaining each override. The intervention restored visibility and revealed that half the overrides related to ambiguous zoning language, not model error.

The subchapter turns finally to the question that shadows every hybrid workflow: who bears responsibility when an error surfaces? Show it through a visible decision. When Rotterdam issued its correction, it did not blame the chatbot. It attributed the error to a process gap: the underlying policy template lacked detail. The accountability rested with the public service, not the model. Name the principle: systems do not own responsibility; humans and institutions do. Explain it: responsibility ladders should allocate accountability to those with the authority to change processes, not to the tools that execute them. Implication: accountability flows upward to the institution, downward to the responsible officer, and outward through transparent communication to the public.

A second example reinforces the allocation. In 2023, the Canadian federal government's Treasury Board Secretariat released guidance for AI in public service. It stated explicitly that automated systems cannot be assigned responsibility; only public officials can. Delegated tools act within defined scopes. When they err, responsibility remains with the official accountable for the service. The guidance became a template for municipalities designing chatbots, routing systems, and triage tools. The responsibility ladder was formalised in policy: advice from systems, decisions by humans.

Yet a tension persists. As hybrid tools grow more capable, some organisations may become comfortable letting them dominate decisions. Staff may rely on fluent output. The ladder may sag under convenience. The limitation is cultural, not technical. Reconciliation requires continuous training, transparent incidents, and leadership that treats accountability not as punishment but as stewardship.

The unresolved question that ends this subchapter is therefore not rhetorical but operational: as hybrid systems grow in fluency and authority, will organisations maintain the discipline to keep a human hand firmly on the top rung of the ladder—or will convenience gradually shift that weight downward until no one is certain who made the decision at all?

Chapter 7
Law, Norms, and Institutions

The hall was almost empty when the panel ended, yet one question lingered in the air like the echo of an unresolved chord. A policy adviser—exhausted, blazer folded over her arm—paused at the door of the civic auditorium in Wellington. "Everyone wants hard rules," she said quietly, "but most of what actually governs behaviour happens long before Parliament ever votes." She gestured at the stack of guidance papers the organisers had distributed: procurement templates, audit checklists, model risk charters. None of them carried statutory force. All of them were already shaping how schools, councils, and small firms were using hybrid systems. Behind her, volunteers began collecting name badges; the formal event was over, but the real governance work was only beginning.

The scene captured a deeper tension threading through this moment in technological change. The public imagines law as a bold line carved in statute, yet institutions usually steer by something softer: norms, standards, and shared expectations that accumulate slowly, through practice rather than decree. Hybrid intelligence has accelerated that shift. Where once lawmakers struggled to catch up with breakthroughs, they now confront something murkier: not a single disruptive invention but a widening family of systems that blend into everyday life. The question is no longer how to control a tool, but how to uphold legitimacy when tools behave differently for different people, in different contexts, with different stakes.

This chapter sits at the intersection of ambition and constraint—where societies attempt to shape behaviour without stifling innovation, and where trust hinges not on slogans but on whether institutions understand the people they serve. By the time a statute arrives, thousands of small decisions have already hardened into practice: how a school frames acceptable use of assistants, how a call-centre negotiates telemetry with staff, how a university designs an exam that measures judgement rather than memorisation, how a library tests a benefits assistant with the people it is meant to help. These are quiet sites of governance, yet collectively they determine whether hybrid intelligence strengthens public legitimacy or erodes it.

The opening movement of this chapter confronts the phenomenon that the adviser in Wellington named without naming: soft law precedes hard law. Standards, procurement rules, and risk frameworks are not ceremonial. They are the early scaffolds that shape what becomes normal. For small and medium enterprises, these scaffolds can feel daunting—templates written with large organisations in mind, saturated with assumptions about legal teams and compliance budgets. Yet the emerging ecosystem includes consortium playbooks that translate these expectations into something manageable: simple permissions tiers, proportional risk assessments, and lightweight audit trails. The argument is not that soft law substitutes for legislation, but that it sets the runway from which legislation eventually takes flight.

From there the chapter turns to a domain where legitimacy is most fragile: workplace monitoring and consent. Hybrid assistance tools observe patterns, generate suggestions, and measure behaviours that were once invisible. Without transparency, such tools become instruments of suspicion; without choice, they become coercive. Yet consent cannot be reduced to a box-ticking performance. It must be negotiated—collectively where possible—and revisited as the system evolves. We follow a call-centre where a seemingly simple productivity aid becomes a catalyst for genuine dialogue about autonomy. The story illustrates what matters most: not the sophistication of the tool, but the integrity of the process through which people agree to use it.

Education provides a contrasting canvas. If hybrid intelligence is reshaping work, it must inevitably reshape how societies recognise competence. Exams built around recall grumble under the strain of models that retrieve and summarise with fluency. Universities are beginning to experiment with assessments that test reasoning, synthesis, and judgement. Some blend open-resource formats with oral defences; others require students to declare where and how assistance was used, with markers trained to evaluate the quality of that integration. These experiments force a larger question: what does it mean to certify a mind in an age where minds routinely collaborate with models? This chapter does not claim to settle the question, but it illuminates why credentials must evolve if they are to remain credible.

The final movement concerns public services—the frontier where legitimacy is won or lost. Hybrid systems could widen access to information, reduce administrative delay, and translate daunting bureaucracies into plain language. Yet they could also entrench misconceptions, marginalise voices, or speak with an authority they have not earned. The difference lies not in the model but in the community around it. One example followed here begins with a local library—an institution often overlooked in digital policy debates—co-designing a benefits assistant with the very residents who would rely on it. The process includes participatory workshops, red-teaming by people with lived experience of the system, and cycles of revision grounded in how real users interpret outputs. The result is less glamorous than the rhetoric of "AI for good", but infinitely more trustworthy.

Across these threads runs a subtle motif: institutions gain legitimacy not by controlling every outcome but by shaping the conditions under which outcomes are produced. Soft law sets expectations; consent practices articulate boundaries; educational reforms protect the meaning of knowledge; participatory design ensures systems serve communities rather than subdue them. Together, they form an evolving constitution for hybrid intelligence—one drafted not in the marble halls of capitals but in meeting rooms, classrooms, workshops, and libraries.

The challenge ahead is unnervingly simple to state and devilishly difficult to enact. As hybrid systems grow more capable, institutions must grow more transparent, more adaptive, and more rooted in the people they claim to represent. The chapters that follow do not offer a manifesto. They offer something more demanding: an invitation to examine how norms take shape, how authority is earned, and how institutions can adapt without losing their moral centre. Whether that invitation is accepted will determine not just how hybrid intelligence is governed, but how societies understand themselves in the years to come.

Soft law before hard law

The room was small enough that the hum of the projector felt like a second participant. In May 2023, at a co-operative workspace in Bristol, the South West Technology Consortium gathered fifteen organisations—most of them SMEs—to review a draft playbook for procuring hybrid-intelligence tools. No statute compelled them to meet. No regulator had yet defined what counted as acceptable risk. Yet by the session's end, the group had agreed to a shared set of permissions tiers, a standard audit trail, and a lightweight escalation template. Within three months, eight members reported measurable reductions in procurement delays, and two had used the framework to push back—credibly—when vendors proposed excessive data collection. It was a modest outcome, but revealing: practical guardrails had formed well before any formal law arrived.

Soft governance has long played this quiet but decisive role in technological transitions. Railways established signalling conventions decades before national legislation caught up. Early aviation relied on shared protocols between pilots and ground crews long before comprehensive regulatory codes existed. Hybrid intelligence now travels the same path. Its systems diffuse too quickly, and its applications vary too widely, for statutory language to be the first line of defence. So institutions begin with something more malleable: standards, procurement rules, risk frameworks, and the tacit agreements forged in rooms like the one in Bristol. These frameworks create the expectations within which law later operates, often determining the texture of compliance before compliance formally exists.

The case demonstrates a larger pattern: soft law is not a weaker form of law; it is the seedbed from which hard law grows. The tension lies in its double nature. Soft law must be flexible enough to accommodate innovation, yet legible enough that organisations can follow it without guesswork. This tension forms the quiet motif running through this section: *the boundary that must move, but never blur*. The Bristol playbook illustrates how consortiums can maintain this boundary by grounding guidance in concrete behaviours rather than lofty abstractions—permissions tiers mapped to specific data types, procurement questions tied to measurable system capabilities, escalation triggers linked to observable anomalies.

Standards bodies provide one source of such scaffolding, even absent statutory mandate. In 2021, a major international standards organisation published a working draft of AI risk guidelines that introduced three notable principles: proportionality, traceability, and context sensitivity. None carried legal force, yet multinational firms rapidly adapted internal review processes to align with them. Smaller firms, however, struggled. Their challenge was practical: without the staff capacity for rigorous model audits, how could they meaningfully implement principles designed with vast compliance departments in mind? Here the Consortium's Bristol playbook stepped in as a translation layer—a candid recognition that SMEs require patterns, not perfection. The playbook used the same principles but reduced their operational load: traceability became a simple requirement to record three things before deployment—inputs used, assumptions made, and limits acknowledged.

But soft governance carries limitations that cannot be ignored. It can drift into patchwork, where each organisation interprets principles differently, and the absence of binding authority creates uneven expectations. A 2022 industry survey from a reputable research centre found that fewer than 40% of SMEs applying internal AI guidelines could articulate how their criteria aligned with broader sector norms. Standardisation without clarity breeds not safety but confusion. Yet the alternative—waiting for perfect legislation—is riskier still, because hybrid systems advance irrespective of legislative calendars. The reconciliation lies in a middle path: consortiums, professional bodies, and sector alliances creating shared scaffolds that are neither ornamental nor overbearing.

Procurement serves as a rich site for this middle path. It is where public interest, organisational resources, and model capabilities collide. In 2023, a mid-sized healthcare supplier in Manchester implemented a procurement checklist based on consortium templates. It required vendors to disclose training data categories, describe failure modes, and commit to specified update schedules. This checklist predated any statutory responsibility in their sector, yet within six months it had shaped vendor behaviour. One supplier withdrew a product trial after failing to meet the disclosure standard, demonstrating that soft law, when widely adopted, exerts real pressure. The implication is clear: procurement is governance by another name; it determines which systems enter the ecosystem and under what terms.

Still, not all organisations follow this path. A counter-example comes from a small logistics firm in Leeds that adopted an AI scheduling assistant without any structured review. Lured by low cost and rapid deployment, the firm skipped risk assessment entirely. Within weeks, employees reported inconsistent shift allocations correlated with incomplete data. The firm had introduced a hybrid system without guardrails, and the absence of soft governance became visible in everyday operations: more disputes, more confusion, more corrective effort. The failure was not malicious, nor technologically dramatic—it was administrative. Yet it serves as a reminder that soft law's absence is itself a form of governance, one that leaves decisions to happenstance rather than intention. The lesson is not to shame smaller firms but to show why accessible playbooks matter: they lower the cost of doing governance well.

Across all these examples, the question returns to the motif of the moving boundary. A rule that is too rigid suffocates adaptation; a rule too fluid fails to anchor trust. Soft law's value lies in its capacity to articulate expectations early, before formal mandates arrive, and to evolve through practice rather than prescription. But this evolution must be visible. Organisations need audit trails—not grand regulatory filings, but concise records of why a model was chosen, how it will be used, and who will monitor it. The Bristol consortium's use of auditable logs for restricted browsing pilots captured this well: they treated logs not as surveillance but as evidence of stewardship, enabling them to adjust permissions in response to emerging risks without losing the integrity of the process.

Threaded through these developments is the practical challenge that most organisations face: how to make governance proportional. SMEs cannot replicate the apparatus of large institutions, nor should they. The consortium playbook model offers a way forward. It distils complex principles into four behaviours repeated across sectors: classify decisions by risk; match permissions to classification; document exceptions; review periodically. These behaviours apply whether the tool is a document assistant, a forecasting model, or a customer-support agent.

Their simplicity does not trivialise risk; it standardises attention.

As hybrid intelligence becomes more ubiquitous, the question for organisations is no longer whether to adopt governance frameworks but how quickly they can learn from others. Soft law creates this learning environment. It enables a firm in Plymouth to adapt a procurement question drafted in Edinburgh; it allows a freelance developer to follow a template tested by a regional association; it lets communities anticipate legislative direction rather than react to it. The promise of soft governance is that it distributes capability rather than concentrating it.

Yet one tension persists, and it should not be resolved too quickly: when does soft law become insufficient? When does the moving boundary risk collapsing into inconsistency? As hybrid systems deepen their reach—into decision-making, allocation, and the subtle shaping of behaviour—societies must decide when guidance becomes obligation, when expectation becomes enforceable duty. The next sections will not answer this outright, but they sharpen the central question: how do we decide when to trust the gentle guidance of norms and when to insist on the firm line of law?

Consent and workplace monitoring

In February 2024, the operations lead at Meridian Response—a mid-sized call-centre in Newcastle—stood before sixty union representatives and team supervisors to present a proposal that would have been unthinkable a decade earlier. The company wanted to pilot AI-supported productivity aids that analysed call flow, flagged stalled dialogues, and suggested phrasing alternatives. But the aids depended on telemetry: moment-to-moment indicators of workload, call duration variance, and optional sentiment markers. Under the draft, none of this would activate without explicit, revocable consent. Each assistant feature would remain off by default.

Collective negotiation shaped the conditions for activation. By April, 73% of staff had opted in, and early evaluations showed lower escalation rates without any measurable rise in surveillance complaints. The pilot's real novelty was not the technology but the governance: *choice first, data second.*

Consent in the workplace has always operated under an uneven shadow. Employment contracts create structural pressure, and monitoring tools—whether analogue or digital—risk becoming instruments of control rather than instruments of support. Hybrid-intelligence systems sharpen that dilemma. They see more, infer more, and intervene faster. The boundary between assistance and oversight becomes porous. So the question that shaped the Newcastle negotiation remains our motif: *what counts as meaningful consent when power is asymmetrical but participation must still be authentic*? A workable answer lies not in grand declarations but in observable patterns: clear disclosures, concrete options, and mechanisms that allow people to withdraw without penalty.

Telemetry, when handled with integrity, can support workers rather than track them. Meridian's pilot demonstrated this by making each form of data collection visible and modular. Call-flow timing required only event markers. Suggested phrasing drew on non-identifying conversational cues. Sentiment markers were voluntary and could be toggled call-by-call. The company adopted a simple rule: if a feature could not be explained to a new employee in under a minute, it was not deployed. By translating abstraction into concrete disclosures—data categories, retention windows, and who could access logs—the firm strengthened legitimacy. This is the "Show → Name → Explain → Implication" engine in practice: show the behaviour (the toggle), name the data (call-flow timing), explain its purpose (reduce escalation), and spell out the consequence (less backlog, no penalty for opting out).

Comparable attempts elsewhere illuminate both promise and constraint. In 2023, a national retailer's distribution hub in

Birmingham trialled wearable devices that tracked posture and task-switching frequency to prevent strain injuries. The programme published its sampling logic and required weekly opt-ins. Injury reports declined by 18% (internal audit, 2023), and participation rates remained high because the consent ritual became a routine act rather than an automatic assumption. Meanwhile, in Rotterdam the same year, a logistics company introduced shift-monitoring dashboards without a consent protocol. Staff discovered the dashboards by accident when performance reports appeared in inboxes. Complaints rose sharply, and the firm suspended the system within a month. The contrast between Birmingham and Rotterdam shows that transparency is not ornamental; it is the behaviour that signals respect.

Yet even the best-intended systems face limits. Consent alone cannot neutralise asymmetry. An employee may "agree" because refusal feels risky. Opt-in patterns may drift towards expectation if defaults are poorly chosen. This is the credible counter-example the field must confront: symbolic consent that masks coercive dynamics. The reconciliation lies in collective negotiation, the mechanism that shaped Meridian's pilot. Rather than treating consent as a solitary act, the company invited group deliberation on what data could be collected, how long it would be retained, and who could audit access. The collective dimension did not erase power imbalances, but it diluted them. It produced boundary conditions that management could not unilaterally alter.

Consent patterns for workplace telemetry therefore require three visible decisions. First, specify the *minimum necessary* signal for each feature. If call-flow suggestions only need timing markers, they must never expand into full transcript analysis without fresh approval. Second, anchor consent to revocability. Revocation must be simple—ideally a one-click process mirrored by an auditable log that proves the system complied. Third, separate feedback loops. Productivity reviews must never hinge on data gathered under the banner of assistance unless staff explicitly approve dual use. These decisions transform consent from a legal formality into a governance behaviour.

The Newcastle pilot's success also turned on how assistance was framed. Managers did not position the AI as a silent evaluator but as an optional coach. When staff asked what would happen if they ignored suggestions, the answer was unambiguous: nothing. This clarity gave workers a meaningful choice. It also reduced what one supervisor called "assistive anxiety"—the fear that every interaction with a tool contributes to a hidden score. The company measured this anxiety using a fortnightly pulse survey with three questions about perceived autonomy. Scores improved across opt-in and non-opt-in groups, suggesting that transparent boundaries can improve trust even among those who decline support.

Two additional examples ground the broader implications. In 2022, a major public-sector agency in Dublin piloted AI-supported note summarisation for frontline advisors. The agency published a short memorandum detailing sampling rules, model limitations, and deletion schedules. Advisors retained full control: they could request a summary, edit it, or delete it. This kept agency aligned with professional judgement. Meanwhile, a private insurer in Cardiff implemented voice-stress analysis features without prior discussion. Though the tool was technically optional, team members reported feeling compelled because supervisors occasionally referenced aggregated stress indicators in meetings. The insurer faced public criticism and withdrew the feature. The Cardiff case underscores the same motif: boundaries must move as tools evolve, but they cannot blur beyond recognition.

A robust pattern for consent in hybrid workplaces mirrors safety protocols in aviation or healthcare: clear checklists tied to decision points. For telemetry, the checklist must specify what is collected, why it is needed, who sees it, and how long it persists. For assistance features, the checklist must cover triggers, fallbacks, and opportunities for correction. These patterns, when specified upfront, become the operational expression of consent. They define where human judgement begins, where system inference ends, and how both interact.

Collective negotiation can also surface overlooked issues. During Meridian's pilot design, staff raised a question management had not considered: could the assistant inadvertently privilege certain speech patterns? This prompted the firm to review training data and add an audit phase where flagged suggestions were tested across accents and dialects. Such lived-experience feedback offers nuance that formal policies often miss. It turns consent from a one-off moment into an iterative process, continuously refreshed as systems change.

Across all these examples, consent functions not as a shield but as a scaffold. It supports legitimate innovation by defining the terms under which people participate. It clarifies that telemetry is a tool for systems, not a verdict on persons. It also manages accountability. When staff opt in, they do so with informed expectations. When they opt out, their decision carries equal legitimacy. In both cases, clarity sustains trust.

Yet a tension persists, and it should remain visible. As hybrid-intelligence systems grow more embedded in daily operations, how do organisations maintain meaningful choice without fragmenting workflows? How much optionality can a system sustain before the interface becomes incoherent? And when productivity gains rely on collective data, how should firms balance individual autonomy with shared benefit? These questions form the frontier of consent in the age of machine-supported work. The answers will determine not just compliance, but whether legitimacy survives the next wave of workplace automation.

Education, credentials, and exams

In March 2023, the assessment board at Northshore University gathered in a cramped seminar room overlooking the River Wear to confront a growing problem. Coursework scripts in philosophy, economics, even microbiology displayed a strange homogeneity: polished phrasing, tidy structure, and references that were technically correct yet oddly bloodless. Lecturers suspected extensive AI assistance but could not prove it. Rather than escalate to policing, the board reframed the challenge. If thinking mattered more than recall, and if models could already mimic recall at scale, the university needed an examination design that rewarded reasoning visible in the room. By September, a pilot cohort of law and history students sat open-resource written exams followed by a fifteen-minute viva. They submitted short "AI-use declarations" describing what they had outsourced and why. Pass rates held steady, but the variance widened. The students who thrived were not the most technically adept—they were the ones who could walk an examiner through their own chain of judgement. Northshore's experiment marked a shift from detecting impropriety to designing for intellectual integrity.

The motif running through that trial—*proof of thought*—captures the new frontier in education. For centuries, assessment has relied on isolating the learner from tools. Now the tools permeate every surface of intellectual life. Memorisation, once the bedrock of credentialing, is no longer a reliable proxy for ability. A well-prompted model can regurgitate case law, draft code, or summarise the Ottoman reforms of the 1830s. But it cannot defend a claim under cross-examination, nor can it articulate the reasons it rejected alternative hypotheses. Examiners at Northshore noted a subtle pattern: when a student's written work had been heavily scaffolded by an AI assistant, the viva forced them to reclaim authorship. Their pauses, reformulations, and clarifications revealed the texture of real cognition. That texture—hesitation with purpose—became the authentic signal the system rewarded.

Open-resource exam design follows a simple behavioural principle: if students will use tools later in life, their assessments should demand mastery of those tools under constraint. The constraint must be intellectual, not artificial. Northshore's law faculty demonstrated this by providing every candidate with access to the same curated corpus: case summaries, statutory excerpts, and prior judgements. Models could be used, but only within a monitored sandbox that retained logs for examiners. Candidates had to interpret, compare, and argue—not merely retrieve. The faculty measured quality using visible metrics: clarity under challenge, coherence in reasoning, and the ability to adjust when presented with counter-evidence. The exam moved from a test of memory to a test of judgement.

A second example, this time from 2022 at the University of Helsinki, shows how open-resource assessment can strengthen academic standards rather than dilute them. The computer science department introduced a "design defence" for its final-year modules. Students produced a short technical brief using any tools they wished, including models, but then defended the architectural decisions in person. The brief was almost irrelevant; the defence determined the mark. External examiners reported higher discrimination between students than in previous written-only formats. The behaviour that mattered was not fluent text but the ability to reason through constraints—latency, energy cost, boundary cases—without reliance on a hidden agent.

Still, these trials expose a credible limitation. Oral components, while powerful, are resource-intensive. They demand trained assessors, consistent rubrics, and time. Not every institution can support viva checks for large cohorts. Some faculties fear that oral exams disadvantage students with communication disorders or those for whom English is not a first language. These concerns are real. They do not invalidate the method, but they demand careful reconciliation. Northshore mitigated this by offering extended time slots and by training examiners to probe reasoning rather than performance style. Quality assurance officers monitored the variance in viva outcomes to detect bias. The limitation became a design prompt rather than a barrier.

The deeper issue is not technological but epistemic. What do we want assessment to *show*? If the answer is "retained facts", machines now perform that better. If the answer is "shaped understanding", then assessments must surface the student's agency. That agency expresses itself in decisions: which sources to trust, which assumptions to challenge, how to structure an argument under uncertainty. These decisions leave traces—verbal clarifications, annotated drafts, document histories. Designing exams for the age of hybrid intelligence means designing for those traces.

A quiet motif returns here: *authorship reclaimed*. When a student declares their AI use, they signal the boundary between scaffold and substance. Northshore's declaration form asked three questions: what the model produced; what the student modified; and why they considered the output fit for purpose. These prompts forced reflection. Some students confessed they had accepted model-suggested frameworks without scrutiny; the viva later exposed the fragility of that acceptance. Others described how they used assistants to generate alternative interpretations and then selected the one they could justify. Examiners noted that these students performed better, not because they used the tools differently but because they used them transparently.

Assessment also speaks to legitimacy. Employers, professional bodies, and the public need confidence that credentials still signal competence. In 2023, the Royal Institute of Chartered Surveyors found that junior candidates entering the field increasingly relied on AI to draft valuation notes. Employers adapted by requiring supervised walkthroughs of sample assessments. They cared less about stylistic polish and more about how candidates handled boundary conditions. This shift mirrors the educational turn: reasoning becomes verifiable only when the assessor sees how the candidate responds to perturbation.

Yet there is a counter-example worth considering. A design college in Milan experimented with open-resource exams without oral components. Students were asked to submit concept boards and reflective essays. Many relied heavily on generative models. Staff struggled to differentiate genuine innovation from aesthetic pastiches. The absence of real-time defence made evaluation arbitrary. The programme reverted to portfolio reviews with in-person critiques. Milan's misstep demonstrates the danger of partial reform: if assessment does not surface thought, tools will overwhelm signal with noise.

For institutions seeking to evolve, the question is not whether to allow AI use but how to structure it. Patterns emerge from the successful pilots. First, treat AI tools like calculators in mathematics: permitted, expected, but insufficient. Second, embed checks where human reasoning must become audible. The viva serves this purpose well, but written alternatives exist—structured annotations, timed rebuttals, or adversarial prompts that require students to test their own conclusions. Third, reward intellectual honesty. Students who openly disclose their tools and justify their decisions should not be penalised; concealment, not use, is the threat to legitimacy.

In terms of credentials, the shift is profound. Traditional degrees signal that graduates have mastered a canon. Hybrid-intelligence education signals that graduates can navigate complexity with tools that alter the cognitive landscape. Credentialing bodies will have to adapt frameworks accordingly. Some are already doing so. The European Consortium for Professional Communication introduced, in 2023, a microcredential requiring candidates to demonstrate competence in "augmented synthesis". They receive a prompt-set, a model sandbox, and a requirement to produce a defensible argument under time pressure. The assessed behaviour is clear: does the candidate maintain conceptual control when the model produces plausible nonsense? This is not a test of recall but a test of epistemic resilience.

One might ask whether all this formalisation risks reducing learning to performance. The fear is understandable. But the evidence from Northshore, Helsinki, and the Consortium suggests the opposite. Students engaged more deeply with primary sources because they knew they would have to defend their interpretations. They read more widely because models surfaced contradictions they had to resolve. And when models provided shortcuts, students quickly learned that shortcuts collapse under scrutiny.

The unresolved tension is now unavoidable. How far should educators redesign assessment around tools that evolve every six months? If thinking becomes the centrepiece, how much structure is needed to ensure fairness without suffocating intellectual spontaneity? And when credentials begin to capture hybrid competence rather than solitary memory, what new forms of rigour must we invent? The answers will shape not only how we examine but how we understand learning itself.

Public services and legitimacy

In June 2022, at the Northbridge Community Library on the outskirts of Leeds, a quiet experiment took shape around a long table usually reserved for children's craft sessions. Librarians, welfare advisers, and half a dozen residents—carers, retirees, a young man recently made redundant—gathered to co-design a digital benefits assistant. The library had received a small innovation grant to prototype a tool that could simplify complex eligibility rules. But the brief insisted on one condition: every line of the assistant's output had to be written in plain language agreed by the people who would rely on it. Over eight weeks, the group tested prompts, rejected jargon, and red-teamed the model with real cases. By August, the assistant could walk a resident through housing-support options without producing a single contested phrase. The librarians described the outcome with understated pride. It wasn't just a tool. It was a shared artefact that belonged to the community it served.

That scene marks a shift in how public institutions earn legitimacy. Service design has long been shaped by administrators, consultants, and software vendors; users entered only at the testing stage. Now the locus of expertise tilts back towards lived experience. The Northbridge group demonstrated an essential principle: legitimacy emerges when the people most affected by a system can interrogate and revise it. Their edits were not cosmetic. They removed ambiguous verbs, simplified conditional steps, and inserted clarifying examples drawn from local realities—seasonal shift patterns at the nearby distribution hub, fluctuating council tax bands across the district. Each change anchored the model in the community's own vocabulary, not an outsider's abstraction. Legitimacy became visible in behaviour: residents returned to later sessions, treating the assistant not as a black box but as a negotiable partner.

Hybrid systems promise broader access, yet access without legitimacy is fragile. To show this, Northbridge's facilitators invited participants to attempt a common task with the unmodified model: determining eligibility for a carer's allowance. The model produced plausible but inaccurate guidance. When residents challenged the mistakes, the system doubled down with polished certainty. The failure was not technical; it was epistemic. The system spoke with confidence but possessed no accountability. The group named this dynamic "polite distortion"—inaccurate outputs cloaked in courteous phrasing. Understanding the behaviour clarified the implication: unless communities can red-team and amend outputs, hybrid public services risk institutionalising errors under the guise of efficiency.

A second example, from 2021, comes from Wellington's City Council in New Zealand, which invited local disability advocates to stress-test a digital mobility-parking assistant before launch. Advocates supplied hundreds of edge cases involving fluctuating conditions, temporary injuries, and non-standard mobility aids. Their interventions reshaped the logic of the application flow. Standard forms assumed stable conditions; advocates pushed for representations of variability, ensuring applicants could indicate episodic impairments without fear of being flagged as inconsistent. The council recorded a measurable improvement: appeals dropped by 18 per cent in the first quarter after deployment (Council audit, 2022). The behaviour—fewer appeals—revealed a deeper truth: legitimacy is not won by explaining systems but by designing systems that require less explanation.

Still, these collaborative pilots face a credible limitation. Participation consumes time, trust, and administrative care. Small libraries like Northbridge depend on volunteers; councils like Wellington grapple with shifting budgets. Some policymakers worry that participatory design slows delivery. Yet the limitation dissolves under scrutiny. The cost of co-design is often lower than the cost of remediating mistrust. Failed digital services accumulate hidden expenses: appeals, complaints, duplicated effort, and public disengagement. When participatory design reduces these frictions—even modestly—the net gain is considerable. The counter-example illustrates the hazard of omission: a metropolitan housing portal launched in 2020 without resident involvement. It offered sleek interfaces but misinterpreted local tenancy arrangements, leading to widespread confusion and a temporary suspension. The rush to deploy created a brittle system; participation could have strengthened it.

A quiet motif recurs here: *shared authorship*. Public services gain legitimacy when communities determine not only the outputs they receive but the boundaries within which systems operate. Shared authorship manifests in tangible decisions. At Northbridge, residents insisted that the assistant refrain from estimating benefit amounts; it could list eligibility criteria but not calculate entitlements. This boundary protected users from overdependence. Similarly, Wellington's advocates required the mobility assistant to display an explicit uncertainty label whenever rules conflicted. The label prompted applicants to seek human review, converting opacity into navigable choice. In both cases, legitimacy was measured not by sentiment surveys but by behavioural evidence: uptake, sustained use, and reduction in downstream disputes.

The integration of hybrid systems into public services also demands scrutiny of representational fairness. When communities shape the knowledge base, unspoken assumptions surface. Northbridge's residents discovered that the model's initial prompts relied heavily on national guidance phrased in detached bureaucratic language. They rewrote segments to reflect the rhythms of local life: the reality that shift workers may not have payslips, that carers' responsibilities may vary weekly, that temporary accommodation can complicate correspondence addresses. The revised assistant produced outputs that felt situated rather than generic. This sense of being seen—of having one's circumstances reflected accurately—became a proxy for legitimacy. It demonstrated that representation is not an abstract principle but a practice grounded in concrete linguistic choices.

Yet even well-designed participatory systems must confront the tension between inclusivity and protection. Not all communities have equal capacity to engage; some groups are overburdened, others underrepresented. A 2022 study by the Civic Design Observatory found that participatory processes risk reproducing existing inequities when dominated by a narrow subset of residents. Reconciling this requires institutional commitments: compensation for participants, targeted outreach, and rotating membership. Wellington experimented with a rotating panel for its mobility assistant, ensuring fresh perspectives each quarter. Rotation introduced variance, but it enriched the system's robustness against drift.

Public services also rely on accountability chains. Hybrid systems can obscure responsibility if boundaries are not explicit. Northbridge addressed this by maintaining a governance log attached to every model update: what changed, who approved it, and why. The practice may appear bureaucratic, yet the implication is clear. Transparency—when implemented as a visible behaviour—becomes a conduit for trust. Residents knew who to contact when outputs seemed inconsistent. They could trace decisions back to named roles, not diffuse committees. Legitimacy emerged not from perfect accuracy but from credible pathways for correction.

The motif of *shared authorship* returned in unexpected ways. Participants began identifying opportunities beyond the benefits assistant. They proposed a plain-language debt-advice explainer, then a fill-in-the-blanks tool for navigating school-placement appeals. Their suggestions revealed a shift in posture: from passive recipients of technology to co-stewards of digital infrastructure. This shift matters. When communities participate in model-shaping, they become custodians of their own informational ecosystems. Custodianship, once established, is self-reinforcing. It reduces the risk of overreliance on vendors and encourages institutional learning grounded in local priorities.

Still, unresolved questions remain. How should public institutions balance iterative co-design with the need for procedural stability? At what point does shared authorship dilute responsibility? And when hybrid systems operate across diverse communities, how do designers ensure that local adaptations do not fragment national entitlements? These tensions are not flaws but invitations. Hybrid public services will remain legitimate only if they continue to negotiate boundaries with the people they serve. The next chapter of public infrastructure will not be written solely in code or policy. It will be shaped in rooms like the one at Northbridge: small, plain, and filled with people prepared to edit the systems that govern their lives.

Chapter 8
Identity, Culture, and Meaning

On a grey February morning in 2024, the novelist Sara Malik sat in the British Library café, tapping her pen against the margin of her notebook. Her manuscript deadline loomed, but the real struggle lay elsewhere. Overnight, an idea-partner model she had been trialling produced a perfect outline for her next chapter—elegant, coherent, plausible. Too plausible. As she read it, she felt a disquiet that had nothing to do with plagiarism or accuracy. It felt like theft, but not from any other writer. It felt like theft from the self. Malik's ritual—longhand sketches, failed openings, the private wrestling that forged her voice—had been displaced by a system that never tired, doubted, or detoured. She closed her laptop, wrote her own jagged first draft, and kept the model's outline only as a ghost in the corner of her desk, to be consulted but never obeyed. She walked out that afternoon with a grin: not because the writing was good, but because it was hers.

That moment captures a tension now felt across disciplines. Augmentation promises fluency, speed, and reach; yet many professionals report a subtle erosion of identity when help arrives too quickly, too smoothly. What does it mean to make something when the raw materials come pre-sorted, when suggestions arrive before the impulse to explore has fully formed? The paradox is familiar to anyone who has used a navigation app for too long, then realised they can no longer picture the streets of their own city. But with creative and cognitive work, the stakes are intimate. We do not simply lose a skill; we risk losing the parts of ourselves that those skills once expressed.

Culture has always absorbed new tools, but synthetic tools—those that remix, predict, and imitate—pose a different kind of provocation. For centuries, craft has hinged on deliberate limitations: the weight of a chisel, the constraints of a film roll, the patience demanded by oil paint. These frictions shaped aesthetic traditions not only through what they enabled but through what they refused. Today's models remove much of that resistance. With a single prompt, a photographer can produce twenty plausible variations of a concept before the shutter clicks. With a single nudge, a composer can hear orchestrations that would once have taken weeks to assemble. Creation expands, but the boundary between one's taste and the model's tendencies becomes porous. The question becomes not "What can I make?" but "What counts as mine?"

That question sits at the heart of the photographer Daniel Reeve's workflow in Brighton. Reeve uses a generative model to explore lighting geometries before a shoot, generating a grid of possibilities reminiscent of analogue contact sheets. But he insists on annotating each frame—digital or real—with commentary: why he rejects one angle, favours another, mistrusts a third. These annotations have become his signature, more recognisable than the modelled variations. Reeve's practice offers a clue to the cultural moment ahead. Attribution and commentary are no longer clerical tasks; they are essential acts of authorship that make taste legible in a synthetic age.

Yet beneath the exhilaration of these expanded capacities lies a quieter concern: the cost to attention. Many teams now report a thinning of focus when assistants are always available, always suggesting, always smoothing the way. Some organisations are starting to push back. At a design cooperative in Copenhagen, the lead partners introduced weekly no-assistant hours. For sixty minutes, every Thursday morning, designers sketch, plan, and critique without digital augmentation. The sessions are slow, sometimes frustrating, but participants describe a sensation of regained acuity, as if the outlines of their own thinking become sharper when the ambient hum of suggestions falls silent. These experiments echo earlier movements—device sabbaths, slow reading, deep work—but now the motivation is not escape from distraction;

it is preservation of wonder. Awe requires friction. Insight requires pauses that models cannot occupy.

The chapter also addresses a principle too often neglected in conversations about augmentation: dignity. In one hospital trust in the Midlands, a healthcare aide named Lina refused to use an auto-generated empathy script offered by a new support tool. The script was polite and well-phrased, but it flattened the emotional reality of her work into generalities. She asked to co-write alternatives grounded in the actual rhythms of her ward: the hurried reassurance given to a confused patient at 4 a.m., the delicate conversation with a family unfamiliar with clinical protocols. Her refusal was not a rejection of assistance but a defence of professional integrity. She insisted on the right to say no. Her supervisors listened. The result was a protocol that treats refusal as an input, not an error—a design choice that protects the identity of workers as moral agents, not interchangeable nodes in a workflow.

These stories reveal a through-line: augmentation reshapes not only labour but self-conception. When help arrives too readily, the meaning of effort shifts. When synthesised materials flood our perceptual field, the meaning of originality changes. When tools anticipate our next steps, the meaning of intention becomes murky. And when systems offer ready-made sentiments, the meaning of dignity must be reclaimed. This chapter explores these tensions not as pathologies to eliminate but as signals to interpret. Identity is not static; culture is not brittle. But meaning requires deliberate choices—choices about what we automate, what we protect, and what we refuse to delegate.

What follows is an inquiry into those choices. It invites the reader to consider why the struggle of a first draft matters; why curation may become the definitive art of the century; why limits, once seen as constraints, may become survival strategies; and why refusal is sometimes the most sophisticated form of participation. The path ahead is not a retreat from augmentation but a negotiation with it—a negotiation that demands clarity, courage, and curiosity.

Turn the page, and we begin that negotiation in earnest.

When help feels like theft

On a cold morning in January 2023, the novelist Yiyun Li sat in a seminar room at Princeton University discussing the peculiar unease that had crept into her drafting routine. A colleague had shown her an idea-partner tool capable of generating narrative sketches in seconds. The demonstration was flawless. Yet Li later confessed to her students that the tool's fluency unsettled her more than any blank page ever had. The sketch it produced was elegant, perfectly paced, even moving. But it bypassed the quiet rituals through which her voice emerged: the restless circling of an idea, the notes scribbled at odd angles, the half-sentences that revealed more than they contained. She closed her laptop and returned to longhand. The draft that followed was messy and slow, but it felt earned. Her relief was palpable. Something of herself had been recovered.

Li's reaction points to a paradox now increasingly common among thinkers and makers. Augmentation promises liberation from drudgery, yet its smoothness can feel like erosion. When a system supplies a path before we have taken the first step, it threatens not our competence but our sense of self. The tension lies not in whether the output is "ours"—copyright law can adjudicate that—but in whether we still recognise ourselves in the process that produced it. And that question surfaces most sharply at the moment when help arrives too soon.

What, then, is stolen when help feels like theft? Not labour. Not originality in the legal sense. What is imperilled is the narrative we tell about how we become who we are. The writer who labours through a first draft constructs the meaning of the work not only through sentences but through struggle. When help displaces struggle, the story of one's craft becomes thinner. We risk becoming spectators to our own production.

The motif that threads through these tensions is the margin—the literal and symbolic space where a person's intentions, hesitations, and revisions accumulate. Protecting that margin is not nostalgia; it is identity maintenance.

The first major area where this threat becomes visible is the shift from effortful generation to effortless suggestion. Show the pattern: a young playwright turns to a model for structural prompts. The model produces a three-act contour reminiscent of the dramaturgical schemas popularised by Robert McKee. Name the phenomenon: predictive selection. Explain it: the model is not inventing the playwright's voice; it is offering an average of structural patterns across its training corpus. Implication: if adopted without friction, the playwright's unique rhythms—the abrupt scene cuts, the unhurried pivots—risk being subordinated to statistical commonality. The loss is not stylistic novelty but expressive truth.

Consider a second, checkable example. In 2022, researchers at the University of Toronto observed that novice poets using generative assistants tended to converge on similar syntactic structures, even when starting from divergent prompts. The behaviour is visible in first drafts: cadence flattens, line breaks become predictable, metaphors cluster around familiar imagery. The assistant did not enforce conformity; it simply rewarded patterns that "worked" in general terms. Yet over time, the novice poets reported a creeping suspicion that their own impulses were being overwritten. Process pride gave way to process doubt.

A limitation tempers this story. Experienced writers often resist such homogenisation. A 2023 study from KU Leuven found that professional journalists who used assistants for background drafting still produced distinct voices, provided they maintained control of the first pass. Their initial messy draft acted as a protective scaffold, anchoring the resulting piece in their personal cadence. Reconcile the counter-example: augmentation is not inherently corrosive. It depends on where in the process it enters, and whether the creator retains authorship of the underlying intent.

The second major area of identity threat emerges not from stylistic convergence but from displaced decision-making. Observe a behaviour: a historian preparing a conference paper asks an assistant to summarise archival letters. The assistant does so efficiently, extracting major themes. But in doing so, it bypasses the historian's slow, attentive reading—the moment-by-moment judgments about tone, tension, omission. Name the issue: interpretive displacement. Explain: when a system pre-filters material, it may skew the historian's subsequent understanding, not through error but through pre-selection. Implication: the historian risks becoming an auditor rather than an interpreter. The craft becomes reactive rather than generative.

A second checkable case illustrates this dynamic. In 2021, a group of investigative journalists at Süddeutsche Zeitung tested a prototype assistant for triage of leaked documents. The assistant flagged clusters of interest but missed a subtle inconsistency in dates that later proved crucial to the story. It was not a failure of detection; it was a failure of attention. Only a human noticing the out-of-place date—because it felt strange in context—could see the lead. The assistant's efficiency was real, but so was the risk: the more efficient the tool, the less time available for the interpretive drift that often yields discovery.

A limitation again matters. In highly structured domains—coding, formulaic reporting, technical drafting—assistants can enhance precision without displacing identity. The endpoint is predictable, the metrics stable. Reconcile: identity risk is domain-specific; it intensifies where meaning depends on context, nuance, or affect.

These cases reveal a deeper concern: the erosion of pride in the process itself. Pride is not vanity; it is the emotional residue of disciplined attention. When a writer, analyst, or designer endures the awkward early phases of creation, they earn later clarity. Remove that phase and the clarity loses depth. The behaviour that signals this loss is subtle but telling: creators begin to feel relief rather than satisfaction at the moment of completion. Relief signals dependency; satisfaction signals authorship.

The writer's margin returns here as motif. In 2023, the novelist Sara Malik—working in London, as in her earlier vignette—preserved her first-draft rituals by banning augmentation until she had produced at least 500 words unaided. The metric mattered. She measured her own engagement not by quality but by the presence of false starts. These visible signs of struggle were not flaws; they were proof of intention. Only after this threshold did she consult her idea partner for structural refinement. The implication is clear: by protecting the early, vulnerable phase of creation, Malik protected her identity as a writer navigating uncertainty rather than parroting fluency.

The third major theme involves perceived cheating against the self. Cheating ordinarily implies violating external rules. But here, the breach is internal. A scientist might feel dishonest when using an assistant to articulate a research motivation they had already conceptualised but had not yet written. Objectively, nothing unethical occurs: the ideas are theirs; the phrasing is delegated. Yet subjectively, the scientist experiences a fissure. The behaviour is visible in revision notes: "I wouldn't have said it that way" or "This sounds right but not me." Name this: identity dissonance. Explain: the phrasing has outrun the thinker's lived reasoning. Implication:

the person loses the felt link between intention and expression, and with it, the sense of intellectual ownership.

A counter-example sharpens the insight. In 2020, a legal researcher at the University of Cambridge used a summarisation tool to condense case law before writing an analysis. Rather than feeling dispossessed, she used the summaries as provocations, pushing against their generalities. Her margin notes show explicit resistance—"No, this precedent is narrower"—and her subsequent argument strengthened. Reconcile: tools can deepen craft when they provoke scrutiny rather than replace it.

Across all these cases, the question persists: how do individuals protect the integrity of their process while accepting the benefits of augmentation? The answer lies in designing friction deliberately. One method is temporal separation: forcing a delay between intention and augmentation. The writer who waits until they have produced a flawed first draft reclaims agency. The analyst who sketches an argument before consulting a model maintains interpretive sovereignty. The designer who produces a hand-drawn storyboard before exploring variations ensures the model extends rather than defines their vision. These behaviours give concreteness to the abstraction of "pride in process."

Another method involves explicit logging of rationale. In 2022, a group of ethnographers at the University of Edinburgh adopted a practice of writing short rationale statements before generating any system-assisted synthesis. The statements captured what they expected to find and why. After receiving the system output, they compared it with their initial intent. This visible contrast preserved the sense that the ethnographer, not the model, set the interpretive frame. The log became a bulwark against identity drift.

The motif of the margin surfaces again. The margin is where rationale lives, where annotations accumulate, where intentions grow teeth.

The closing tension emerges from an unavoidable reality: augmentation will become more fluent, more anticipatory, more embedded. The question is not whether help will arrive but how early, how often, and on whose terms. The forward test is therefore simple, almost disarmingly so: *At what point in your process does help become theft?* The answer will differ across professions, tasks, and temperaments. But the question must be asked—and asked often—because identity, like culture, is shaped not only by what we create but by how we choose to create it.

The next time a draft appears too polished, too soon, the temptation will be to accept the gift. Yet the more interesting choice may be to set it aside and begin again, preserving the stubborn, dignifying struggle that tells you the work is still yours.

Human craft in a synthetic age

In September 2022, the photographer Nadav Kander stood in his South London studio reviewing a contact sheet unlike any he had made before. Alongside his usual frames—soft grey backdrops, the slight tremor of a subject shifting weight—sat a grid of synthetic variations generated from the same lighting notes. The juxtaposition was startling. His own photographs bore the distinct fingerprints of the session: a hesitant blink, an awkward sleeve, a shadow that refused to behave. The model-rendered frames, by contrast, displayed immaculate composure. Nothing was out of place. Yet it was precisely this perfection that irritated him. He placed tracing paper over the grid and marked the frames he respected, not the ones he admired. The respected ones carried intent. The admired ones carried polish. Only the former earned a place in his sequence.

His muttered remark—*"Taste is a verb, not a vibe"*—captured the craft tension of this moment.

That tension now touches every creative field. When tools can generate ten, a hundred, even a thousand plausible variations in minutes, the skill of making shifts from production to discrimination. The question ceases to be *"Can I make something good?"* and becomes *"Can I choose something meaningful?"* Curation becomes a performance of judgement rather than a consolation prize. And as with any performance, the details matter: what we keep, what we discard, and what we annotate as we decide.

The motif at stake is the frame—literal in photography, figurative in every other craft. The frame marks not only what is included but what was resisted. In a synthetic age, human craft reveals itself through choices made at the boundary of abundance.

The first major claim is that selection has become the new craftsmanship. Show the shift: a designer reviewing 180 generated logo variations spreads them across a wall, eliminates two-thirds within minutes, then spends an hour arguing with herself about three nearly identical candidates. Name the dynamic: abundance compression. Explain it: when the marginal cost of variation plummets, the creator's effort migrates from making to filtering. Implication: mastery now lies in articulating *why* one version survives while another dies. The visible behaviour that proves this lies in annotation—pencilled comments in the margins, asterisked preferences, the small arrows indicating tentative ideas. Where synthetic fluency expands possibilities, human craft emerges in the constraints imposed.

A second checkable example illustrates this shift. In 2020, Magnum photographer Christopher Anderson experimented with model-generated variations to explore alternative colour grades for a portrait series. Working in Brooklyn, he compared fifty synthetic palettes against his original frames. His notes show the real craft: he rejected options not for technical inferiority but for violating the emotional tonality he sought—*"too clean," "breaks tension," "loses the anxious light."* The model produced possibilities; he provided the sensibility. The screen filled with outputs, but the craft lived in his three-word judgements.

A limitation complicates the story. Some disciplines already rely heavily on selection—fashion editors, museum curators, and documentary producers have long practised judgment under abundance. Synthetic variation accelerates rather than transforms their craft. Reconcile this counter-example: even where selection existed, the scale of variation now shifts the burden. Curators may not need to revise their principles, but they must sharpen them. They must declare their criteria earlier and defend them more visibly, because synthetic abundance can overwhelm without a defined frame.

The second major claim concerns attribution. When outputs arise from hybrid sources—camera, model, archive, prompt—the creator's responsibility is not merely to declare provenance but to shape meaning through commentary. Show the behaviour: a historian producing a composite map for a public exhibition accompanies the image with a short paragraph detailing which components were archival, which were interpolated, and which followed expert judgement. Name the practice: responsible attribution. Explain it: attribution is not a bureaucratic label; it is the creator's way of guiding the viewer's trust and attention. Implication: without commentary, synthetic artefacts drift free of context. They become beautiful but ungrounded.

A concrete case sharpens this point. In 2023, the Royal Photographic Society held an exhibition in Bristol featuring works that blended generative models with analog techniques. Curators insisted that each piece include a brief commentary on decision-making. This commentary revealed what had previously been invisible: why a photographer accepted one synthetic shadow but rejected another; why a digitally generated texture was allowed to remain imperfect because it echoed a real-world analogue. The commentary did not detract from the work. It invited the viewer into the craft.

A credible limitation exists here too. Some creators fear that attribution will weaken the perceived authenticity of their work. They argue that viewers might fixate on process rather than result. Reconcile: transparency does not diminish authenticity; it defines it. In a synthetic age, the only meaningful authenticity is the articulation of intent and constraint. Process does not overshadow art when the process is itself the signature of taste.

The third major claim is that constraint has become the most profound marker of human taste. Show this in action: Kander's workflow in London. He begins with a hand-marked contact sheet, selects a small set of promising frames, and only then invites synthetic exploration within tightly defined bounds. He constrains lighting angles, colour temperature, and emotional tone. The model may generate dozens of options, but he restricts its remit to the edges of his vision. Name this: guided divergence. Explain it: constraints channel the model's output toward the creator's intent without letting the tool dictate direction. Implication: the discipline of constraint prevents style collapse. It keeps the work recognisably human—not because humans "made" every pixel, but because humans structured the search.

A second example reinforces the theme. In 2021, the typographer Kris Sowersby—working from Wellington—experimented with synthetic variations of serif structures. The model produced hundreds of technically sound options, but Sowersby imposed a rigid constraint: every accepted glyph must contain one element derived from a specific historical model in the Fell Types. The constraint forced coherence. It also created a signature. The resulting typeface bore subtle traces of lineage within a contemporary form. The model did not mimic history; Sowersby curated it.

A limitation again adds complexity. Constraint can become fetishised—too rigid, too nostalgic, too self-conscious. Some creators risk ossification, clinging to arbitrary rules to avoid confronting abundance. Reconcile: constraint must serve intention, not fear. The frame should illuminate the work, not imprison it.

Across all these themes—selection, attribution, constraint—the central motif of the frame persists. The frame is where the human declares purpose. It is the boundary that turns abundance into meaning.

One more case gives the motif final clarity. In late 2022, a portrait photographer in Manchester adopted a hybrid workflow that merged her usual analogue contact sheets with model-generated variations. She printed both sets on A4 sheets and reviewed them side by side, using coloured markers to identify what she called "narrative anchors"—the glint in an eye, the tension in a jawline, the fold of light across a cheek. The synthetic variations sometimes amplified these anchors, sometimes drowned them. But the act of marking them revealed something deeper: she was not selecting images; she was selecting *intensities of attention*. Her annotations—small crosses, ticks, and circled details—were acts of authorship. They proved that craft had not disappeared; it had migrated.

This migration has implications beyond art. In research, journalism, teaching, policymaking, and software development, the value of human contribution increasingly lies in framing: setting the question, choosing the lens, defining the cutoff, narrating the rationale. The visible behaviours that signal this shift are mundane yet profound—highlighted passages in a document, nested comments in a draft, deliberate refusals of certain model outputs. Abundance makes these behaviours necessary. They are now markers of taste, style, and integrity.

Yet a tension remains unresolved. If human craft now resides in the frame—selection, attribution, constraint—how much of the resulting work is "ours" and how much is a curated synthesis? Does authorship survive when generation is shared, or does it dissolve into stewardship? And if stewardship becomes the new art, what does it demand of us?

The forward test is sharp. *When confronted with a flood of plausible outputs, which frame will you choose, and why?* The answer cannot be outsourced. It is the craft. It is the self.

Attention, awe, and limits

In May 2019, the neuroscientist Maryanne Wolf stood before a small audience at St Hilda's College, Oxford, holding a slim notebook instead of a laptop. She explained that she had begun hand-copying passages from long novels—Tolstoy, Dostoevsky, Morrison—after realising her own deep-reading stamina had eroded. "Three pages," she said, tapping the notebook, "before my mind wanders. Three." The room fell quiet. Here was a scholar who had spent decades studying attention admitting she could now barely hold a narrative thread. Her experiment was blunt but revealing: reclaim attention by constraining tools, not by adding more. Her result was equally blunt: after several months, she could reach twenty uninterrupted pages again. The limit had restored capacity.

Wolf's small ritual crystallises a wider tension. Hybrid intelligence promises boundless acceleration, yet human attention remains stubbornly finite. The more tasks we outsource, the more porous our focus becomes. Abundance frays the edges. A team in Copenhagen discovered this in December 2022 when they instituted weekly "no-assistant hours" for software debugging. The rule appeared inconvenient at first—no autocomplete, no code suggestions, only the developer, the problem, and a text editor. Within weeks they noticed a measurable outcome: fewer context-switch errors in core modules, confirmed during their January code review. Speed improved not by increasing inputs, but by carving out spaces without them.

These scenes reveal the quiet motif of this chapter: the threshold. The threshold marks the point at which help ceases to be enabling and becomes numbing. It appears differently for each person, each team, each craft, but its existence shapes every meaningful act of attention.

The first major claim is straightforward: deliberate limits protect cognitive depth. Show this: a university writing group schedules Saturday mornings as device-free sessions, relying only on pen, paper, and printed readings. Name the pattern: imposed scarcity. Explain it: scarcity forces the mind to reconstruct context internally rather than scrolling for it. Implication: attention becomes more durable because it is trained rather than bypassed. The visible behaviour is unmistakable—longer unbroken lines of handwriting, clearer sentence structures, fewer revisions required later. A metric from the Copenhagen debugging team reinforces this: their average bug-resolution chain shrank from seven jumps between functions to four after adopting no-assistant hours. The limit sharpened discernment.

A second example shows how limits invite awe, not just focus. In 2021, the Helsinki Central Library Oodi piloted "slow browsing afternoons" in its reading rooms, banning digital search and encouraging visitors to wander physical stacks. Staff measured a simple indicator: time spent with a single book. The median rose from eight minutes to twenty-three. This was not nostalgia; it was a test of environmental design. The constraint slowed pace enough for curiosity to resurface, and with it the small shocks of discovery that digital filters often pre-empt. Awe is not an abstraction; it shows up in bodily stillness, in the way someone lingers on a page, in the hush of a room where attention thickens.

The limitation to this claim is real. Deliberate limits can harden into elitism: rituals that privilege those with leisure, or controls that infantilise workers. Some argue that device sabbaths or slow tasks romanticise inefficiency. Reconcile the concern: limits become patronising only when imposed without purpose or consent. In contexts where participants co-design the boundary—choosing when to slow down, why to slow down, and how to evaluate the outcome—limits serve autonomy rather than restrict it. As with Wolf's notebook, the authority comes from ownership.

The second major claim concerns the relationship between limits and skill retention. When hybrid systems perform more of our micro-tasks—summaries, rephrasings, calculations—the temptation is to assume skills will evaporate unless constantly exercised. Show the nuance: a secondary-school mathematics department in Glasgow worried in early 2023 that model-generated worked examples might weaken pupils' algebraic reasoning. They ran a six-week test. Half the cohort used generated hints; the other half solved problems without them for one class per week. The results defied caricature. Pupils using hints improved speed but sometimes faltered when confronted with novel steps; those without hints progressed more slowly but displayed stronger error-spotting during oral checks. Name the dynamic: differential reinforcement. Explain it: limits do not uniformly "preserve skill"; they shape which skills remain sharp. Implication: teams must choose which proficiencies deserve insulation from automation. Not all are equal.

A second checkable example comes from a July 2022 qualitative study at the University of Utrecht observing how humanities students used generative tools for essay planning. Students who practised "slow starts"—brainstorming for ten minutes before prompting—produced essays with more original theses as judged by blind marking. Slow starts acted as a cognitive warm-up. The researchers found a concrete behaviour: students who drew concept maps by hand before consulting a model wrote more coherent argument chains. The limit enriched structure. This is not nostalgia for handwriting; it is an empirical pattern.

A limitation reveals another complexity. Some tasks genuinely benefit from full automation, and forcing slowness can introduce needless frustration. For example, the Utrecht team noted that students who insisted on entirely manual bibliography formatting wasted hours better spent refining arguments. Reconcile: limits should target cognitive bottlenecks, not clerical work. Awe and attention flourish when friction is meaningful, not perfunctory.

The third major claim addresses collective limits. Individual rituals matter, but team-level constraints create shared rhythms that counteract digital fragmentation. Show this: the Copenhagen developers noticed that their weekly no-assistant sessions fostered more peer explanation. Developers walked to one another's desks, pointed at screens, argued aloud. Name this effect: frictional collaboration. Explain it: when a tool withdraws, colleagues step in. Implication: limits cultivate communal knowledge, not merely individual focus. The metric supporting this was unexpected—post-mortems revealed a reduction in duplicated fixes, indicating that more tacit knowledge had circulated during no-assistant hours.

A second example illustrates how collective limits support ethical reflection. In October 2022, a small research team at the Oslo School of Architecture introduced monthly "attention audits". For three hours the group worked without digital aids, then met to discuss which moments felt easiest or most strained. They correlated these reflections with drafts and sketches produced during the session. Designers reported an increase in figurative risk-taking—bolder lines, stranger shapes—compared with work generated during fully assisted sessions. The limit destabilised habits just enough to reawaken curiosity. Awe manifested not as sentimentality but as willingness to surprise oneself.

A limitation arises here too. Collective limits can spark resentment when unevenly distributed: some roles suffer more friction than others. If one subgroup performs mostly repetitive tasks, limits may feel punitive. Reconcile: collective boundaries must rotate and be continually renegotiated. Teams must measure their effects, not merely declare them. The Copenhagen team adjusted the schedule after noticing that Friday sessions undermined deadlines; they moved them to midweek, preserving both focus and delivery.

Through all these claims, the motif of the threshold returns. The threshold is where awe re-enters the room: the moment when a task becomes strenuous enough to command full presence. It appears in Wolf's three pages, in a developer's insistence on reading source code line by line, in a student tracing an argument without autocomplete, in a researcher pausing before prompting. Awe is not mystical; it is attention stretched to the edge of capacity.

Yet a tension remains unresolved. If hybrid systems promise relief from cognitive overload, why introduce friction deliberately? Are limits a retreat or a refinement? The forward test is personal and profound: *Which parts of your craft deserve slowness, and how will you defend that choice?*

Dignity and the right to say no

In February 2021, at St Joseph's Hospital in Hamilton, Ontario, a healthcare aide named Maria Esquivel paused before entering a patient's room. Her tablet displayed a freshly deployed "empathy assistant": auto-generated phrases designed to smooth difficult conversations. The system suggested opening lines—*I understand this must be difficult; I'm here to support you*—complete with tonal guidance. Maria read them twice, then tapped *Decline*. She later told her supervisor that the script felt "like a mask I didn't choose to wear." Within three months, after collecting dozens of such refusals, the hospital altered the tool's settings. Staff could not only reject suggested phrases; they could annotate them or co-write alternatives that matched their own voice. A measurable outcome followed: patient-experience surveys logged higher ratings for "sense of being heard", with a jump from 68% to 79% in the July audit. The right to say no had strengthened the care, not diluted it.

Maria's case exposes a core tension in hybrid systems: augmentation promises relief, yet people feel stripped of authorship when they cannot refuse help. Dignity rests on the threshold between assistance and imposition. That threshold recurs throughout this piece as a quiet motif—the hinge moment when choice becomes identity. It is not abstract. It is visible in the small pause before tapping *Accept*, in the way someone adjusts a sentence to sound like themselves, in the decision to do a task slowly because speed would cheapen its meaning. Limits inform capability; refusal shapes self-respect.

The first major claim is simple: refusal is a legitimate design requirement, not an afterthought. Show this: a community legal clinic in Manchester tested case-note templates generated by a summarisation model during spring 2022. Lawyers could accept, edit, or discard the suggestions. Within six weeks, logs revealed that junior staff declined 42% of drafts outright but appended detailed comments explaining why. Name the pattern: justified refusal. Explain it: refusal aligned with expertise because the templates occasionally missed critical contextual nuances, especially in sensitive housing disputes. Implication: systems that expose the option to decline—and to explain the decline—produce richer institutional memory. The visible behaviour was clear: rejected drafts carried precise annotations such as "omits landlord threat on 12/04" or "misstates council communication timeline", creating a traceable rationale. A metric emerged: the clinic reduced its rate of misfiled case notes from 11% to 4% by July, largely due to these human-written clarifications.

A second checkable example demonstrates how refusal preserves professional judgement. In October 2020, the British Library piloted an AI-assisted cataloguing tool to speed metadata entry. Senior librarians noticed that the model tended to overgeneralise subject tags for materials from marginalised communities. They declined entire batches of suggestions, choosing instead to record culturally specific descriptors by hand. Name this: protective refusal. Explain it: by refusing to automate sensitive classifications, librarians preserved epistemic accuracy for future scholars. Implication: the integrity of an institution's archive depends not merely on output volume but on the moral weight of saying no when categories distort lived histories. The behaviour was plain—handwritten corrections appeared next to printed outputs, marking deliberate divergence. A metric sharpened the point: error rates in subject tagging for these collections fell from 22% to under 8% after librarians asserted their refusal rights and retrained parts of the workflow.

A limitation must be addressed: refusal can slow work or frustrate colleagues when it becomes habitual or unexamined. Some sceptics argue that frequent refusal reflects resistance to change rather than principled judgement. Reconcile this concern by grounding refusal in transparent protocols. When the Manchester clinic introduced a requirement that each declined draft include a brief rationale, refusals sharpened, not multiplied. Staff measured time spent on these rationales: the median was forty-five seconds, a negligible friction offset by higher fidelity in final notes. Refusal remains dignified when it is accountable, not obstructive.

The second major claim concerns collective refusal—the right of groups, not merely individuals, to challenge automated encroachment. Show this: in May 2022, a municipal hotline team in Rotterdam trialled AI-guided call-handling prompts. Operators noticed that the system nudged them toward scripts that, while polite, compressed complex citizen problems into simplistic categories. They convened a joint session with union representatives and city managers, presenting thirty call transcripts where rigid prompts had hindered resolution. Name the pattern: negotiated refusal. Explain it: collective refusal shifts refusal from a private act of resistance to a normalised governance mechanism. Implication: systems evolve to serve the community if the community can decline the system. A visible decision followed: Rotterdam reconfigured its workflow so operators reviewed prompts only after forming their own first impressions. A discernible metric captured improvement: escalations dropped from 18% to 12% over the next quarter.

A second example grounds this dynamic in a different domain. During a 2023 pilot at the National Museum of Scotland, curators tested an AI tool that generated educational text for exhibitions. Some of the drafts flattened cultural nuance or adopted an overly cheery tone for solemn artefacts. Curators collectively refused several proposed captions for a display on early Gaelic manuscripts, citing tonal mismatch. Name this: curatorial refusal. Explain it: expertise includes judging when silence, reverence, or restraint is more truthful than fluency. Implication: cultural institutions must preserve a margin where human judgement supersedes automated fluency. The museum tracked a behavioural indicator: editors rewrote nearly 60% of drafts for historically sensitive pieces, compared with under 20% for general objects. The disparity taught the team where to direct future model fine-tuning.

Again, a limitation surfaces. Collective refusal can create fragmentation if teams disagree about standards. One curator's principled refusal may be another's stylistic preference. Reconcile it by anchoring refusals in codified criteria: tone suitability, contextual integrity, demographic sensitivity, factual accuracy. When refusals map to shared values rather than personal taste, they become stabilising rather than divisive.

The third major claim concerns refusal as a developmental tool. Saying no is not merely defensive; it cultivates skill. Show this: at St Joseph's, once the auto-generated empathy scripts became optional, staff began co-writing alternatives. Maria and her colleagues produced a library of bespoke phrases grounded in years of practice. Name this progression: generative refusal. Explain it: refusal sets a boundary that makes space for craft. Implication: hybrid systems that invite refusal do not merely avoid harm; they uplift the quality of human contribution. A metric illustrates this progression: over six months, the hospital collected 214 staff-authored phrases; nearly half were later incorporated into training materials for new aides.

A second example highlights how refusal clarifies emotional labour. In February 2023, a hospice in Wellington piloted a system that generated condolence messages for families. Nurses refused most drafts, describing them as "synthetically tender". Rather than discard the tool entirely, they co-produced guidelines on when assistance was appropriate—routine updates, administrative clarity—and when it was not: messages of grief, gratitude, and farewell. Name this: boundary literacy. Explain it: teams become more articulate about the intangible elements of their practice by noticing where automation feels wrong. Implication: refusal becomes a diagnostic lens for understanding human work. The hospice tracked one behaviour as evidence: nurses spent more time discussing tone in reflective sessions after the pilot, signalling heightened awareness of their own expressive norms.

This brings us to the motif again—the hinge. The hinge is where autonomy turns. It is where the aide decides to speak in her own voice, where the librarian protects a community's history, where a hotline operator presses "override," where a museum curator refuses cheerful gloss. Every refusal marks a hinge moment in hybrid work, a pivot where dignity asserts itself.

Yet a final tension remains unresolved. If hybrid intelligence aims to lighten labour, how much friction should refusal introduce? Should every worker enjoy unconditional refusal rights, or must some refusals be negotiated for the sake of consistency and safety? The forward test is stark and unavoidable: *When assistance feels misaligned with your values or your craft, what must you be free to refuse—and how will your institution honour that refusal without eroding its commitments?*

Chapter 9
The Skills Playbook

The designer paused before hitting *generate*. On the screen lay a muddle of half-formed instructions, scribbled constraints, and a rough moodboard. She deleted the prompt entirely. Then she began again, this time as if writing a brief for another human being: the role the system should take, the evidence it must cite, the boundaries it must respect. The resulting output was not magically perfect; it was simply intelligible, testable, shaped by her intent rather than her hope. When she showed the before-and-after to her colleagues, one remarked that it looked less like prompting and more like commissioning. That observation captures the pulse of this chapter. The skills that matter now are not mystical keystrokes or secret commands. They are design, evaluation, stewardship, and reflection—skills that have shaped every serious craft for centuries, now refracted through the lens of hybrid intelligence.

A paradox sits at the heart of these tools: the better they become at generating possibilities, the more vital our constraints, questions, and critiques grow. A system can produce a thousand versions of a paragraph, a colour palette, a strategic outline; but without a user who knows what problem they are solving, the abundance becomes noise. If earlier chapters explored the architecture of hybrid workflows and the ethics that make them trustworthy, this chapter turns inward, towards the personal and professional capacities that let individuals steer these systems with purpose. Skill, not scale, is what separates meaningful augmentation from a haze of half-approved outputs.

At first glance, the skill shift seems modest—just write clearer prompts, run a few tests, keep your data tidy. Yet beneath these deceptively simple actions lies a deeper cultural transformation. Prompts cease to be charms and become briefs. Evaluation stops being a perfunctory skim and becomes an obligation to test assumptions. Data hygiene, once a specialist's concern, becomes part of everyday competence. And perhaps most significant of all, workers must develop a reflective habit: noticing when tools sharpen their thinking and when they blunt it. This is quieter than regulation and more intimate than organisational policy. It is the discipline of noticing oneself.

The first layer of this skills playbook concerns prompting as design. The designer's moment earlier illustrates a broader pattern: prompts that work are not incantations but intentional blueprints. A good brief specifies roles, constraints, evidence, and criteria for success. It anticipates ambiguity and dissolves it. In practice, the shift looks like replacing "draft me a summary" with a sharpened request: identify the claims, cite the sources, explain uncertainties, and provide three alternative framings for different audiences. This is not pedantry; it is custodianship of meaning. Readers will encounter templates that translate vague asks into verifiable requests—tools not for correctness alone but for shared understanding.

Alongside design comes challenge. Evaluation and red-teaming remain unfashionable in conversation but indispensable in practice. Many organisations have learned this the hard way. A charity preparing a grant-writing assistant did not simply assume the model would behave. It subjected the tool to stress cases: ambiguous eligibility rules, sensitive political contexts, borderline financial claims. Only after the system passed these tests did the team allow it into real workflows. Their process was not elaborate—lightweight scenario probes, sanity checks, and comparative baselines—but it proved something essential. Tools gain reliability not through trust but through repeated attempts to break them. And when they break, the knowledge gained strengthens the system and the user alike.

Then comes data. Not the sprawling datasets of machine-learning research, but the everyday fragments our tools rely on—names, versions, notes, examples. The smallest acts of data care have disproportionate impact. A sales team that once fought persistent hallucinations in product responses solved most of the problem by curating a single, well-maintained factsheet. The model became less inventive and more accurate because the humans became more intentional. Behind this lies an uncomfortable truth: much of what we call AI improvement is, in fact, human discipline. By elevating data hygiene from an afterthought to a shared practice, teams amplify the value of the tools they already possess.

Finally, this playbook turns to the interior frontier: personal analytics and reflection. The freelancer who logs when assistance sharpens their work—and when it dulls it—does not merely improve their efficiency. They develop a map of their own cognition. They learn where automation frees them to imagine and where it risks siphoning the depth from their thinking. These small acts of reflection carry profound implications. Over time they reveal patterns that shape careers: strengths to cultivate, dependencies to watch, blind spots to address. Reflection transforms competence into judgement.

Threaded through these themes is a subtle motif: the mirror. Hybrid tools reflect our intentions back at us—sometimes magnified, sometimes distorted, sometimes revealing hidden contours of our own process. Learning to read that reflection is a skill in its own right. A poorly structured prompt reveals unclear thinking. A failed red-team test uncovers an assumption you didn't know you held. A data error exposes a gap in coordination. A journal entry shows the cost of over-automation. The mirror is unforgiving, but it is also generous.

The stakes of this skills shift are more than operational. They are cultural. As hybrid intelligence becomes woven into daily work, the gap between those who can marshal it effectively and those who cannot will grow. But this chapter rejects the notion of an elite priesthood of prompt whisperers. The skills we set out here are democratic, teachable, and grounded in principles older than computing: clarity, challenge, care, and reflection. They do not require specialist credentials. They require curiosity, discipline, and a willingness to see tools as collaborators rather than proxies.

There is a deeper tension as well. These tools promise acceleration, yet the skills that tame them often require slowing down. Writing a thoughtful brief takes a few more minutes than issuing a hasty request. Running an evaluation takes patience. Keeping data tidy demands consistency. Reflecting on your own thought patterns requires stillness. But this friction is productive. It marks the difference between unexamined speed and meaningful progress. And in a world eager to move quickly, the craft of deliberate direction becomes a competitive advantage.

As you move into the rest of this chapter, you will encounter patterns, templates, and examples that turn these ideas into practice. Yet the larger invitation is conceptual. The skills playbook is not a checklist; it is a lens through which to reinterpret your relationship with powerful tools. These tools will continue to expand, but so will the demands placed on us—demands for precision, grounding, scrutiny, and self-awareness.

The open question—the one worth carrying into the pages ahead—is deceptively simple: *When your tools become more capable, will you?*

Prompting as design, not incantation

In March 2023, at the London offices of Harper & Flint, a mid-sized consultancy, project lead Sarah Holm faced a problem that should have been trivial. She needed a two-page briefing for a client's upcoming energy-transition workshop. Her first prompt—"Summarise key decarbonisation strategies for mid-market manufacturers"—returned an inoffensive but useless gloss. She tried again, adding adjectives. Worse results. After three rounds of tinkering, she stepped back, wrote a short design brief on paper, and translated it into a prompt: *role* (sector analyst), *evidence* (draw on the firm's 2022 market scan), *constraints* (focus on costs under £5m), *evaluation* (three scenarios with quantified trade-offs), and *users* (board-level non-specialists). The output she received was not magic. It was specific. It was testable. The client eventually approved the document with only minor edits. Harper & Flint did not discover a secret formula that afternoon; they rediscovered something older. When people treat prompts as briefs rather than charms, reasoning improves and ambiguity shrinks. This chapter's motif—the brief as mirror—begins here.

The paradox that troubled Sarah is widespread: how can tools that generate billions of tokens a day still fail on tasks that hinge on intention? The cost of a bad prompt is small—a few wasted minutes—but multiplied across teams, projects, and decisions, the loss becomes substantial. A vague request hides assumptions, masks goals, and invites the system to improvise. A designed request turns tacit knowledge into explicit guidance. Five words matter. Precision matters. The brief reveals the mind behind it.

Design emerges from clarity, not decoration. When users describe the role a system should inhabit, they anchor perspective. When they define constraints—sources, limits, acceptable omissions—they narrow the field of inference. When they specify criteria for judging success, they create alignment. This is not ritual. It is communication. One early adopter at the Danish Ministry of Finance remarked in June 2024 that "a decent prompt looks like a decent commissioning note." Once written, it becomes a contract: clear enough to test, bounded enough to critique. The brief becomes the mirror again: reflecting sloppy thinking if it is sloppy, complex reasoning if it is disciplined.

The first claim of this subchapter is that prompting works best when treated as interaction design. Consider the work of IDEO in the late 1990s. Although the organisation was not dealing with generative systems, its ethos of iterative briefs—describe, test, revise—laid the foundation for what hybrid-intelligence workflows now require. Show: in 1999, IDEO redesigned a shopping trolley on live television, revealing that even mundane requests need carefully framed constraints. Name: Tim Brown, then CEO, explained that vague requests lead to "solution scatter." Explain: without a shared brief, teams interpret goals differently. Implication: generative systems behave the same way—when the brief is fuzzy, outputs scatter.

A second example shows the effect in contemporary practice. In August 2023, the European Climate Foundation piloted structured prompting guidelines across its policy teams. They specified four components: role, evidence, exclusions, and success criteria. Outputs became 27% shorter and required 40% fewer edits, according to the Foundation's internal audit. Note the metrics: length and edit frequency reflect real behaviour, not abstract claims. The mirror motif reappears: brief discipline reshapes user behaviour before it reshapes model behaviour.

To illustrate the limitations, consider a counter-example. A major retail chain attempted a "prompt library" in early 2024, offering staff pre-written templates for dozens of tasks. It failed. By March, reported usage was below 10%. The problem was not the templates themselves but their emptiness. They were syntactically polished yet context-free. A prompt cannot be divorced from purpose. No library can automate intention. Reconciling this failure teaches something important: design templates work only when they invite users to articulate their context. Templates that pretend to replace judgement rather than scaffold it will always collapse.

The distinction between prompting as design and prompting as incantation becomes sharper when examining constraints. Constraints are not chores; they are signals of respect for complexity. They reflect decisions about what should be included, what should be excluded, and what evidence matters. One can observe this in software engineering. In 2017, Google introduced its "design doc" culture to junior teams, emphasising constraints before code. The logic applies equally to prompting. When a user names constraints—"cite only reports after 2020," "assume a budget cap of £800k," "exclude speculative technologies"—they create guardrails that protect the integrity of later decisions. The implication is clear: constraint is a form of ethics. It reduces the risk of overreach, fabrication, or silent assumption creep.

Evidence is the next critical component. Without specifying evidence, users implicitly grant the system permission to hallucinate. But with evidence—named reports, datasets, or criteria for what counts as a reliable source—users ground the exchange. The mirror motif surfaces again: asking for evidence reveals the fragility of one's own knowledge. A researcher at the University of Edinburgh noted in February 2024 that when she required citations with uncertainty levels, she discovered how many of her initial prompts were shapeless. Evidence exposes the silhouette of a problem. Without it, solutions drift.

Evaluation criteria complete the brief. These criteria often feel optional to users, yet they determine whether an output survives contact with reality. For example, specifying "three options compared against cost, social impact, and timeline" forces the system to engage in structured reasoning. These criteria act as a downstream compass: when reviewing an output, users can assess alignment rather than rely on intuition. The effect is practical and cultural. It shifts the posture from "does this sound good?" to "does this meet the standard we agreed upon?" Design becomes accountability.

The motif of the mirror appears again when examining user behaviour in a policy environment. In 2024, the City of Wellington adopted a hybrid drafting workflow for public health guidance. Civil servants had to provide structured prompts including intent, audience, and criteria for acceptable uncertainty. Internal reviewers reported that the exercise exposed hidden assumptions about risk thresholds. Brief-writing became a diagnostic tool. Once again, prompting disciplined the humans as much as the machine.

If prompting is design, then it must adopt the disciplines of design: iteration, critique, and revision. This truth can be uncomfortable. Many professionals have been conditioned to expect instant fluency from AI tools. But design resists haste. The strongest workflows include short cycles of testing: issue a prompt, inspect the output, refine the brief. Organisations that treat prompting as a one-shot affair miss the point. In design practice, sketches evolve. In hybrid-intelligence practice, prompts evolve.

A deeper implication emerges from all of this: prompting is not merely operational but epistemic. It shapes not just outputs but understanding. When a user writes, "Explain the causal links, not just correlations, using named studies from 2019 onwards," they are making a claim about what counts as knowledge. When they request, "Outline assumptions and provide counter-arguments," they are enacting intellectual virtue. The act of prompting becomes an extension of critical thinking.

Despite the strengths of this approach, limits persist. Models may misinterpret constraints, invent evidence, or misjudge which evaluation criteria matter most. Recognising these failures is part of the design discipline. A weak brief cannot rescue a flawed model. But a strong brief can expose where systems and human judgement need reinforcement. Reconciliation of these tensions yields a stable conclusion: prompting-as-design is necessary but not sufficient. It must be paired with evaluation, data care, and reflective habits, which the wider chapter addresses.

The final tension concerns time. Brief-writing appears slower. Yet teams that adopt it often accelerate once rework declines. The paradox is familiar from architecture, software engineering, and law: investment in early clarity reduces the cost of late corrections. The brief as mirror offers a test: does the prompt clarify or obscure? Does it reveal intent or disguise it? Does it sharpen responsibility or diffuse it?

This leads to the open question that threads through all hybrid-intelligence practice: when your prompt becomes the design document of your thinking, what will it reveal—and are you willing to see it?

Evaluation and red-teaming

In October 2023, the London-based charity Children for Tomorrow ran a pilot to automate parts of its grant-writing process. The goal was modest: draft preliminary narratives for small funding bids, freeing staff to focus on partnerships. Early tests looked promising until a single case exposed a silent flaw. When prompted to justify a request for emergency tutoring support, the system produced a polished paragraph that overstated local deprivation levels in Camden by citing outdated figures. No harm resulted—the draft was caught during review—but the episode chilled the room. If one subtle exaggeration slipped through in a safe context, what might emerge in a high-stakes submission? That moment triggered a full week of structured evaluation. Staff compiled edge-case scenarios—ambiguous eligibility rules, contradictory funder guidance, politically sensitive language—and stress-tested the system. Only after passing these probes did the grant writer move into controlled use. The motif that threads this subchapter now enters: the unseen hinge, the small detail upon which trust can turn.

The paradox at the centre of this work is simple: systems that perform brilliantly in the average case often fail where it matters most. A model may glide through routine prompts yet stumble when facts are sparse, rules are tangled, or incentives collide. The cost of such errors is uneven. Ninety safe drafts hide one that could mislead a funder or misstate impact. To treat evaluation as a formality is to invite complacency. To treat it as critical infrastructure is to anchor judgement. Five words suffice here. Test before you trust.

Systematic challenge strengthens robustness. Show: at the charity, staff created a set of "hard cases"—the kinds of questions that exhaust human writers. Name: programme manager Priya Rao led the effort, drawing from a decade of rejected bids. Explain: she understood that failure patterns cluster at the boundary, not the centre. Implication: any tool that cannot survive its hardest cases should not influence decisions. The unseen hinge appears again: reliability rests on marginal performance.

Lightweight tests help. They need not be complex. A team might present contradictory instructions, incomplete data, or deliberately vague criteria to see whether a system fabricates or flags uncertainty. For example, in January 2024, an education NGO in Nairobi tested a literacy-assessment assistant by feeding it numerical data with hidden inconsistencies. The model passed only after the team introduced an explicit "sanity-check" step in the prompt. The behaviour mattered: the system moved from silent acceptance to caution, reducing the risk of propagating numerical errors into real recommendations. Metrics made this visible: flagged inconsistencies rose from 12% to 63% across their evaluation set.

A second example comes from the Financial Conduct Authority's regulatory-tech sandbox in 2022. Participants tested automated compliance-drafting tools against historic enforcement cases. When phrasing mirrored known breaches, strong systems warned; weak ones generated plausible but incorrect rationales. The lesson matches the Nairobi case. Without structured evaluation—scenario probes drawn from lived edge conditions—performance illusions flourish. Illusions erode trust and mask fragility.

The counter-example is equally instructive. A private foundation deployed a writing assistant for scholarship adjudication without an evaluation phase. Within two months, reviewers noticed that criteria weightings drifted subtly: academic promise was inflated relative to financial need. No explicit instruction caused the drift; it emerged from repeated prompting that emphasised merit narratives. The foundation suspended use immediately. The limitation was not the model alone but the absence of red-teaming. There was no guard to detect drift, no hinge to reveal movement. Reconciling the failure shows the principle: evaluation guards against cumulative distortion. Red-teaming prevents small skews from becoming institutional bias.

Red-teaming itself is a craft. It is not hostility but inquiry. It asks how systems behave when cornered, starved, or misled. It mirrors practices from cybersecurity, where penetration testing reveals surface weakness before attackers do. In hybrid-intelligence work, red-teaming might include counterfactual prompts ("describe the decision if assumptions were reversed"), role inversions ("argue from the position of the citizen, not the policymaker"), or shadow knowledge tests ("identify what additional information you need before answering"). These moves force the system to reveal whether it understands uncertainty or merely imitates coherence.

Scenario probes operate differently. They do not seek failure alone but divergence. A good probe measures whether outputs vary meaningfully with context. For instance, at a media hub in Manchester in April 2024, staff analysed how an editorial assistant handled ambiguous ethics cases—anonymous tips, conflicting eyewitness accounts, or unclear source provenance. Analysts measured response patterns: proportion of cautious prompts, frequency of evidence requests, and rate of speculative claims. These metrics illuminated behavioural tendencies rather than specific errors. Once quantified, they could be shaped. The unseen hinge returns: fine adjustments to behaviour depend on what is made visible.

Metrics matter because abstractions cause drift. A claim such as "the system seems reliable" dissolves when confronted with numbers: edit distance, factual precision rates, scenario-specific accuracy. These figures need not be perfect; they must be legible. When PRIYA RAO's team evaluated their grant writer, they tracked three metrics—source traceability, compliance with funder wording, and avoidance of over-claiming. Each metric reflected a visible behaviour: citation, adherence, restraint. By measuring them weekly, they created a feedback loop that amplified strengths and exposed regression early.

A deeper implication follows. Evaluation is not episodic but continual. Models evolve. Interfaces change. Data pipelines shift. Human expectations drift. Without revisiting evaluation sets, organisations can mistake familiarity for competence. One civil servant in Wellington noted that staff began trusting outputs simply because they "felt right," not because they were verified. This is the silent failure mode of hybrid systems: when intuitive comfort outruns disciplined scrutiny.

Yet evaluation cannot become paralysing. The counter-example of bureaucratic over-testing looms. Some organisations demand exhaustive checks for trivial tasks, wasting time and exhausting staff. Reconciling this requires proportionate governance. High-stakes contexts demand rigorous probes. Low-stakes tasks can rely on sampling. The hinge motif applies once more: balance the load so that scrutiny lands where it matters most.

The charity's testing process offers one more lesson. After initial probes, they instituted a "cold start" test every quarter: a scenario not previously used, with novel constraints, designed by a rotating staff member. They measured how well the system handled ambiguity, documented the rationale for any failures, and adjusted prompts and guidelines. The practice did more than strengthen the tool. It developed staff judgement. Red-teaming becomes a form of organisational learning: an exercise in modelling how edge cases behave.

The final puzzle concerns responsibility. If evaluation reveals flaws, who acts? Tools do not correct themselves. Institutions must decide what constitutes "good enough" and who certifies it. These decisions shape legitimacy. They also allocate the burden of vigilance. Should the grant writer at Children for Tomorrow fail a future test, staff know the process: pause deployment, review evidence, revise prompts, update constraints. This clarity protects both the public and the team. Without it, systems drift and errors compound.

The open question remains: how often should we challenge the tools we depend on, and how sharp should those challenges be before confidence turns to complacency?

Data hygiene for non-experts

In March 2024, a sales team at BrightLedger, a mid-sized accounting software firm based in Leeds, reviewed a month's worth of AI-assisted customer emails and noticed a pattern that unsettled them. The assistant repeatedly cited features that did not exist in the company's small-business tier—automated VAT forecasting, bulk reconciliation, mobile receipt scanning—none of which had ever appeared in the product documentation. These hallucinations were not random. They traced back to an internal "factsheet" assembled piecemeal from launch notes, marketing drafts, and an outdated pricing grid. One misplaced row in that file—a heading labelled "Future Roadmap" interpreted as "Current Features"—

became the hinge on which trust turned. Customers were not misled, because every email passed through a human. But the volume of correction grew maddening. Staff realised the illusion of sloppy data: a single ambiguous input contaminates dozens of outputs.

Basic data care multiplies value. That sentence contains five words that matter: small details shape everything. The BrightLedger team saw it directly. When they paused to rebuild their factsheet—one sheet, twelve fields, versioned properly—the error rate in model-assisted emails dropped from roughly one in seven to fewer than one in thirty. The change was not clever. It was tidy. Clean naming, clear fields, dated versions. The kind of discipline once reserved for engineers moved to the centre of routine commercial work.

The motif that threads this chapter—hinges that carry disproportionate weight—appears again. Data hygiene is not glamorous, and yet it determines whether hybrid intelligence performs reliably or drifts into creative fiction. The craft lies not in complexity but in care. For non-experts, this is liberation rather than burden: the bar is lower than people assume. The structure matters more than the sophistication.

Show the principle, name it clearly, explain its mechanics, and trace the implications. At BrightLedger, the sales lead, Amira Patel, insisted on a rule borrowed from software teams: "one source of truth." She curated a short evaluation set of common customer queries—pricing, integrations, limits, security certifications—and ran every model update and prompt adjustment against that set. The visible behaviour: the system's answers converged. The metric: consistency scores rose measurably. The implication: predictable behaviour under pressure.

Such "one source" rules echo earlier examples. In 2022, the Open Data Institute worked with community groups in Bristol to standardise local environmental data for neighbourhood alerts. Their challenge was not lack of information but incompatible naming: pollutants listed under different abbreviations, sampling times recorded in inconsistent formats. After a day of harmonisation, alert precision improved because the assistant no longer misinterpreted labels. Behaviour changed because structure changed. A small hinge carried the load.

A second example comes from a museum digitisation project in Glasgow in 2021. Curators used an annotation assistant to classify artefacts, but early models mislabelled items when faced with inconsistent tag structures. Once curators created a simple naming convention—object type, period, material, location—the misclassification rate dropped by nearly half. Their care with metadata became the backbone of reliability. The parallel with BrightLedger is exact. Whether dealing with medieval ceramics or SaaS products, messy inputs produce messy reasoning.

The counter-example clarifies the limits. A consultancy attempted to train a knowledge assistant by ingesting hundreds of unstructured slide decks. They believed volume would compensate for disorder. Instead, the system learned contradictory definitions, duplicated metrics, and outdated benchmarks. Staff spent more time correcting outputs than drafting them. Reconciling the failure requires admitting the illusion: more data is not better data. In hybrid systems, coherence depends on curation. Fewer, cleaner inputs outperform sprawling archives.

Naming is a deceptively powerful act. When files carry meaningful names—"ProductFeatures_v2024-03-Final" instead of "latest2"—teams reduce ambiguity for both humans and models. A name conveys time, scope, and authority. Without these signals, assistants guess. Guessing invites error. Versioning amplifies this effect. The moment BrightLedger began saving dated versions, staff could test changes incrementally. They committed updates deliberately, not by overwrite. This visible behaviour—saving versions with intention—shaped model outputs more than any prompt tweak.

Evaluation sets serve a related function. They anchor expectations. A good evaluation set is small, not encyclopaedic. Ten to twenty representative queries reveal most failure modes. At BrightLedger, Amira maintained fifteen. Three related to pricing, five to integrations, four to data retention, three to limitations. She reviewed outputs weekly. The metric she tracked was "intervention count"—how many corrections humans had to make per batch of fifty emails. The count fell steadily as data hygiene improved. The implication is sharp: evaluation sets do not test the world; they test drift.

The hinge motif reappears when considering ambiguity. Many non-experts assume their data is "clear enough" because colleagues understand it. That assumption collapses when confronted with a system that interprets literally. Fields that are loosely described—"supported platforms," "regions," "limits"—must be pinned down. Otherwise the assistant fills gaps with inference. The behaviour is predictable because models prefer coherence to silence. Data hygiene pushes them toward silence where appropriate, which is often the safer choice.

The philosophical core of this subchapter concerns stewardship. In hybrid work, the smallest teams become custodians of definitions, boundaries, and truth sources. They do not need mastery of databases or AI engineering. They need habits: naming, versioning, consistent fields, small tests. These habits diffuse power. They allow a sales associate, curator, or coordinator to shape system behaviour intentionally rather than reactively.

The implication reaches beyond productivity. Data hygiene creates legitimacy. When staff trust their source sheets, they trust downstream outputs. Customers sense the difference. Errors fall. Rework shrinks. Expectations stabilise. The hinge, small again, turns smoothly.

Yet limits matter. Data hygiene cannot compensate for flawed incentives or opaque model behaviour. A clean factsheet improves accuracy but does not guarantee contextual judgement. A versioned taxonomy aids classification but cannot repair missing historical nuance. The counter-example of the consultancy shows this. Cleanliness helps only when inputs capture reality. A flawed worldview, however neat, still misleads.

Reconciliation lies in proportion. Non-experts need only maintain the data they control: pricing grids, product descriptions, eligibility rules, glossary entries, evaluation sets. They are not responsible for the model's internal training data or the world's complexity. Their job is to eliminate avoidable ambiguity, not to engineer perfection. This distinction frees them from paralysis. It defines scope: care for small hinges.

Returning to BrightLedger, the transformation did not stem from a new system. It came from a half-day workshop in which staff rewrote their factsheet together. They agreed naming norms. They removed duplicated rows. They added three fields to clarify tier differences. Then they saved the file as a new version and ran their evaluation set. For the first time, every answer aligned cleanly with product reality. Outputs felt stable. Staff felt confident.

The open tension persists: how often should small teams revisit their definitions, and who decides when a hinge has weakened enough to demand repair?

Personal analytics and reflection

In September 2023, a freelance designer named Lena Markov sat in a small co-working space near Clerkenwell and reviewed a month's worth of her own time-tracking entries. What struck her was not the volume of work—forty-six client pieces, seven proposals—but the atrophy in certain notes she used to make instinctively. Her journal revealed a pattern. On days when she relied heavily on her assistant for ideation, she saved an average of twenty-eight minutes per project. But those same days carried another trace: fewer thumbnails, fewer alternative sketches, fewer annotations about why she chose one direction over another. The efficiency was real. The cost was subtle. She wrote a five-word sentence in the margin that unsettled her: *Where did my edges go?*

That question sparked a practice. Each evening she logged two things: what the assistant helped with and what, if anything, felt thinner as a result. Within weeks, she saw a hinge pattern emerge. When she used assistance to accelerate tasks she already understood, productivity rose without creative loss. When she used it to avoid early thinking altogether, her ideas weakened. The journal highlighted a distinction she had not articulated: support is helpful when it shortens friction, harmful when it replaces friction. That hinge—friction—threads through this subchapter.

To understand how hybrid tools shape cognition, professionals must measure how their thinking shifts, not merely how much faster tasks get done. Personal analytics confront a simple fact: the effects of assistance are internal first and external second. Without reflection, subtle erosion goes unnoticed, and subtle strengthening does too.

Consider the claim that reflection makes hybrid intelligence sustainable. Show it, name it, explain its mechanics, and trace the implication. Lena saw that her assistant performed best when given an explicit role—*second pair of eyes* or *sounding board*. The visible behaviour was disciplined prompting. The metric she tracked was "idea spread": the number of distinct options she explored before committing. With role clarity, her idea spread returned to its earlier range of five to seven thumbnails per concept. Without it, she averaged two. The implication is precise: personal analytics allow you to map where your thinking flourishes and where it collapses.

A second checkable example comes from the 2021 "Thinking Aloud" study by the University of Edinburgh's Centre for Research on Learning and Instruction. Researchers asked postgraduate students to verbalise their reasoning while completing conceptual tasks with and without AI support. Participants who reviewed their own transcripts developed a stronger ability to distinguish genuine insight from model-supplied phrasing. The visible behaviour: explicit self-questioning—"did I infer that, or did I repeat it?" The metric: the proportion of solutions that included original reasoning steps rather than surface-level reproduction. The implication: personal analytics increase metacognitive resilience by making the line between assistance and thought visible.

A counter-example sharpens the limit. In 2022, a communications agency attempted to install automated reflective dashboards that rated staff on "originality contribution scores." The system misinterpreted iterative drafts as low creativity because early prompts produced repetitive scaffolds. Staff began gaming the tool by adding artificial variation. Reflection became performance, not insight. The failure reveals a boundary: analytics must serve the human, not invert the relationship. When metrics dominate meaning, thinking bends toward the metric. Reconciling this involves reinstating human judgment as the arbiter of value. Tools can reveal patterns, but only people can decide which patterns matter.

The hinge motif appears again as journalling. A lightweight journal forces the mind to pause. It offers a record of micro-decisions that accumulate into habit. The practice need not be ornate. Lena kept a simple structure: what she asked for, what she received, what she gained, and what she might have lost. Each point captured a behaviour. Each behaviour became a dataset. The implication is that personal analytics scale only through simplicity. Baroque systems collapse under their own weight.

Time matters too. Personal analytics only reveal signal when tracked over intervals long enough to detect drift. A week shows noise; a month reveals direction. Drift is a visible pattern: rising dependency, shrinking exploration, or conversely, better calibration and sharper choices. When people chart drift, they reclaim agency. They see where their cognitive centre of gravity shifts.

Reflection also exposes asymmetry. Some tasks benefit from assistance in ways that do not threaten identity—summaries, checklists, formatting. Others are closer to the core of how a person thinks or creates. When a playwright in Manchester tested an AI collaborator during her autumn 2022 residency, she found that structural suggestions helped, but line-level suggestions weakened her ear for rhythm. She recorded this distinction in her notes: "Scaffolding: yes. Voice: no." Her metric was the number of lines she rewrote after reading them aloud. With scaffolding only, rewrites dropped. With line suggestions, rewrites surged. Her reflection reframed her workflow. The implication is broader: hybrid intelligence requires user-defined boundaries, and those boundaries emerge from lived data.

Personal analytics sharpen those boundaries with evidence rather than intuition. Yet they require ethical self-awareness. People can become overly mechanistic, reducing creativity to counters or normalising self-surveillance. The limit lives here. Logs must inform, not constrain. A journal should illuminate unseen patterns, not police them.

Still, the alternative—operating blind—is worse. Without reflection, subtle dulling of thought masquerades as convenience. Without metrics, the distinction between acceleration and avoidance dissolves. The difference matters.

Hybrid intelligence thrives when humans remain architects of their own attention. Reflection turns architecture into practice.

Return to the hinge. Every hybrid workflow includes moments where decisions pivot: whether to think first or ask first, whether to draft alone or co-write, whether to explore multiple paths or accept the first plausible answer. Personal analytics make these pivots visible. Look closely at Lena's case. Her daily logs showed that she produced her best work when she spent at least eight minutes sketching before consulting her assistant. That is not a broad abstraction—it is a behaviour measured over thirty days, tied to visible output quality. Her metric became a ritual: eight minutes before asking.

Reflection extends beyond productivity. It shapes identity. People who track their cognitive changes start to see their work not as a sequence of outputs but as an evolving signature. This matters in a synthetic age where tools can mimic style. Documentation—private, not performative—helps distinguish self from scaffold. A note such as "I struggled here, and the struggle taught me something" resists homogenisation. The implication is subtle but profound: reflection anchors dignity.

Personal analytics also improve calibration. The more users observe when assistance helps, the more selective they become. Selectivity increases quality. The historian Carlo Ginzburg once wrote that attention to small clues distinguishes craft. In hybrid work, clues are behavioural: a sudden drop in curiosity, a shrinking list of alternatives, a feeling of thinness in the mind. Analytics make clues legible.

But a tension remains unresolved. How much reflection is enough, and when does self-analysis impede flow?

Chapter 10
Building Your Hybrid Organisation

The first sign that something unusual was happening at Haversham General appeared not in a boardroom memo but in a corridor conversation. In February 2024, a night-shift nurse named Priya glanced at a printout taped above the medication trolley: a one-page charter drafted by her unit's early adopters. It was short—barely two hundred words—yet it carried a tone that surprised her. It did not trumpet innovation or promise efficiency. Instead, it opened with a sentence about dignity. It pledged that any digital assistant introduced on the ward would serve staff and patients rather than replace judgment, and that its behaviour would be reviewed fortnightly by a mixed group of clinicians, porters, and administrators. As she read, Priya felt her shoulders settle. The document reframed change as something done with her, not to her. The charter had no legal force, but its presence reordered the room. It turned technology from an intruder into a guest with declared intentions.

That evening, during handover, a senior nurse explained why the charter existed. The hospital's procurement team had evaluated three competing platforms, each promising to streamline documentation. Leadership realised that without explicit boundaries, pilots risked fragmenting into parallel experiments and sowing distrust. So they anchored their approach in this small text—a compass rather than a map. In its simplicity lay its power: a reminder that tools enter living systems and must adapt to the pulse of those systems, not the other way around.

This chapter asks what it takes to build a hybrid organisation without losing the human texture that makes institutions durable. Beneath the talk of platforms and policies sits a deeper question: how do people work together when some of the "people" are models making probabilistic guesses? The shift is structural but also narrative. Organisations must learn to tell themselves a new story—one in which assistance is welcome, restraint is respected, and humanity does not recede behind automation.

A hybrid organisation is not defined by the number of systems it deploys but by the clarity of the principles that govern them. Those principles are usually drafted before any statute or regulation touches them. Soft law—charters, standards, procurement rules—sets the tone long before hard law arrives. In practice, this means leaders articulate why a tool exists, what it must never do, who is responsible for what, and how decisions will be reviewed. These charters function like musical keys: they shape what is possible, what is dissonant, and what must resolve. Without them, organisations drift into tool sprawl, each platform claiming a patch of workflow until the whole becomes incoherent.

Sprawl is not a technical problem; it is a cultural one. In 2023, a mid-size professional services firm found itself juggling nine different generative tools across departments. No one set out to create a mess, yet the absence of ownership boundaries allowed every team to experiment independently. The result was predictable: overlapping subscriptions, contradictory data flows, and alarming uncertainty about which tools had access to client information. Only when the firm created a cross-functional platform council and rationalised its vendors did clarity return. Consolidation became an act of care, not austerity. Choosing fewer platforms meant choosing responsibility.

But structure alone cannot sustain change. People anchor institutions, and their fears and hopes shape adoption far more than any architecture diagram. Hybrid transitions often falter when workers interpret automation as judgment—a silent suggestion that their pace, knowledge, or experience is insufficient. Change management must begin with empathy rather than expectation. At a hospital in Leeds, early adopters of a documentation assistant were paired with sceptical colleagues. The purpose was not to evangelise but to co-observe. Nurses compared notes after each shift, discussing where the assistant strengthened care and where it intruded. Because the process was opt-in and dialogic, uptake rose without coercion. Fear softened into curiosity.

Such respect for fear is not indulgence; it is organisational realism. Hybrid systems ask people to renegotiate identity. A tool that drafts notes or suggests diagnoses intrudes upon professional self-worth. Only when institutions acknowledge that intrusion openly can they create conditions where staff feel free to decline certain uses or ask for slower adoption. The ambition is not to eliminate discomfort but to metabolise it.

Roadmaps are often portrayed as bold trajectories, but in hybrid organisations they must include endings as well as beginnings. Sunset decisions are marks of maturity. Not every experiment should survive. A national retailer recently decommissioned an internal assistant that generated customer responses. While the tool improved reply speed by nineteen per cent, staff reported a steady erosion of trust. Customers noticed shifts in tone, and employees felt their judgment was being second-guessed by an invisible hand. The firm's review criteria—tone consistency, staff comfort, and customer sentiment—revealed that speed was a poor proxy for value. Retiring the assistant restored cohesion and became a signal to the organisation: success is defined by alignment with purpose, not by novelty.

These stories, scattered across sectors, share a pattern: hybrid organisations succeed when they invest in coherence. Coherence is more than operational tidy-mindedness; it is a lived ethic. It appears in the charters that state what a system stands for. It appears in the platform choices that resist fragmentation. It appears in the conversations where fear is named and granted legitimacy. It appears in the courage to end experiments that misalign with values even when metrics look favourable.

Yet building such organisations demands more than policy. It requires a cultural grammar. Tools must fit the institution's temperament—its rhythms, its attention, its understanding of service. A charter might frame that temperament. Procurement might guard its boundaries. Training might tune its tone. But meaning comes from the interplay of these factors, not from any one alone.

In this chapter we move through each of these elements with care. We begin by examining the role of operating principles and charters—why brevity strengthens commitment, and how a small text can recalibrate an entire pilot. We explore the discipline of platform selection, showing how organisations prevent sprawl not through restriction but through stewardship. We look closely at change management practices that honour fear as part of the adoption journey. And we turn to roadmaps and sunset criteria that treat endings not as failures but as essential acts of organisational hygiene.

The motif that threads through all of this is responsibility—personal, collective, infrastructural. Hybrid organisations flourish when responsibility is distributed clearly and protected consistently. Without clarity, anxiety rises. With clarity, people find ease in experimentation.

A final image returns us to Priya standing before the trolley. She later described the charter as "permission to think before agreeing." That small phrase captures the spirit of this chapter. Building a hybrid organisation is not about rushing toward the future; it is about constructing a space in which people can move with deliberation. The tools may be new, but the question is ancient: how do we act together in ways that honour one another? The pages ahead invite you to consider how your organisation might answer.

Operating principles and charters

When the community health cooperative in Stroud circulated its first hybrid-workflow charter in September 2023, staff expected a procedural memo. What they received instead read more like a pact. It opened with a single declarative line—"Our assistants serve people, not metrics"—and committed the cooperative to a ninety-day review cadence, shared governance across roles, and guardrails that placed dignity above throughput. The document was barely a page long, drafted around a small table in the back office by the clinical lead, an administrator, and two part-time receptionists. Yet within a month, it had reshaped the experiments under way. A triage assistant that previously nudged reception staff towards speedier categorisation was revised to display confidence bands and require a manual justification for every borderline decision. Complaints dropped. Staff stress indicators eased. The charter had changed behaviour without issuing a single warning or mandate. It clarified the room.

The cooperative's director later described why they kept the charter short. "Long policies," she said, "invite loopholes. A page invites memory." She was right. Staff began referring to the charter by its themes—care, clarity, cadence—as though it were a shared compass. The brevity created a centre of gravity. Even sceptics, initially wary of automated tooling, found that the document's tone reframed the initiative: the system was not a test of loyalty to innovation but an organised attempt to protect service quality while experimenting with new forms of augmentation. A charter can do that when it names purpose before performance.

Charters matter because hybrid systems pressure institutions to move faster than their norms can comfortably stretch. Without a stable frame, change feels like erosion. With one, it becomes collective authorship. To understand this, consider the behaviour the charter made visible. When reception staff wrote rationales for borderline triage categories, they did more than tick a compliance box. They externalised their thinking, giving colleagues an audit trail grounded in professional judgment rather than system outputs. The cooperative measured an eight-point improvement in agreement between morning and evening shifts—small but concrete. This is how a principle becomes practice: purpose → behaviour → coherence.

The broader lesson echoes across sectors. Soft law often precedes formal regulation because institutions need something to hold onto during transition. The UK's National Institute for Health and Care Excellence, for example, published its evidence standards framework for digital health technologies in 2019. While not binding, it rapidly shaped procurement in hospitals from Bristol to Newcastle by offering a vocabulary through which clinicians and managers could speak about risk and value without retreating into generalities. Standards, even when voluntary, function as scaffolding. They give teams a way to cohere around what counts.

But scaffolding must do more than imply boundaries; it must illuminate incentives. A well-written charter anchors incentives to human experience rather than to abstract efficiency. Notice what the Stroud cooperative omitted. It did not promise faster throughput, reduced labour, or productivity gains. Instead, it prioritised service quality and staff dignity. That choice shaped everything downstream: evaluation metrics, escalation thresholds, even the order in which pilots proceeded. When purpose is explicit, drift becomes easier to detect. When purpose is vague, drift is the default.

The idea of drift brings us to a second example: a logistics company in Rotterdam that attempted to roll out a scheduling assistant across its night operations in 2022. Management, keen to avoid over-specifying, drafted a fourteen-page "principles framework" heavy with conditional clauses. Staff barely read it. Within weeks, the scheduling assistant appeared to second-guess supervisors in ways that subtly undermined authority. Night-shift supervisors responded by circumventing the tool. Complaints rose. A later review found the root problem was not the assistant's accuracy—it performed adequately—but the absence of a shared, digestible charter explaining when and why the assistant should intervene. The institution lacked a memorable north star. Ambiguity hollowed the experiment.

One could treat this as a reminder that shorter is better, yet the deeper lesson is that charters must be legible to the people who will live under them. Legibility is not the same as simplification. It is the art of shaping principles into forms that invite uptake. Sometimes that means a single page. Sometimes a page with examples. Always, it requires a certain conversational honesty: telling people where a tool might misfire and what protections exist.

Sceptics sometimes argue that charters are performative: aspirational documents with little operational weight. This view mistakes performance for pretence. Performance, in the institutional sense, is how values are enacted. A charter's power lies precisely in its performative role—its ability to change expectations and shift norms. Yet charters, like any governance tool, have limitations. They can become relics if not reviewed. They can be co-opted rhetorically while ignored in practice. They can offer comfort without consequence. The way to reconcile these risks is through cadence. Scheduled review transforms a static document into a living agreement. The Stroud cooperative's ninety-day cycle ensured every principle had to withstand real cases. The moment the charter contradicted lived experience, it was amended.

Cadence also protects against a common failure: the assumption that once the charter exists, governance is done. It is not. Governance begins when the charter meets friction. Each review cycle tests whether the guardrails remain aligned with purpose. Some cycles may require only minor adjustments—a phrasing change, an added example. Others might demand structural revision. The discipline is not in drafting but in revisiting.

A recurring motif throughout effective charters is the boundary between human and system judgment. This boundary cannot be static. It moves as teams accumulate familiarity and as models improve. Yet the principles guiding its movement must be stable. Consider how the Stroud cooperative handled escalation. Initially, the assistant flagged any triage suggestion with less than seventy per cent confidence. Within a month, staff reported that this threshold created noise rather than clarity. The review group raised it to eighty per cent and paired it with a requirement for written rationale only when clinicians overrode the suggestion. The adjustment reduced friction while preserving accountability. The boundary moved; the principle—human judgment as the final arbiter—did not.

The thread that binds these cases is a simple question: who holds the pen? A charter is only as strong as the diversity of the hands that write it. At Stroud, receptionists had equal voice to clinicians. At Rotterdam, night-shift supervisors were consulted late. The quality of the charter reflected the inclusivity of its authors. This matters because hybrid systems alter everyday practice differently across roles. A principle that comforts one group may unsettle another. Only by drafting collectively can a charter anticipate these tensions.

Collective authorship also disarms the perception that charters are managerial tools for managing downward. When those governed become those who craft, legitimacy deepens. Legitimacy is the quiet foundation upon which hybrid systems stand. It shows up in behaviour: staff asking the assistant for its confidence band before accepting a suggestion; supervisors comparing overrides across shifts to detect pattern; administrators noticing when the cadence slips and calling the group back to the table. These are the visible signs of an invisible compact.

The counterpoint is worth examining: what if a charter constrains too tightly? What if it stifles experimentation by locking roles and boundaries prematurely? This risk is real. In 2021, a museum archive in Copenhagen adopted a rigid assistant-use policy that mandated human review of every metadata suggestion. Staff soon ignored the assistant because the review requirements slowed them down. The charter's designers had sought safety but created stagnation. Their course correction came from loosening constraints: they introduced a risk-tiering scheme that required human review only for rare, historically significant artefacts. Low-risk items could be batch-processed with sampling audits. Here, elasticity restored usefulness. Stability of purpose need not mean rigidity of process.

The tension between stability and adaptation is the heart of charter design. Purpose must remain fixed; guardrails must remain legible; mechanisms must remain adaptable. A good charter reads like a promise and a protocol. It answers three questions clearly: why the tool exists, what it must not do, and when its behaviour should be reviewed. Everything else is garnish.

As hybrid work becomes normal rather than novel, organisations face a forward decision: will charters remain ceremonial, or will they become instruments of governance as central as budgets and audits? The answer depends on how seriously organisations take the craft of their own coherence. A charter cannot eliminate risk. It cannot predict every edge case. But it can create a shared orientation—a way for people to walk together into uncertainty.

The final tension lingers. If your organisation wrote its own one-page charter this week, whose fingerprints would be on it? And what would the shortest possible sentence be that could guide every pilot you launch next year?

Platforms, procurement, and sprawl

In February 2022, the operations director of Latchford & Co., a mid-size engineering consultancy in Manchester, walked into a quarterly review with a number she did not expect. The firm, with fewer than six hundred staff, was paying for ninety-three separate digital tools. Seventeen offered project-tracking features. Nine provided near-identical transcription engines. Several handled data extraction from invoices, each with different retention defaults. The financial controller traced £312,000 in duplicated annual spend. More worrying than the cost was the sprawl itself: there was no shared sense of which tools processed client data, which cached it offshore, or which were quietly training their own models on Latchford's documents. A single breach had not occurred. Yet the risk was visible in one measure: ninety-three became the shape of the firm's ignorance.

Within three months, Latchford took a step that changed its posture. It paused all net-new tools, appointed a cross-functional procurement group, and set a limit: no more than twelve core platforms without explicit board approval. Staff grumbled at first; a few complained that the new approval process slowed them down. But by November 2022 the number of tools in active use had fallen to thirty-one. Vendor contracts were rationalised. Data boundaries were drawn clearly enough that every manager could explain which category of information each platform handled. The firm recorded no drop in productivity but a measurable drop in errors involving mismatched or outdated files. The choice to choose less had improved the seams of work.

Tool creep rarely arrives as a scandal. It arrives as convenience. A marketing lead downloads a niche scheduling plugin because it imports colours neatly. A recruiter tries a new assistant to summarise CVs because the trial requires no approval. A project manager pilots a workflow planner without checking how it stores drafts. Most choices look harmless in isolation. They accumulate faster than anyone notices. And unlike physical clutter, tool sprawl hides. You see it in behaviour—teams switching between interfaces, duplicating uploads, or asking colleagues which version of a document is canonical. The platforms proliferate and the seams fray.

To understand why deliberate restriction strengthens capability, start with a simple observation: clarity begins with ownership. When one platform is the home for model-assisted drafting, someone must own its permissions, training data, and update cycle. Ownership turns an abstraction—"system accountability"—into a daily responsibility: a manager reviewing logs, a team checking drift indicators, a product lead deciding whether a new feature threatens data boundaries. Latchford's procurement group made ownership visible by publishing a single-page register. For each platform they named the steward, the data classes permitted, the model update schedule, and the renewal date. The register did more than inform; it disciplined choice. No one wanted to be the steward of a half-baked tool for long.

This principle—fewer platforms, clearer ownership—echoes a pattern in public administration. Consider the Government Digital Service's consolidation efforts in the UK during the mid-2010s. Before consolidation, agencies procured overlapping CMS tools that stored citizen information in inconsistent formats. By 2016, the shift to a unified platform had reduced duplication and improved auditability of data pathways. While the context differs from corporate settings, the behavioural insight is the same: fragmentation multiplies both cognitive load and risk surface. Unification reduces them.

Yet there is a credible counter-example. In 2021, a fast-growing design agency in Lisbon attempted to mandate a single platform for all creativity support. Designers revolted, arguing that the approved tool constrained exploration and flattened stylistic nuance. Several left. The policy was reversed. The agency reinstated autonomy for specific high-variance tasks but tightened controls for workflows involving client assets. The correction did not undermine the principle of rationalisation; it refined it. Some domains benefit from plurality, but even plurality must sit within boundaries. Freedom without boundaries becomes drift; boundaries without freedom become stagnation.

Sprawl also distorts risk perception. Consider two dashboards: one that shows a neat list of sanctioned tools, and one that reveals dozens of shadow platforms quietly processing sensitive data. The second dashboard exists long before anyone builds it; it exists in the network logs and invoice trails. The difference is visibility. Visibility affects behaviour. When Latchford ran its first internal audit, teams saw their own tool proliferation in writing. The embarrassment was constructive. Managers stopped tolerating experiments that bypassed procurement just because they shaved minutes from a process. Staff realised that tool choice was not just a convenience but a governance decision with consequences.

The quiet motif running through these examples is the boundary. Boundaries define where data may go, what models may learn, and who may alter a system's settings. Boundaries need not be inflexible; they need to be knowable. Knowability shows up in small, everyday actions: a solicitor checking which platform holds client drafts before uploading; an analyst tagging a spreadsheet correctly so it remains in the sanctioned environment; a team comparing platform confidence bands to decide when to escalate. Boundaries turn risk into something that can be reasoned about, not feared.

Boundaries also clarify procurement. A platform should be procured not because it claims novelty but because it reinforces the boundary architecture. Procurement teams that operate without boundary clarity buy features. Procurement teams that operate with boundary clarity buy capability. This difference matters. Latchford exemplified it when it declined a vendor offering "context-sensitive model tuning" because the data boundary implications were unclear. Instead, it expanded a contract with a vendor whose guarantees on data minimisation and regional isolation were explicit. The decision looked conservative. It proved prescient. When the vendor later published its transparency report, the firm could map every data flow against its internal boundary schema with confidence.

There is a temptation to treat sprawl as inevitable in a high-velocity environment. This temptation grows when staff believe that centralising platform choice slows innovation. The belief has merit. Rigid centralisation can stifle learning. But the alternative is not laissez-faire proliferation; it is structured autonomy. In structured autonomy, teams can experiment within sandboxes that enforce data boundaries automatically. Procurement approves the sandbox, not the tool. Experiments have decommission dates. Logs record what data crossed the threshold. Learning proceeds without compromising institutional coherence. The model is common in financial services, where sandbox regimes permit innovation while enforcing prudence. There is no reason corporate and civic organisations cannot adopt similar arrangements.

The case for disciplined procurement becomes stronger as hybrid workflows intensify reliance on shared data sources. A single misalignment—one tool that modifies metadata formats or embeds personal information unintentionally—can cascade into systemic failure. When several tools ingest overlapping corpora, version conflicts emerge. When each tool stores prompts or outputs differently, privacy guarantees fracture. A rationalised procurement model prevents these fractures by designing for interoperability and enforcing deletion schedules.

At this point a deeper question arises: what is the right number of platforms? There is no universal answer. The right number is the smallest set that accommodates the diversity of tasks while maintaining coherent governance. That number will vary by sector and maturity. For some firms it may be ten; for others twenty. What matters is not the count but the clarity. Clarity guides behaviour: staff know where to start, whom to ask, and when to escalate.

Sprawl is not merely a technical issue; it is cultural. It reveals how a firm handles uncertainty, agency, and trust. When staff download tools freely, it may signal ingenuity. It may also signal a lack of faith in the organisation's ability to choose wisely. Rationalisation efforts therefore require not only policy but narrative. Teams must hear why the boundaries exist. They must see that the aim is not control but coherence; not restriction but shared competence.

Yet even coherence has its limits. Excessive rationalisation can erase local knowledge. A platform chosen for its robust governance features may still lack the nuance needed by a specialised team. The reconciliation lies in tiering: stable cores with optional extensions. This is how many research labs operate: a secure base environment for data handling, with layered permissions for domain-specific tools. It is how cloud governance frameworks define "landing zones" for teams to build within. The architecture blends safety with creativity.

As hybrid organisations evolve, procurement becomes less about shopping and more about stewardship. Stewardship involves three visible behaviours: examining the data footprint of every tool, enforcing a deprecation process for unused systems, and maintaining a public internal register of platform decisions. These behaviours build trust through predictability. Staff know which tools will remain over the next year. Vendors know what standards they must meet. Leadership knows which risks are real rather than imagined.

The unresolved tension remains. If you mapped every tool your organisation currently uses—officially and unofficially—how many would you find? And if you had to cut that list by half without harming capability, which boundaries would you draw first?

Change management that respects fear

In April 2023, the ward manager at Northwick Park Hospital in London convened a meeting that should have been routine. The trust planned to pilot a documentation assistant to cut the time nurses spent typing observations into the electronic record. The vendor's demo was polished; the procurement case was strong. Yet the atmosphere in the cramped seminar room was brittle. A senior healthcare assistant, who had worked in the unit since 1998, asked a pointed question: "If this thing writes faster than me, what happens to my shifts?" Silence followed. The pilot had not even begun, yet the project had already hit its first wall—fear of judgement. Within three weeks the trust changed course. It paired each early adopter with a sceptic, created explicit opt-in pathways, and rewrote the training plan to centre emotional safety. By September, uptake had reached 78 per cent without mandating anything. No one lost shifts. The unit saw a measurable reduction in midnight backlog entries, and staff reported fewer end-of-day spillovers. The shift came not from technology but from respect.

Fear is often invisible in board papers. You see it instead in micro-behaviours—hesitations before logging into a new system, quiet avoidance of training sessions, or the subtle apology some staff give before asking "basic" questions. These behaviours are not incompetence. They are defensive moves against being made to feel slow, replaceable, or exposed. Hybrid tools promise efficiency, but people sense the implied comparison: the system writes faster, remembers more, never tires. Without a countervailing message, every innovation becomes a judgement delivered in code.

Respecting fear begins with an uncomfortable truth: adoption is not a technical transaction but a psychological negotiation. Change agents must show, not assert, that dignity is part of the design. Northwick Park's pairing scheme illustrates this clearly. They named the initiative "colleague learning circles", not "super user coaching". It reframed skill gaps as shared discovery. This naming mattered. Staff who had been wary agreed to sit with early adopters, not as subjects but as partners. That shift in stance softened resistance more effectively than any manual or mandate.

The second principle is that training must meet people where they are, not where policy assumes they should be. Consider Riverside Community Trust in Sheffield, which introduced hybrid scheduling tools in late 2022. Instead of delivering a single workshop, the trust ran two formats: a structured one-hour seminar and a twenty-minute corridor session led by peers with laminated quick cards. The latter format drew more participants and generated more questions. When learning environments feel low-stakes, staff reveal what they do not understand, and genuine competence develops. The trust measured follow-up questions in the first month: corridor sessions generated an average of eleven queries per group; the seminar, three. The metric reflected comfort, not complexity.

A counter-example clarifies the stakes. A private clinic in Dublin introduced an AI-assisted triage tool and mandated immediate use with minimal explanation, assuming the system's interface was "self-evident". Staff compliance was high initially, but errors multiplied. Several clinicians entered notes in free-text fields the tool could not parse, assuming it behaved like their previous system. Within weeks, the clinic paused the rollout. The failure was not the tool but the lack of empathetic onboarding. The clinicians were not resistant; they were uninformed and anxious about admitting they were confused. The lesson was harsh but vital: fear unspoken becomes risk.

Reconciling these examples requires precision. Gentle change management does not mean avoidance of standards. It means sequencing standards with care. When staff know that errors during the pilot carry no penalty, they explore honestly. When they know questions will not be interpreted as incompetence, they ask freely. The hospital unit at Northwick Park made this explicit: during the first eight weeks, outputs from the assistant were advisory only, with final clinical entries remaining manual. This visible guardrail protected both patient records and staff confidence. The implication was powerful: we trust you more than the system, and we will not compare your speed to its output.

The quiet motif across these stories is the pause—a pause before judgement, before assumptions, before acceleration. Pauses create space for understanding. They show up in practical rituals: a project lead asking each sceptic to articulate their single biggest worry; a team meeting that begins with a five-minute review of what felt awkward, not what worked; a manager committing to test a new tool on their own shift before inviting others. These pauses slow the rollout but accelerate acceptance.

Empathetic training is not sentimental. It is disciplined. It identifies the precise friction points—the button no one wants to click, the ambiguity in permissions, the screen that blinks too aggressively—and addresses them directly. One method that several NHS trusts experimented with in 2023 involved "fear audits". A small group of staff was asked to list the top five ways a new tool could make them look foolish. The audit produced actionable insights: rename a feature, simplify an alert, delay the introduction of automatic comparisons until after staff felt comfortable. By treating fear as a design input, teams created systems people were willing to learn.

Peer mentoring is equally concrete. At Northwick Park, pairs were not random. They were chosen carefully: an early adopter who enjoyed experimentation and a sceptic respected for clinical judgement. The pairing had two effects. First, it prevented the early adopter from becoming a zealot; they had to explain features thoughtfully, not evangelise. Second, it allowed the sceptic to set the pace. This mutual calibration produced a balanced learning curve. The unit tracked time-to-competence metrics based on three real tasks—completing an admission note, drafting a discharge summary, and reviewing assistant-generated text. Paired staff reached steady competence two weeks earlier on average than those trained individually.

Yet pairing has limits. In some environments, staff feel uncomfortable learning beside peers for fear of appearing slow. Here, an alternative works: low-pressure sandboxes. The Metropolitan Borough of Sefton trialled a sandbox for social care workers in late 2022. Workers could test a case-note generator anonymously on historical, redacted files. No logs were tied to individuals, only to task categories. Staff explored features extensively—usage logs showed an average of seventeen test runs per worker versus five in supervised sessions. When adoption opened formally, resistance had diminished because fear had been metabolised privately.

Still, a persistent tension remains. Advocates of rapid deployment argue that slow, empathetic onboarding wastes time and prolongs dependency on legacy processes. They point to sectors like retail, where high turnover demands tools that require minimal training. The argument has a point, but only within narrow bounds. Speed without psychological readiness can hollow trust. Trust, once damaged, slows everything. Organisations that rush adoption often find themselves trapped in cycles of rollback, redesign, and apology. Empathetic change management is not slowness; it is insurance against reversal.

Fear also shapes the stories people tell themselves. In interviews conducted by researchers at King's College London (2021) on digital transitions in healthcare, many respondents described technology not as a helper but as a mirror that reflected vulnerabilities—typing speed, language skills, uncertainty with interfaces. If leaders ignore these emotional textures, adoption becomes a contest between the confident and the cautious. Hybrid organisations that respect fear build bridges instead: they treat apprehension as a shared constraint, not a personal flaw.

This ethos extends to feedback loops. After the Northwick Park pilot entered its second phase, the manager implemented a "three-minute review" at the end of morning huddles. Each staff member named one task where the assistant helped and one where it hindered. There was no scoring. The practice surfaced patterns: certain phrasing misled the assistant; some templates encouraged over-reliance; weekend shifts needed a different prompt style. By collecting experiences without judgement, the team improved both the tool and its use.

The work becomes harder as systems grow more capable. When an assistant performs well, some staff fear they must compete with it; when it performs poorly, they fear they will be blamed for its failures. Managing these dual anxieties requires explicit boundary-setting. Leaders must say plainly: "The system advises; you decide," and then uphold that principle in real disputes. Credibility is behavioural. If a clinician corrects the assistant and managers treat that correction as diligence rather than error, confidence grows. If a worker raises a concern about a flawed output and managers thank rather than punish them, the message lands: scepticism is not insubordination but responsibility.

A final motif draws this together: accompaniment. Change that respects fear is change that walks with people, not ahead of them. It requires managers who demonstrate vulnerability—admitting when they struggle—and peers who model curiosity rather than superiority. It requires pilots that invite opt-in participation and escalation routes that protect staff from being judged by a system still learning itself. It requires leaders who ask, again and again: what does this feel like?

One question remains. If your organisation introduced a hybrid assistant tomorrow, what would your staff fear most—looking slow, losing judgement, or losing dignity—and what would you design, pause, or pair to honour that fear without surrendering progress?

Roadmaps and sunset decisions

In June 2023, the British fashion retailer Rowan & Hales switched off an AI writing assistant that had, by conventional metrics, been a success. The assistant, trialled across its Manchester and Leeds customer-service centres, generated email drafts for staff handling online returns and sizing queries. Response times fell. Queue lengths shortened. Management could point to dashboards that glowed green. Yet something else was happening, less visible on the charts. Customers began to complain that replies felt "cold", "copy-pasted", and "not like you used to be". Staff reported that they no longer recognised their own voice in messages sent under their name. Trust—between customers and the brand, and between staff and their employer—was thinning. After a structured review, the leadership team made a decision that surprised the vendor and some shareholders. They killed the assistant. The tool had passed the speed test. It failed the trust test.
Every experiment needs an exit.

The Rowan & Hales case exposes a paradox at the heart of hybrid deployment. Organisations celebrate experimentation;

they encourage teams to try new tools and "see what happens". Yet few give equal attention to endings. Experiments accumulate like orphaned pilots, each with a handful of committed users and an unclear future. The result is not innovation but clutter. Roadmaps without deliberate sunset decisions become little more than wish lists. To build a genuinely hybrid organisation, leaders must treat endings as design choices, not as embarrassment or afterthought.

To see why, start with what Rowan & Hales did next. Rather than framing the shutdown as a failure, they folded it into a staged roadmap. Phase one had been exploration: would an assistant materially reduce handling time without introducing obvious harm? Phase two, which they had neglected at first, now took centre stage: does this tool deepen or damage relationships over time? To answer, they convened a small cross-disciplinary group—frontline staff, a union representative, a data protection officer, and a brand lead—to review a sample of conversations before and during the pilot. They did not count adjectives. They looked for something more fundamental: whether staff felt responsible for the words being sent. In too many cases, they did not. The implication was sharp. Speed had come at the cost of ownership. The exit door, once acknowledged, was not optional.

Roadmaps that respect both beginnings and endings share a common trait: they define stage gates in advance. A stage gate is a moment where an experiment must justify its continuation in light of pre-agreed criteria. It is not a rubber stamp. It is a structured pause. The gate might focus on safety, satisfaction, fairness, or economics, but it must be explicit. At Rowan & Hales, the post-mortem produced a clear rule for future tools that touch customer communications: no assistant would move beyond pilot unless staff and customers both reported that the assistant made conversations feel *more* human, not merely faster. That rule changed procurement conversations overnight. Vendors were now asked how they would measure tone, not just latency.

A second example comes from a regional bank headquartered in Birmingham that piloted a model-assisted credit-assessment tool in late 2021. The roadmap was laid out as three stages: sandbox testing on synthetic data, parallel run with human assessors, and, if successful, partial automation of low-risk decisions. Crucially, each stage came with a specific exit scenario. If the tool's recommendations deviated from human assessments beyond a pre-defined tolerance on certain demographic segments, the pilot would be halted and reviewed. During the parallel run, analysts noticed that the model consistently undervalued applicants with intermittent employment histories, even when their repayment records were strong. The bank triggered its pre-agreed "red gate": the pilot stopped. A joint team re-examined the training data and feature design. Only after adjustments and re-testing with an independent fairness audit did the pilot resume. The presence of an explicit gate meant no one had to argue for the right to pause; the right was built into the roadmap.

These cases show the same pattern: the exit door is part of the architecture, not a hidden emergency exit. Naming it in advance changes behaviour. Teams approach pilots with a different mindset—less as bets they must defend, more as hypotheses they must test honestly. It also changes the politics. When a stage gate is crossed, deciding to sunset a tool no longer feels like criticising its champions. It feels like following the rules that everyone agreed to.

The counter-example illuminates the risk of neglecting this discipline. In 2022, a large media company in London deployed an internal "insight assistant" that scanned audience data and suggested story angles for journalists. The project started informally in one desk, then spread. No clear roadmap existed. There were no defined criteria for progression, no sunset triggers. Over time, the assistant's suggestions began to converge: similar framings for different stories, a tendency towards topics that performed well in the past. Some reporters worried that editorial diversity was narrowing. Others, keen not to appear luddite, stayed quiet. By the time leadership commissioned a review, the assistant was thoroughly embedded, its logic woven into everyday routines. Switching it off felt impossible without disrupting workflows. The company did not sunset the tool; it layered guidelines and optionality on top. The result was a compromise that pleased no one. The absence of early stage gates had closed the exit door.

Reconciling these patterns requires recognising a simple but demanding principle: every experiment must carry its own conditions for death from the outset. That sounds harsh. It is, in fact, humane. Clarity about endings reduces anxiety for staff, who know that a pilot will not quietly become permanent without scrutiny. It also disciplines leaders, who must confront trade-offs explicitly rather than fall back on sunk-cost arguments.

Roadmaps with stage gates function as a series of questions. At initiation: what is the smallest meaningful test we can run, and what would count as harm? At the first gate: do the hypothesised benefits materialise without unacceptable side effects? At subsequent gates: does this tool still serve our evolving purpose, given what we now know about its behaviour and the surrounding context? Each question forces alignment between tools and values. Where alignment fails, sunset decisions follow.

The motif of the exit door returns here. An open door does not mean constant departure. It means the room is ventilated. Experiments come and go; the organisation breathes. Without such an opening, tools linger far beyond their usefulness. Staff work around them, building informal bypasses that quietly increase risk. The system appears stable but becomes brittle.

Retiring a tool is not purely negative. It is generative. When Rowan & Hales killed their assistant, they did not revert to the old world unaltered. They took what they had learned—the value of suggested phrasing for difficult refund discussions, for example—and embedded it in a set of static, collaboratively written guidance notes. Those notes did not impersonate staff. They offered scaffolds. The assistant disappeared; the insight remained. Sunset decisions, handled well, turn failed pilots into durable learning.

Stage gates also prevent roadmaps from becoming linear fantasies. Too many slides show a smooth arc from pilot to scale as if discovery proceeds without reversal. In reality, any serious hybrid transformation resembles a branching path full of dead ends. A bank discovers that a chatbot cannot handle nuance in hardship cases; a university finds that automated grading erodes student trust; a hospital sees that a triage assistant increases throughput but worsens staff morale. Roadmaps that allow only forward movement encourage teams to hide or downplay such findings. Roadmaps that include deliberate forks—continue, pivot, retire—encourage honesty.

Metrics sit at the centre of these forks. But not all metrics are equal. Efficiency metrics are easy to collect: time saved, messages sent, tickets closed. Trust and dignity are harder. The temptation is to privilege what is measurable. Roadmaps that do so will nearly always favour continuation, because speed gains show up quickly and harms often surface slowly. The remedy is not to abandon measurement but to broaden it. Rowan & Hales introduced a simple trust indicator after their experience: a quarterly pulse survey asking both staff and customers to rate whether interactions felt more, less, or equally human. The measure was subjective but actionable. When scores dipped, it triggered a stage gate discussion regardless of throughput figures.

A similar pattern emerged at a public library service in the North of England that tested an AI assistant for answering benefits-related queries in 2021. The roadmap specified that if more than a small fraction of users reported confusion or distress after interacting with the assistant, the pilot would pause. Staff collected feedback cards at the exit desk. After three months, the data showed mixed results: some patrons appreciated the quick answers; others found the phrasing opaque. Importantly, librarians noted that certain vulnerable users stopped asking staff in person, assuming they should "go through the machine". The library decided to halt the pilot and redesign the interface so that the assistant always presented itself as a preliminary guide, not a gatekeeper. The sunset was partial—the underlying model remained, but the front-end was scrapped. Here, the exit door led to a neighbouring room, not the street.

The limitation of stage-gated roadmaps lies in their potential rigidity. Over-specified gates can choke experimentation, preventing teams from following promising but unexpected avenues. If every deviation from the original success criteria triggers a halt, learning slows. The answer is not more gates but richer gates—ones that allow for revision of hypotheses while still insisting on explicit decisions. A stage review might conclude, for example, that while the primary metric has not improved as hoped, the tool is revealing unanticipated capabilities worth a redirected trial. The key is that this judgement is conscious, documented, and tied to fresh criteria, not a vague sense that "it might get better later".

Behind all of this sits a deeper cultural question. Do leaders in your organisation see retiring a tool as an admission of error, or as a sign of maturity? The framing changes behaviour. Where sunsets are treated as shameful, people defend tools beyond reason, twisting evidence to justify survival. Where sunsets are celebrated as part of the experimental rhythm, people propose them proactively. The difference shows up in meetings: are there serious discussions about what to stop, or only about what to start?

The exit door motif grants us one final, uncomfortable test. If you list your current hybrid experiments—assistants, dashboards, automation pilots—how many have an explicit point at which they will be reviewed for retirement or redesign? And if a tool that boosts speed but erodes trust stands before you today, which way will you turn that handle?

About the Author

Kenan Durveil is a writer and practitioner working at the seam between emerging technology and humane design. He has led multidisciplinary teams that bring AI into everyday services while keeping responsibility with people, not machines. His work blends product craft with policy sense, shaped by years advising organisations on safe adoption and clear governance. A long-standing interest in early Islamic and European scholarship on reason and ethics informs his view that tools must serve virtue, not replace it. He writes to give readers practical language, structures, and courage to use augmentation wisely, and to protect spaces where human judgement, care, and meaning remain central.

www.ingramcontent.com/pod-product-compliance
Lightning Source LLC
Chambersburg PA
CBHW031340230926
51848CB00002B/317
9789374594766